GREEK LITERATURE
FOR THE MODERN READER

GREEK LITERATURE
FOR THE
MODERN READER

BY

H. C. BALDRY

*Professor of Classics in the
University of Cape Town*

CAMBRIDGE
AT THE UNIVERSITY PRESS

PUBLISHED BY

THE SYNDICS OF THE CAMBRIDGE UNIVERSITY PRESS

Bentley House, 200 Euston Road, London, N.W. 1
American Branch: 32 East 57th Street, New York 22, N.Y.

First printed   1951
First paperback edition 1959
Reprinted   1960

First printed in Great Britain at The Carlyle Press, Birmingham, 6
Reprinted by offset-lithography by Jarrold and Sons, Ltd, Norwich

CONTENTS

PREFACE

THIS book is a general introduction to ancient Greek literature, mainly intended for the increasing number of readers who know no Greek and have little acquaintance with ancient history, but who nevertheless derive enjoyment and satisfaction from the many excellent translations of Greek authors now available in English. All quotations are given in translation, and no knowledge of the ancient world is taken for granted. I have not tried to write a work of scholarship, although I hope that scholars may find some interest in points of emphasis or interpretation. Nor is this a text-book. My aim was not to achieve completeness or objectivity (which, if it were possible, would be very dull) but merely to write a history of Greek literature as I see it. This personal and perhaps arbitrary approach will be apparent in my answers to some of the problems which confront anyone who attempts such a task.

Where is a survey of ancient Greek literature to end? Authors continued to write Greek, sometimes with distinction, throughout the Roman period. Are they to be included? Because this book is already long enough, and discussion of these later writers would involve the whole history of Rome, I have stopped at the 'Alexandrian' age after which Roman domination of the Greek world begins.

Which of the documents that survive from ancient Greece can be called 'literature'? Should all the philosophers be included? And the medical writers? And the mathematicians? In antiquity there was no clear dividing line. A modern writer on the subject must draw one, and his decision must be arbitrary. I have written about Xenophanes, but scarcely mentioned Parmenides or Empedocles; discussed some of Plato's dialogues at length, but said very little about his late works, and still less about Aristotle.

Even within the confines of literature proper and of the period before Roman domination, how is space to be allotted? Where is emphasis to be placed? Here I have been guided by the interests of the modern reader, or rather, perhaps, by what I imagine his interests ought to be. My most serious omission is the orators of the fourth century B.C., whom I have passed over in a couple of pages.

What of the great controversies which haunt the historian of Greek literature—the Homeric question, the origins of tragedy and comedy, and the rest? To deal adequately with any one of them would require a volume in itself. Rather than touch on all the various views without doing justice to any, I have in each case given the view which seems to me most reasonable, most suited to the approach I have adopted in the book as a whole.

If this general survey has any particular thesis, it is the simple and by no means original idea (elaborated in more detail in Chapter II) that the various forms of Greek literature can best be understood by studying them against the historical background in which they arose. Although literary form and technique is more difficult to observe in translation, I am convinced that the best way to approach ancient authors is to see *how* they wrote before examining *what* they wrote; and the first question of all is to consider *why* they wrote as they did. Hence this book is much concerned with discussion of the emergence of forms—epic poetry, for example, or drama or the dialogue—from the environment in which they came into being. But forms cannot, of course, be dealt with in the abstract, in isolation from the works in which they were used. The main subject-matter of this volume, as of any other history of literature, is the actual documents themselves and what we know of the authors who wrote them. To this most of the book (Chapters III-X) is devoted. At the beginning I have put two chapters which seemed likely to be useful preliminaries, though they involve some slight overlapping with what comes later: a brief sketch of Greek history, placing emphasis on those aspects which seem most relevant to the development of literature; and a series of questions and answers which attempts to remove some of the general difficulties that face the modern reader. If the result of the whole is to increase the reader's comprehension and enjoyment of Greek literature itself, my purpose will be amply fulfilled.

H.C.B.

CAPE TOWN
May 1950

ACKNOWLEDGMENTS

THANKS are due to George Allen & Unwin Ltd., and to Oxford University Press, New York, for permission to quote from Professor Gilbert Murray's translation of Menander's *Rape of the Locks*; and to Oxford University Press for the many extracts from the *Oxford Book of Greek Verse in Translation*, for the lines from Jowett's translation of Thucydides, and for those from Sir William Marris's translations of Homer.

Rawlinson's translation of Herodotus, no longer copyright, is published by John Murray.

CHAPTER I

OUTLINE OF HISTORY

ANCIENT Hellas had no frontiers. It was the region where the Greek language was spoken, where Greek civilisation and culture arose and prospered and died away: a region which varied from century to century, but never coincided with modern Greece. During the years when most of the Greek literature now extant was produced, Hellas included not only the Aegean Islands and the Southern parts of the peninsula we now call Greece, but to the East, the coastal fringe on the other side of the Aegean; to the West, Sicily and Southern Italy. Most of the land within this area contained only small pockets of cultivable soil where communities could become established, separated from each other by formidable mountain barriers. The principal means of contact and intercourse between them was the sea, across which men could sail with land always in sight. Greece today is a land unit, but in antiquity it was the sea that gave Hellas its unity, bringing Crete and Athens, Syracuse and Byzantium within a single whole.

When and how did civilisation first emerge in this area? The ancient Greeks' own views on the point belonged to the sphere of legend rather than of history. For factual evidence we are dependent on the sensational discoveries made since about 1870 by archaeologists, who have brought to light a great civilisation of which the Greeks had only shadowy memories—first at Troy and Mycenae, then at Cnossos in Crete, then at other centres. The material objects unearthed in these places are our only certainty. Turn to the question who put them there and when, to problems of racial origins or religious beliefs, of the economic, social, or political organisation of society in these early times, and we are in a realm of conjecture where deductions drawn from the archaeological remains and from Egyptian and Hittite records must be combined with inferences from the Homeric poems and other literary sources to build up a shaky structure of theory. Nevertheless, on the main outlines of the story general agreement has been reached.

For the first stages the focal point is the island of Crete. The earliest centres of human culture, the Nile Valley and Mesopotamia, had already advanced some distance towards civilisation when Crete began to follow in their footsteps, passing from the stone age to the use of metal, from village life to the building of towns. But whereas Mesopotamia and Egypt were river civilisations, the inhabitants of Crete inevitably became seafarers. By about 1500 B.C. their island and its lesser neighbours were the centre of a sea empire which dominated the Eastern Mediterranean and traded as far West as Spain. The great seaport of Cnossos had domestic architecture and art, roads, bridges and drainage, which Greek cities a thousand years later could not equal. But about 1400 B.C. came disaster—whence or how we do not know. Cnossos was destroyed, and Crete soon no longer controlled the surrounding seas. The emphasis in our narrative must now shift to the mainland.

Archaeology shows that during several centuries before the fall of Cnossos cities had been growing up on the mainland almost comparable in splendour with those of Crete, but in some ways very different. Cretan towns, for example, had been unfortified, but Mycenae and other mainland settlements had massive fortifications and—like the cities of later Greece—were on sites chosen for defence against attack. Behind the various differences, it is believed, lies a clash and fusion of cultures, a combination of civilisation introduced from Crete with the way of life of migrants or invaders who came down into Greece from the North—people whose ultimate origins lay in the inland grass plains of Europe, far removed from the conditions they found round the shores of the Aegean. Probably these 'Achaeans' (a name which originally belonged to one section, but was applied to all) overran the Southern regions when they were already 'Cretanised'. But however the fusion took place, it was far advanced, if not complete, when Cretan power declined and Mycenae and her neighbours entered upon their greatest days. Its ultimate sequel was one which has been repeated elsewhere when semi-civilised and civilised peoples have come together— not a regime of great stability or permanence, but a 'heroic age' full of change and flux. In Greece and the Aegean the closing centuries of this second millennium B.C. were a time of warring expeditions and migrations of peoples, of piracy and plunder, until fresh waves of more primitive immigrants came from the North, bringing with them the use of iron. This 'Dorian invasion', as it became commonly known, overran most of Greece and threw the whole Aegean area into a confusion which brought the glories of the Bronze Age to an end.

It is in the heroic age that we can first reconstruct a picture of the organisation and life of society—a picture built up partly from archaeological evidence, but chiefly from the *Iliad* and *Odyssey*. At the head of each small community stood the hereditary big chief or 'king'. Inferior to him in power and property, yet of the same class, were 'nobles', some of whom formed his personal retinue. War, piracy, plunder, hunting, feasting were the favourite occupations of this ruling class. From them was drawn the council of 'elders' who discussed all problems and whose decisions—nominally, those of the king himself—were announced for approbation or disapproval to the common people gathered in the market-place, or to the assembled army in time of war. Some of the common people were craftsmen—smiths, potters, leatherworkers, workers in wood or stone. The majority were

3

small farmers or peasants. At the bottom of the social ladder were slaves—in no great numbers as yet—and 'hired men' who were often worse off than the slaves. For the purpose of war against a common enemy the various petty kingdoms, each framed on more or less this model, united in a loose military federation which reproduced the same kind of organisation on a larger scale. The king of one community headed the confederacy, with the other kings as his vassals and members of his council of war, while the common folk formed the rank and file of the army and came together to hear what their rulers decided.

There is obviously little room for literature in this picture. In the songs with which minstrels entertained the feasting nobles lay the roots, as we shall see, from which epic poetry grew in later centuries. But from all the period before the 'Dorian invasion' no literature survives, nor is there reason to suppose that any then existed. The specimens of Cretan writing unearthed by archaeologists are still undeciphered, but they look like accounts or inventories. The Achaeans probably spoke an Indo-European language which later developed into Greek, but the chiefs—and, presumably, the people—were illiterate. Yet to tell the story of Greek literature and leave this period out would be to play *Hamlet* without the Prince of Denmark, for the exploits of these early times became the stuff out of which Greek poetry was made, part of the mental furniture which both poets and public shared. Many things happened to the original facts in the intervening centuries. Events spread over many generations were telescoped into a few years. They were exaggerated and glamorised by time, distorted to suit vested interests, mingled with folk-lore and mythology, until it was impossible to distinguish the hard core of fact from the layers of added fiction. But in the days when first Crete and then the Achaeans dominated the Aegean scene, in the wars and expeditions of the Heroic Age, lay the historical reality behind the mass of legend used by poets,

4

playwrights, even prose-writers—Theseus and the Minotaur, the voyage of the Argonauts, the Siege of Thebes and the Siege of Troy, the wanderings of Odysseus, the homecoming of Agamemnon. History came full circle when the study of Greek poetry led archaeologists to unearth the ruins of Troy and Cnossos and Mycenae.

The upheavals that followed the 'Dorian invasion' brought a Dark Age to Hellas. Only after two or three centuries can we begin to watch the course of events once more, and now our chief source of light is no longer archaeology, but ancient records and the statements of ancient historians. The uprooting, the migrations, the intermingling of peoples are over. The little Greek-speaking world, now enlarged by the addition of a fringe along the Eastern coast of the Aegean, is settling down into the pattern which is to persist until Alexander the Great and even after him— a collection of small, scattered communities, in each of which the town dominates the patch of cultivable land around it. At this stage these 'city-states' have little contact with each other, although they share the same gods and speak dialects of the same language. The sea, like the mountains, acts for the present as a barrier between them, and the unity of the Heroic Age has disappeared. But the structure of society within each community has undergone no fundamental change. The nobles, now settled landowners rather than marauding chiefs, still maintain their position, and the only important shift of power has taken place within the ruling class itself: because the need for a single war leader is no longer so great, the king's power has been retrenched and his property cut away till all the noble families are on more or less the same level. This is the age of aristocracies, which kept alive the dim memory of their more adventurous ancestors and continued to celebrate their exploits in song. It was in Ionia, on the Eastern shore of the Aegean, that aristocracy reached the greatest heights of culture, and it was there that the minstrel's stories at the nobles' feast were transformed into epic poetry and brought into being the *Iliad* and the *Odyssey*.

The influence of the noble families remained a strong force for many generations. But their absolute rule could not last. Even at the height of their ascendancy, the cause that was to undermine it was already there—the inadequacy of the soil, which was the dynamic behind many of the changes in Greek history and one of the primary reasons, strangely enough, for the brilliance of Hellenic civilisation. 'Greece', says Herodotus, 'always has poverty for a mate'.[1] Few of the Greek communities possessed enough land to maintain more than a very limited population. In societies where a minority owned big estates, it was the small farmers and peasants who felt the pinch of land-hunger. Something of their hardship is reflected in the *Works and Days* of the poet Hesiod. But the land shortage ultimately created other forces working against aristocracy beside peasant unrest and peasant revolts.

Different states solved their land problem in different ways, with different social and political results. Sparta, for example, conquered the neighbouring region of Messenia and eventually became like a military camp in enemy territory, turning from a cultured aristocracy to a disciplined military regime which made her the foremost land power of Greece. But the commonest answer to the need for *lebensraum* was emigration. During the eighth, seventh, and sixth centuries B.C. the Greeks settled round the shores of the Mediterranean and the Black Sea (to use Plato's phrase) like frogs round a pond. 'Colonies' were sent by one city-state or another to every patch of coast from the Crimea to Cyrenaica, from Cyprus to Marseilles, where there was land to cultivate, a safe site for a town, and no considerable power to keep the newcomers out. In most instances the primary motive was the desire for land, but the results of this great colonising

[1] VII, 102.

movement went far beyond the colonists' original intentions. It led to a rapid increase in intercourse across the seas, in trade between mother-city and colonies and generally between state and state. More trade led to greater production of manufactured goods. And as at the same time the Ionian Greeks on the East of the Aegean made closer contact with their inland neighbours and learned from them (among many other things) the use of money, commerce and manufacture began to come to the forefront alongside agriculture to play an important part in the pattern of Greek life. Ionia led the way, but many parts of the Hellenic world were affected by the change. Technical advances were numerous, and not least among them was the increase which trade caused in the use of writing, with all its manifold consequences for the history of literature.

It was the political results of this economic and social development, originating in the shortage of land, that brought the decline and fall of the landowning aristocracies. A new type of rich man arose, who was more concerned with commerce than with agriculture, and whose wealth lay in movable goods rather than in land. Many of these merchants and manufacturers came from among the nobles, others from lower in the social scale. But whatever their origin, their interests necessarily clashed with those of the nobility. Here was a cleavage which, combined with the discontent of the peasantry, could become a powerful cause of social conflict, a powerful force for social change. Amid the struggle 'tyrants' arose, as the Greeks called them: ambitious and usually wealthy individuals, often disgruntled members of the aristocracy itself, who in one way or another seized the opportunity of the moment and rose to power. Although the word 'tyranny' later developed a bad sense which it has retained until today, most of the 'tyrants' did great service to their states. They consolidated the strength and patriotism of the community. They instituted or reorganised games and religious festivals, set up

7

great public buildings, issued new and better coinage, attracted poets and artists from elsewhere to their courts. And in doing all these things they broke the power of the nobles, loosened their grip on the religion and the minds of the common people, and prepared the way for further political advance.

The period of aristocracy and of the 'tyrannies' which brought it to an end filled several hundred years and lasted till about the close of the sixth century B.C. In Ionia, it was an era of brilliant cultural and intellectual renaissance. Yet from all this, after Homer and Hesiod, remarkably little literature has survived. We shall find that the extant remains, though they mirror clearly enough the conflicts and changes of the day, are no fair reflection of the amount of literature that was produced, or of the advances that were made in literary form. After the time when the development of epic reached its climax came the age when choral song, encouraged by nobles and 'tyrants' alike, rose to the greatest heights of elaboration and sublimity—an achievement represented today only by the odes of Pindar. A new individualism generated by the clash of social forces brought the poetry of personal emotion into being, now known to us only through the most meagre fragments. Still more vital for the history of human culture, the new spirit in Ionia led to the beginnings of science and the beginnings of prose literature. And at Athens, as we shall see, 'tyranny' set the stage for the rise and growth of drama. Though little of Greek literature as we now have it dates from these centuries, a knowledge of them is essential for understanding of the whole.

The rule of the 'tyrants' rarely lasted longer than two generations. When assassination or expulsion had removed them, the political vacuum which they left was filled in new ways. With the breaking of the power of the aristocracy the old struggle between landowner and peasant no longer dominated the scene. The issue

8

which developed now within most of the city-states was one that lasted throughout Greek history—the clash between the rich and the poor, the few and the many. In some states the few, the *oligoi*, kept control, and oligarchy was the prevailing regime. Elsewhere the common people, the *demos*, triumphed, and established and maintained democracy. Some communities experienced first one form, then the other.

In the course of time this conflict grew to such dimensions that it could separate cities into groups on what would now be called 'ideological' lines, could even become a more compelling force than loyalty to the state. Yet it was not the main cleavage within society. More fundamental, more taken for granted, and therefore comparatively rarely mentioned in literature, were two deeper lines of division: first and less important, the difference between citizens, who could own land, and *metics*—aliens from other states who resided within the community, engaged in manufacture and trade, paid taxes and gave military service, but possessed no land and exercised no political rights; second and most vital, the distinction between free man and slave. Slavery, a small factor in the life of the community before the Dorian invasion, had increased during the age of aristocracy and tyranny until now it was the basis—and the curse—of Greek economy. When we read about wars in ancient Greece, we must not forget that slave dealers followed the armies to buy the prisoners taken in battle. When we admire the glories of fifth-century Athens, we must include in the picture the fact that a slave market was held there once a month. Ancient authors rarely focus our attention on such points. Most of them were citizens of high birth and considerable wealth, often inclined to despise 'the mob' and decry democracy. A few were *metics*. None were slaves. The slave was voiceless, but he was always there.

To illustrate these developments and divisions from various

9

city-states would be a lengthy task, and fortunately in sketching the historical background to Greek literature there is no need to attempt it. Nearly all the extant literature produced in the fifth and fourth centuries B.C. came from democratic Athens, which advanced to the forefront when Persian invaders conquered Ionia and brought the brilliance of Ionian culture to an end. So to Athens we must now turn.

In her early history Athens and the surrounding territory of Attica had passed through much the same phases as other states. Monarchy (Theseus was the greatest of her legendary kings) had given place to aristocracy—the rule of landowners who oppressed the peasants and reduced many of them to serfdom or slavery. Commerce began to develop, and those who drew wealth from trade joined the peasantry in hostility to the nobles' regime. Early in the sixth century Solon, some of whose verses we still possess, made an attempt to solve the conflict by compromise, but the struggle was too bitter. In 560 B.C. Pisistratus, himself a member of a noble family, seized power and made himself 'tyrant'. It was Pisistratus who laid many of the foundations of Athens' future greatness, in literature and art as well as commerce and politics. It was he who instituted or raised to fresh splendour the recitation of the Homeric poems at the city's great festival of Athena, and enriched the festival of Dionysus with the first performances of tragedy. Pisistratus was succeeded by his son, Hippias, but the regime of the 'tyrants' came to an end in 510 B.C. When they had been driven out, constitutional reforms introduced by Cleisthenes finally broke the grip of the nobles. The beginning of the fifth century found the citizens of Athens well on their way towards full democracy. But before they could reach it they had to pass through an ordeal which brought them both disaster and glory—the Persian Wars.

The Persian invaders who had conquered Ionia some fifty years earlier were part of a great expansionist movement which had grown in the East under the domination of the Persians and their kings. Not only Western Asia up to the Ionian seaboard but also Egypt was brought within the Persian Empire. A revolt among the Ionian cities was crushed, and presently the Persians turned their attention to the Greek mainland, where the city-states made only half-hearted attempts to combine against them. Athens bore the brunt of the fight. A small force sent by king Darius was defeated by the Athenians at Marathon. A far larger expedition organised by Xerxes was checked at Thermopylae, routed at Salamis and Plataea. When the Greeks finally emerged victorious, which state had the major share in their land successes was a matter of dispute, but there could be no doubt that the Athenians, under the leadership of Themistocles, had been fore-most in defeating the Persian fleet. When the struggle was over, much of their land had been devastated and their city burnt, but they were unquestioned leaders of the Greeks at sea. To complete the defeat of the Persians they placed themselves at the head of a naval confederacy which during the following decades, in spite of the opposition of conservative aristocrats like Cimon, was gradually transformed into an Athenian Empire.

These middle decades of the fifth century B.C., commonly associated with the leadership of Pericles, were the greatest period in Athenian history. The contributions from her allies towards the common cause against Persia, now turned into tribute from subjects, combined with the rich slave-worked silver mines of Attica to give her wealth such as no Greek state had known before. Some two hundred cities were included in her Empire. The forty thousand or more adult male citizens among her population of about 300,000, freed from many of the ordinary labours of daily life by the use of slaves and the distribution of pay from the state treasury, could devote much of their time to politics, and through their Assembly and Council and executive officials controlled the conduct of affairs in both peace and war.

Magnificent new buildings glorified the Acropolis which the Persians had ravaged. Traders and tourists flocked to Athens from other states. In the great theatre of Dionysus citizens and visitors gathered to watch the tragedies of Aeschylus, Sophocles, and Euripides, and the comedies of playwrights whose works are now lost. Among the aliens who found a home in the city was Herodotus, historian of the Persian Wars.

Athens was now both intellectual and commercial capital of Greece. But complete mistress of Hellas she could not become. In 431 B.C. the rising tension between Athens and the states outside her Empire, led by Sparta, flared up into the Peloponnesian War, which for twenty-seven years tore Greece in two—a conflict which was an ideological struggle between democracy and oligarchy as well as a clash between groups of states. A peace treaty was signed in 421 B.C., but hostilities did not stop for long. A few years later the disastrous fate of a great Athenian expedition to Sicily tipped the balance definitely in favour of Sparta, and by 404 B.C. her victory was complete. This exhausting struggle brought more than defeat to Athens. As the years passed and the strain increased, the unity which had held rich and poor together in prosperous days gave way to violent internal conflict, and from now on, although democracy triumphed, strife between the classes was never far beneath the surface. In the minds of the citizens the stress of war also hastened other processes which otherwise might have taken place more slowly—the breakdown of tradition, the decline of faith in the old religion, the growth of scepticism, rationalism, individualism. The Athenians believed that these trends were introduced from outside by the Sophists, itinerant teachers of many subjects and above all of rhetoric—a product of democracy which from these small beginnings became the chief influence on Greek prose literature. But if the Sophists sowed the seed, it found ready soil among many of the Athenians themselves, including some of the greatest writers and thinkers of the day—Euripides, the tragic poet; Thucydides, the historian of the Peloponnesian War; Socrates, a vital figure for the history of Greek literature though he wrote nothing himself. The reaction against these new tendencies found its chief spokesman in Aristophanes, whose comedies satirised and caricatured them all.

When the Peloponnesian War ended, the great days of Athenian literature were by no means over. If the fifth century had produced the finest poets, it was the fourth that brought prose writing, especially oratory and philosophy, to maturity, the fourth that saw Isocrates, Demosthenes, and a dozen others carry the technique of eloquence to the highest perfection, while Xenophon produced works on many topics, Plato developed the philosophic dialogue on the lines he had learnt from Socrates, and Aristotle began the systematic exposition of philosophy and science. Yet it is clear that this fourth century did not sustain the brilliance of its predecessor, that Athens never again rose to such intensity of intellectual effort and achievement. To a large extent this deterioration was due to the exhaustion and devastation brought about by the struggle against Sparta, to loss of population through the war and the plague that came upon Athens soon after hostilities had opened. Another cause was the disappearance of her Empire and the tribute she gained from it. But look at the problem against the wider background of ancient history as a whole, and the phenomenon of the city's rise to pre-eminence and subsequent decline falls into place as part of a longer and more universal process—a tendency towards expansion, towards the opening up of new areas and the creation of larger political units, which began early in the life of the city-state and continued till it reached its climax in the Roman Empire. This trend coincided with the rise of a merchant and manufacturing class, a bourgeoisie, to replace the landed aristocracy as the dominating factor in ancient society. It coincided with the growth of a slave economy, and it is probably here that the chief cause for such a development is to be found. Because the wages of free workers could never rise much above those of slaves, and because slavery made any kind of trade union organisation to raise wages impossible, a society based on slave labour suffered from chronic under-consumption, continually unable to absorb all the goods which it produced. Once slavery had reached considerable proportions in industry, the inadequacy of the internal market led to a constant search for markets elsewhere.

In its economic aspect the Athenian Empire in the fifth century was a product of this expansionist process. In the fourth century the effects of the general trend became more evident. Large new areas began to come within the orbit of Greek commerce and Greek civilisation, most of them, significantly enough, under autocratic rule: to the North, Thessaly and Macedon; to the East, Caria; while in the West 'tyrant' Dionysius and his son built up a temporary empire for Syracuse. Greek links with Persia became more numerous, and the Persian king and his satraps now played a leading role in Greek politics. Most important of all was the change that came over the structure and organisation of Hellenic society itself. An expanding world, a world gradually coalescing into a single economic unit, could not be permanently divided into separate sovereign city-states. The highest development of the city-state form had come at the moment when the citizens, still maintaining their common traditions and their unity, gained the greatest benefit from trade, travel, and intercourse with other communities. This was the culmination reached by Athens in the time of Pericles. But we have seen that even then the fabric was crumbling, undermined by the wider, more sceptical, more individual outlook with which the Sophists were associated. The fourth century was marked by new groupings of states, by experiments in federalism, by talk—in Plato's *Republic*, for example—of drastic political

14

change. Greek civilisation, as a modern writer[1] has put it, was 'ripe for universality'—ready to become one world, with a common economy and a common culture, with no fundamental divisions except the cleavage between rich and poor and the still wider gap between free man and slave. In an age that knew nothing of representative government only a single absolute ruler could bring such a world to birth. Towards the end of the fourth century this autocrat emerged—not from any of the old city-states, which had striven in vain to gain ascendancy over each other, but from Macedon. Like the Achaeans who had united Hellas perhaps a thousand years earlier, this new conqueror came from the North.

The Macedonians were Greek in origin, but had been cut off from Hellas proper for so long that the Greeks regarded them as foreigners, 'barbarians'. Only in the fifth century B.C. did their kings begin to enter Greek politics and encourage the adoption of Greek ways. Contact increased as Macedonian trade with the outside world developed and Greek artists and poets—Euripides, for example—were persuaded to visit the Macedonian court. This growing power to the North became a threat to the Southern regions of the Greek peninsula when King Philip II, who ascended the throne in 359 B.C., unified Macedon itself, annexed some of the neighbouring areas, created a professional army with a national spirit, and so made this kingdom a stronger military and economic force than any Greek city-state. Philip's conquest of the city-states was achieved by a brilliant combination of force and intrigue. At Athens Demosthenes fulminated against him in some of the most impassioned flights of Greek oratory, calling on the citizens to lead Greece against Macedon as they had led her against Persia more than a hundred years before. But the clock could not be put back. Philip had his fifth column in Athens, as elsewhere—men of property who were prepared to

[1] Glotz, *Greek City*, p. 384.

accept alien rule as a means of preventing social revolution. The story reached its climax at the battle of Chaeronea in 338 B.C., when the city-states were decisively defeated. A federal Hellenic League was formed at Corinth under Philip's leadership and allied with Macedonia. Existing constitutions were to be maintained. There were to be no confiscations of property, no new divisions of land, no wholesale emancipation of slaves. Philip announced his intention of making war against Persia, and was elected general with supreme powers.

Philip was assassinated two years after Chaeronea, but his plan was more than fulfilled by his son Alexander, who in twelve spectacular years overwhelmed the East and carried Greek military power—and Greek commerce and culture—to the river Indus and to the upper waters of the Nile. Alexander's brilliant campaigns brought the gradual expansion of the Greek world to a sudden and explosive climax, completing by force that merging of the Eastern Mediterranean and the Middle East which had already been partially achieved by trade. His early death in 323 B.C. left his armies masters of a vast extent of territory, in which new cities that he had founded—Alexandria in Egypt, for example—were growing up to rival and outstrip the old. The regions of this great area were linked together by bonds of commerce, by the penetration everywhere of the Greek trading class, carrying the Greek language and some measure of Greek culture with them wherever they went. But the political unity which Alexander had imposed did not last. Twenty years of struggle for power between his generals ended in the division of his Empire into three great kingdoms: Macedon, with most of the old city-states as its dependents; Egypt; and Syria, which included most of the Eastern portions. Egypt and Syria, although the vast majority of their populations were non-Greek, were dominated by the Greeks and brought within the sphere of Greek trade. In this 'Hellenistic' age, as it is usually called, the sea was still the key to history. Egypt and Syria, like Macedon, became naval powers, and all three continually fought each other for control of the Eastern Mediterranean; and while they were distracted by these wars, more and more minor principalities or cities or groups of cities took the opportunity to break away and gain independence for themselves. All alike were weakened by internal conflict—in Egypt and the East, revolts of the native population against the Greek minority; in Hellas proper, bitter class struggles among the Greeks themselves. It is not surprising that in the second century B.C. the Hellenistic world could not resist for long the impact of the growing power of Rome.

In many ways it was a world more like our own than the earlier centuries had been. Science made great advances. Literature, lacking the vital national inspiration which the greatest days of the city-state had given it, now reflected the individualism and the increasingly cosmopolitan outlook of the day. Primarily this was an age of prose, but among the small surviving remains it is verse literature that is most prominent: the realistic comedies of Menander produced in the closing years of the fourth century B.C. at Athens, still the chief home of the drama and of philosophy; the varied poetry written in the third century at Alexandria and elsewhere by Callimachus, Apollonius, Theocritus and other poets who all bear the same 'Alexandrian' stamp. These are the last considerable writers of Greek literature before the history of ancient Hellas as an independent entity draws to a close.

LIST OF DATES

(Many of these are conjectural or approximate. Authors' dates
denote their *floruit*—i.e. about their fortieth year.)

B.C.	HISTORY	B.C.	LITERATURE
3400	Bronze Age begins in Crete		
1500	Height of Cretan power. Rise of Mycenae		
1400	Destruction of Cnossos. Supremacy transferred to mainland		
1235	Traditional date of Theseus at Athens		
1184	Traditional date of fall of Troy		
1050	Dorian invasion. Ionians settle East of Aegean		
		900–800	*Iliad* and *Odyssey*
770	Beginning of colonisation		
753	Traditional date of founding of Rome	750	Hesiod
670	First 'tyranny'		
630	Sparta quells Messenian revolt	625	Alcman writes choral song at Sparta
		600–580	Sappho and Alcaeus
		600–550	Beginnings of science in Ionia. Growth of prose literature
594	Reforms of Solon at Athens		
546	Persian conquest of Asiatic Greece		
546–527	Pisistratus' 'tyranny' at Athens	534	Beginnings of Attic tragedy

B.C.	HISTORY	B.C.	LITERATURE
508	Cleisthenes' reforms inaugurate democracy at Athens	486	Official contests in comedy begin at Athens
		485	Aeschylus
490–479	Persian Wars	485	Birth of Protagoras, the first Sophist
		482	Pindar
479–454	Creation of Athenian Empire		
461	Pericles in power	456	Sophocles
		445	Herodotus
		444	Euripides
		429	Socrates
431–404	Peloponnesian War	420	Thucydides
		410	Aristophanes
		396	Isocrates
		390	Xenophon
		388	Plato
359–336	Philip king of Macedon		
		344	Aristotle
338	Battle of Chaeronea		Demosthenes
336–323	Alexander king of Macedon		
331	Foundation of Alexandria		
		302	Menander
		270	Theocritus
		265	Callimachus
		255	Apollonius
210	Beginning of Roman conquest of Greece		

CHAPTER II

SOME QUESTIONS ANSWERED

EVERY stage of civilisation (including our own) has its own mental furniture, its own ways of thought. Those living within that stage are usually unconscious of their assumptions. Those outside it—in space or time—find them strange and difficult to understand. So it is with ancient Greece and the modern reader. The vast majority of the Greeks were unaware of their own attitudes of mind, and in classical scholars familiarity with the assumptions that underlie ancient culture may breed the same blindness to their existence. But the layman often finds it all too obvious that Greek literature takes for granted practices and ideas very different from his own. It is this that makes so much of Greek literature puzzling, difficult, strange, only half intelligible to the modern mind. The purpose of the present chapter is to clear up some of the puzzles and difficulties, to answer some of the problems which confront the ordinary twentieth-century reader when he turns to Homer or Herodotus or Sophocles. We must put on the right spectacles before we begin to read.

Perhaps it will be as well to start with a question which is fundamental for the whole approach adopted in this book.

Is it true that Greek literature was so closely related to the life of Greek society?

At first reading of many Greek authors the point may well appear doubtful. Like the Parthenon and its sculptures, they seem far from the madding crowd, not close to its heart and mind. Modern writers have often praised their universality, the eternal quality which puts them outside place and time. How can such works be linked with a local and transient environment?

Study these 'eternal' masterpieces further, and the answer becomes clear. The link existed: but it was different from the link which commonly binds the written word today to the circumstances amid which it is produced. Ancient literature was not often topical. Although we shall see that it had much to do with special occasions in the life of the community, it was not often consciously and deliberately related to a particular situation and a particular need. It could rarely be labelled 'propaganda' in the narrow sense, rarely possessed the flavour of the modern newspaper or political pamphlet. Homer, Herodotus, Thucydides seem to have a lofty impartiality far removed from our twentieth-century war of words. But because their connection with the life of their time was less conscious, it was not less deep. To understand the difference, to see where the bond between literature and society lay in ancient Greece, turn to an inherent distinction between Hellenic and modern civilisation—one of the ways in which the Greek environment was more primitive than our own.

Ours is a specialised world. The division of labour caused by industrial technique colours our whole way of living—and of thinking. But in ancient Greece, amid a comparatively simple material economy based on cheap slave labour, specialisation was slow to develop. The individual citizen was a citizen first, a potter or olive-grower—or poet—afterwards. This homogeneity of society influenced every phase of the Greeks' experience, every product of their culture. Not least, their literature. Whereas today writers are 'men of letters', specialists in their craft, and literature, however 'topical', tends to be a thing apart, separate from the rest of living, the Greeks knew no such dividing lines in their pattern of existence. Poets, playwrights, orators were regarded as possessors of inspiration which other men lacked, but otherwise as citizens (or *metics*) like other craftsmen. Here is the key to their connection with their environment. They did not write *about* the events and ideas of their generation as something divorced from themselves. Very often their subject-matter was remote legend or abstract philosophy. But because they were not separated from their fellows each was in some sense a mouthpiece of his age. There is little isolated 'self-expression' in Greek literature. Writers do not turn their backs on the community to probe the individual ego, nor do they seclude themselves in mysticism unrelated to normal life. Whether they conform with their environment and the prevailing outlook or rebel against it, it is always within that sphere that their ideas move. That is the reason why their work so closely reflects each phase in the development of society, the reason why there is no literature for which 'background study' is more profitable than for that of Greece.

The attitude assumed, but rarely stated, by Greek writers themselves was made more explicit by their critics, for though until the Hellenistic age literary criticism as a specialised technique was undeveloped and professional critics were a breed yet unborn, judgments on literature and estimates of its value—literary criticism in the widest sense—played a bigger part in Greek history and culture and thought than in our own. When Pisistratus wanted to stabilise his regime, to spread both at home and abroad the belief that Athens merited the national leadership of Greece, he brought poetry to the city. A century and a half later Plato—no mean poet himself—fears that poets may upset the stability of his ideal state, and lays down that they must be expelled. The assumption accepted by tyrant and critic of tyrants alike—that literature deeply affects society and is something with which society must concern itself—was universally taken for granted by their fellow-citizens. A community which allowed the minds of its children to be debauched by comic-strip sensationalism would have been shocking to the Greeks. 'Art for art's sake' was not merely unknown among them: the idea would have been (as a modern scholar[1] has said) 'either monstrous or simply unintelligible'. When in Aristophanes' *Frogs* Aeschylus asks:

Pray, tell me on what particular ground a poet should claim admiration?

Euripides replies:

If his art is true, and his counsel sound; and if he brings help to the
nation
By making men better in some respect.[2]

No one in the audience was likely to disagree. Art and literature were for society's sake, and society had the right—and duty—to pass judgment on them. The formal product of this outlook was a custom which may well have had its origins in primitive days: the literary competition—not merely a feature of Attic drama, but a practice pervading all Greek literature, from the legendary struggle between Homer and Hesiod to Aristophanes' battle between Aeschylus and Euripides, from the singing contests of Theocritus' peasants to the lists of best orators and poets and historians drawn up by his contemporaries. The idea that he must face his fellow-men as judges of his work (*kritai* was the Greek word) crystallised for the Greek author the need for keeping close to the tastes and traditions of his generation.

Emphasis on this general connection between literature and society in Greece does not mean that each individual author and each particular work can be fully explained merely by relating them to the circumstances from which they emerged. In any age the bonds which link a particular writer to his environment are

[1] Sikes, *Greek View of Poetry*, p. 48.
[2] Ll. 1008-10. Tr. Murray (George Allen and Unwin, Ltd.).

far too subtle and complex for the historian of literature to disentangle. But in dealing with the various forms or techniques of literature, with their origin and development and decline, the task is not so difficult. *How* people write can be much more easily related to their historical background than *what* they write. The special importance of this point for ancient Greece will become clearer in the course of answering a second question:

How was Greek literature produced?

Translations of Greek literature are commonly said to be 'from the original', and by the 'original' we mean the printed volume of Greek text which can be bought in a bookshop and from which the translator works. The term is a misnomer. Although the words in the volume of text may be close enough to those the ancient author once used, in other respects both text and translation are far removed from the real 'original' as it was first given to the world. Study the details of the distinction, and many seeming difficulties disappear.

First, the difference in technique. Not only was all Greek literature created before the days of printing: much of it came into being before even writing was a common practice. Dictation to a number of slaves eventually became the regular method of reproducing a book, but even in the fourth century B.C. copies were usually made one by one, and few editions reached double figures. Before 500 B.C. there was virtually no reading public. If written versions of poems existed, they were the closely guarded property of a privileged few: literature reached a wider circle only by word of mouth. Throughout the classical period few works were produced primarily as books for readers: poetry and even prose were normally composed as material for performance and presentation, not for the study and the armchair; to be sung with music and even dancing, or recited, or read aloud, not to be read silently in private. The word *musikē*—the craft over which

24

the Muses preside—means neither music nor poetry, but both, and the scansion of Greek verse by length of syllable is proof of music's influence on the whole poetic art. 'Literacy' in the modern sense was no essential for literary enjoyment. The Greeks were no worshippers of the written word. Mouth and ears, not pen or printing-press and eyes, were the channels for communication of the author's thoughts—a situation restored in some measure by the radio today.

This in itself had profound effects on literature, and the Greeks were not altogether the losers in the comparison. Behind the straightforward style of most Greek authors and the simple clarity of their language—merits which even translations partly reveal—lies the need for being understood at first hearing: the obscurity of parts of Thucydides, who, as we shall see, wrote primarily for readers, is an exception that proves the rule. Singing and recitation led to development and elaboration of rhythm: if the eye was less practised than ours in following the written word, Aristophanes' jokes about poetic diction and metre show that the ear was sharpened to catch subtleties which would be lost on a modern audience—just as the memory did not atrophy like that of a modern student once examinations are things of the past. But there is another more positive side to the picture. The background to the creation of literature for performance rather than for reading was something more than technical backwardness.

Literature, as we have seen, was part and parcel of the normal existence of the ancient Greek community. But it was connected above all with special occasions in that existence. Modern man picks up a novel or perhaps a volume of poetry when he 'has nothing else to do': for the Greek, most poetry and some prose was not an entertainment for hours of idleness, but a vital experience at times which called for 'heightened language'. Often it was linked with ritual. Some recent writers may well be correct in arguing that one branch of Greek verse—choral song—was the prototype of all, that the poetry of the Greeks and of every other people evolved from the magical rite in which music and dancing combined with song to rouse emotion to its highest pitch and concentrate attention on the desired end. Greek poetry's prolonged association with music may go back to such primitive beginnings. The epic recitation, the choral or dramatic performance may be sober and sophisticated descendants of the beating drum and tribal dance. But in the historical period literature is connected with all sorts of occasions, religious and secular, great and small—epic with the chieftains' banquet and later with great popular festivals; choral song with ceremonies of many kinds, from marriage processions to the victorious athlete's homecoming from the Games; drama with the festivals of Dionysus; oratory with political happenings, clashes in the law courts, burials of the dead, Panhellenic gatherings at Olympia.

More than one feature of Greek literature can be traced back to this association with ceremonies or outstanding events. To poetry it brought a heightening of language which in some poets more than counterbalanced the simplicity demanded by writing for the ear rather than the eye. To most literature it gave added stateliness and dignity. But above all it affected the division of literature. This background of the occasions for which most Greek poetry and prose were written is the main explanation both of their division into various forms, and of the connection between those forms and the phases of social and political development amid which they arose.

Here again Greek literature takes us back to an age before specialisation was the rule. The books in our libraries today are classified according to both form (drama, fiction, poetry) and subject-matter (geography, chemistry, gardening). The same categories exist in the minds of writers and help to shape their work. By the Hellenistic age this double division had come about in the ancient world, but before Aristotle separation by subject-matter was hardly recognised, certainly possessed no systematic basis, no technical terms. The dividing line between literature and philosophy, non-existent till Aristotle, has to be artificially and arbitrarily drawn in every account of Greek literature, including this book. Distinctions between ethics and theology and history and politics were as slow to emerge and as ill-defined as the difference between manufacturer and trader, engineer and mathematician. A Pindaric ode or a Platonic dialogue faces us with a bewildering mixture of topics and themes. But turn to division by form, and the picture is completely different. The remains of Greek literature fall into formal categories with ease and precision. The classification of music is perhaps the nearest modern analogy. Just as orchestral music can be subdivided into symphonies and concertos with various instruments, or chamber music into sonatas, trios, quartets and the rest, so we can go further than splitting up the works of Greek authors genus by genus: often each genus has its species—the various particular types of choral ode or speech. This pattern too must have been taken for granted by writers, so that everything they composed accorded with it. It is the connection between each of these patterns and the type of occasion for which it was produced that constitutes the clearest link between Greek literature and society —the link on which stress is laid in this book. It is significant that most of the main forms of literature which ancient Greece created were forms suitable for performance before an audience: in verse, epic poetry, choral song, tragedy and comedy; in prose, the speech and the dialogue. Contrast our most typical modern form—the novel, natural product of an age of readers.

The changing background of Greek history brought the different types of literature into being. Thereafter they were affected by a conservatism which we shall find again in discussing ancient religious ritual. Each form, once it had emerged out of a particular phase in the life of society and the sort of occasion to which that phase gave prominence, tended to become established, stereotyped, a convention which all writers should follow—a model usually accepted as a guide, occasionally rebelled against as a restraint. Epic, already a conventional form before the creation of the *Iliad* and *Odyssey*, took them as its norm and standard ever afterwards. The conservatism of public opinion regarding tragedy—especially the form and technique of tragedy—is voiced by Aristophanes: even Euripides did not break away. Oratory soon developed its own rules, laying down the proper arrangement, style and diction of a speech. Even the use of different dialects for different branches of literature was conventionalised. In every branch of literature formal imitation was a virtue, not a sin. It is this adherence to an accepted model, an accepted technique, rather than any innate instinct, that is mainly responsible for the 'sense of form' in Greek literature and in all Greek art. Yet the various forms could be adapted to new needs, and in their remoulding, as in their birth, changing circumstances were the principal force at work. Few of the conventions of literature became mere relics of earlier days. The majority must be seen as traditions handed down from the past, but continually reshaped by the present. So out of popular dance and song evolved the elaborate texture of the choral ode; out of fifth-century drama, the comedy of the Hellenistic age. In later chapters I shall describe the conventional forms of Greek literature as each existed at its highest point of development, but it must not be forgotten that each had its own story of birth and growth and maturity and decay.

We have seen how Greek literature was originally produced. It seems natural to pass on from the question of production to that of transmission.

How has Greek literature survived until today?

In many instances it is not only a question of survival, but of transformation. How have works first published orally become the printed volumes we use now?

The answer is twofold. First, by being written down. Then, by the making of copies. Both stages have left their mark on our remnants of Greek literature. Each must be considered separately.

Transition from the spoken to the written word took place in different ways for literature of different types. Sometimes it occurred when oral material, more or less traditional, was gathered together and recorded for the first time: obviously through selection and arrangement the recorder had much to do with giving the result its permanent form. There can be little doubt that this was the source of some of the minor remains of Greek poetry, and of much that is now lost. Many scholars go so far as to see the *Iliad* and *Odyssey* and the poems attributed to Hesiod as products of such a process, and describe even Herodotus' book as such a collection, though here the collector was Herodotus himself.

In this first category there is room for endless argument about the manner and order in which each work was composed, about the contributions of tradition and of the individual author towards the final outcome; in some cases, even about the existence of any individual author at all. Very different was the history of poetry and prose produced for particular singular occasions: choral songs, tragedies and comedies, speeches. These—however traditional their character and ideas—were definite creations by a definite author, written down, either before or after the performance, in the form which their creator gave them. But again there are problems involved: doubt and confusion creep into the picture wherever (as often occurred) a play was changed for a second performance and two different written versions were made, wherever publication of a speech was delayed after delivery and the written version could differ from what was actually said.

The third class is more familiar to the modern mind: books written as books, intended for the reading public. From Thucydides onwards if not before, this description fits most non-oratorical works in prose. But even here the similarity to our own practices is not complete. Titles (for example) were not given by the author, but added later by librarians. Many books have come down to us with more than one title, or more than one wording of the same title, and no one can say which is more correct. Where a writer's works have disappeared, the same defect often stands in the way of deciding what he wrote and of classifying the fragments we still possess.

Thus in one way or another the various types of literature reached written form, and were inscribed on the clumsy rolls of papyrus which did duty for books in the ancient world. About their transmission down to the third century B.C. we know little. Copies seem to have been made in haphazard fashion as they were needed, and copyists were far from precise in keeping to what was in front of them. They appear to have had little hesitation over making additions—passages which actors inserted in drama, or poems falsely included in the collection ascribed to a well-known author. Presumably they were equally unscrupulous in deleting what they did not like. It is impossible to tell the extent of the changes made during this early phase of free enterprise in the reproduction of texts. Order was first introduced into the chaos by the scholars of Alexandria, who brought the outlook of the librarian to bear on the material handed down from the past. It was they who worked out methods of 'textual criticism', and attempted to establish an authoritative version of many authors' works. For convenience in classification and cataloguing they invented titles, and fixed the points at which long works should be split up into papyrus-rolls—the division into 'books' which we find in the *Iliad* or the *Republic* today.

The journey from ancient Alexandria to our own library shelves was long and had many different aspects and phases: the adoption in the early centuries of the Christian era of parchment or vellum made from skins in place of the less durable papyrus, of the book form (derived from tablets) instead of the roll, and eventually of printing instead of writing; transmission through copy after copy made by good, bad, or indifferent scholars, whose deliberate alterations of the text were often more harmful than their numerous chance mistakes; the growth of textual criticism into a highly complex technique, aided in recent days by easier means of travel and the use of photography. Our existing manuscripts of Greek literature date from various points in the story: a few, from as early as the last few centuries B.C.; the majority and the most important, from much later. Most of the best are in Italy, where they were brought from further East at the time of the Revival of Learning. Only the past 100 or 150 years have seen the scientific collation of these manuscripts and determination of their family history, till today there can be little doubt that for most authors scholarship has gone almost as far as is now possible in producing an accurate text.

How near is the modern version to the words which Pindar or Aeschylus or Plato wrote? This also we cannot often judge. But on the rare occasions when discovery of an ancient papyrus has provided a means of checking the fruits of scholars' textual labours, the results have proved surprisingly exact. Whether we still read just what Sophocles or Demosthenes wrote we cannot tell. But at any rate our version of them is much the same as that which was read two thousand years ago.

So much for quality. But what about quantity?

What portion of Greek literature do we still possess?

Very little, compared with the original whole. Time has not been much kinder to the literature of Greece than to her architecture and art.

Even if we were less ignorant than we are about the works now lost, it would be impossible to give a precise answer, to work the problem out in mathematical terms. Who shall decide what deserved the name of 'literature' and what did not? But even on a strict view of the use of the word our estimate of the proportion that has survived could go little higher than one per cent. Our richest heritage is from fifth-century Athens, yet probably less than a twentieth of the original Athenian legacy has reached us. Out of hundreds of Attic tragedies we possess only thirty-two. From sixth-century Greece we have little in anything like complete form except the poems attributed to Theognis. From the prolific fourth century, not much more than Plato's dialogues, Aristotle's lectures, and the Attic orators.

Is it the best that has survived? Often there is reason to believe that it is, but by no means always. Chance played a big part in making the selection, whether through the burning of libraries which destroyed thousands of manuscripts or some lucky accident which here or there preserved one. So did practical utility: works on farming or astronomy were always likely to be in demand. Still more important was the approval or disapproval of scholars, librarians, teachers. Few authors survived unless they found a place in the lists of best writers compiled by the learned men of Alexandria. The largest expectation of life fell to those considered suitable for the young—the 'set books' of education in late classical times, copied again and again to be read in schools. We may be thankful that the teachers' choice was not worse.

All this applies to works that have come down to us more or less complete. In addition there are thousands of 'fragments'—a few fairly lengthy, but the majority very short; many from familiar authors, others anonymous or from writers who are mere names. Some of these fragments also are products of chance—the discovery of a mutilated inscription or a torn strip of papyrus. But most of them are brief extracts or quotations made by later writers whose interest was grammar, spelling, peculiar uses of words, strange customs—anything rather than literary merit. Like some modern schoolmasters, these scholars of the past treated ancient literature as if it existed only for its oddities, linguistic and otherwise. We should get a strange picture of some authors whose major works have survived, if we knew them only through the extracts and quotations commentators have handed down to us: clearly 'fragments' are dubious evidence—though often our only evidence—about the character or merit of the multitude of writers whose works are lost.

Something has now been said about the peculiarities of the form of Greek literature, both as it was produced in ancient times and as it survives today. If we turn to its content, we are confronted by a problem which has already arisen in this chapter and which crops up again and again in the study of Greek culture:

Were the Greeks primitive or modern?

The question is more than a debating point: it affects our whole attitude towards Greek literature, our interpretation, our selection of what is significant. Are the masterpieces of the Greeks to be regarded as flashes of exceptional genius amid the darkness of a semi-savage society, or as the products of an enlightened community, the work of intellectual cousins of our supposedly civilised selves?

The discussion is an old one. At one extreme stand those who see ancient Greece as a microcosm of the modern world, who turn to Thucydides for the last word on Revolution and look upon Plato as an up-to-date authority on Communism. For them printing, the steam-engine, the utilisation of electricity, all the technical advances of recent centuries are mere 'external trappings': human nature and its problems remain the same now as in fifth-century Athens. Their *forte* in studying ancient literature is the discovery of parallels with our own day, but their zeal in this search often exceeds their historical sense. They fail to realise that technical development causes profound changes in the structure of society, which have confronted us with issues fundamentally different from those faced by Euripides or Aristotle. Those who treat Greek literature as a mirror of modern times see in it many things which are not there—and miss many things which are.

On the other side in the debate are those for whom it is the researches of the anthropologists, not the columns of our news-papers, that can make the biggest contribution to our under-standing of Greek culture and thought. Their attitude gained its greatest following about half a century ago. While archaeology was throwing new light on the early background and everyday customs—especially religious customs—of the Greeks, anthro-pologists widened their studies of primitive societies existing today. Comparisons and analogies were irresistible. The arid field of classical scholarship blossomed with a new and sometimes riotous growth of totem-poles, bull-roarers, corn kings and spring queens, much of which might well have astonished the ancient Greeks themselves. A check to this seeking after primitive parallels has come from the anthropologists, who have moved towards the conclusion that what is true of one primitive community is by no means necessarily true of another. As more numerous 'primitive' societies—most of them already old—have been studied, the lowest common denominator of primitive cul-tures has shrunk. But there are still those who cannot read Greek poetry without seeing a savage face lurking between the lines.

Put the two views in this extreme form, and clearly both are wrong. Classical Greece was divided from modern times not only by the passage of over two thousand years, but by revolutionary changes in technique and in the organisation of society. On the other hand the main centres of Hellenic civilisation had long outgrown savagery: the earliest extant Greek literature—the Homeric poems—is full of sophistication: Neither the fascination of looking at our own reflection nor the attractive game of anthropological comparisons must divert us from the plain and simple fact that the Greek way of life and thought, the outlook embodied in Greek literature, was the product of the ancient Greek environment—not a hangover from the remote past or an anticipation of the remote future. Nor must the size of Greece make us forget the sharp variations of culture possible in a small area when means of communication were very different from today, or the distance between classical times and our own lead us into the mistake of seeing them foreshortened, of telescoping the centuries and imagining that one label can be applied to a civilisation that had a beginning, many intermediate phases, and an end. Each locality of Greece at each stage in her history had its own conditions and its own outlook. Each work of literature must be seen against its local and contemporary background.

This is the central point, the simple answer to the question 'Primitive or modern?' But history, of course, is not so simple as that.

Surely survivals from the past had a big place in Greek literature?
They certainly did. In every civilisation the legacy of earlier times, even of distant times, plays a large part in the present, in the mind of man as well as in his institutions—a truth that applies to Greek culture even more than to our own. Although the history of ancient Greece is a record of continual change,

although in the theoretical (but not the technical) sphere the Greeks were the most inventive and original of peoples, through their way of life and thought ran a strong conservative strain. Their intellectual advances were made by reinterpreting the old rather than by casting it aside. If innovators were common, they were often frowned upon. The Athenians not only produced Socrates: they also executed him. This conservatism itself seems primitive and tribal, a link with the past. Certainly it strengthened and prolonged the influence of tradition on Greek life, and nowhere shall we find its effect more manifest than in literature.

The prominence of the legacy of the past in the content as well as the form of most Greek poetry is obvious at first reading: its main subject-matter was traditional. Look more closely and we find many things that can only be understood by going back to earlier times, things that reflect not the primitive phase of society, but the complex changes and conflicts on the way from the primitive origins to the highest development of the city-state. The importance of kinship in the organisation of society has left its mark in many places in Greek literature. So has the transition from collective ownership to private property. So have the various stages in the evolution of the status of women. Some scholars claim that there is evidence for the existence of matriarchy in Minoan and Mycenaean times, and that this was superseded by the patriarchal system brought by the invaders from the North. Several phases of development separate these early days from the contrast between feminist theories and far-from-feminist practice in democratic Athens. All this is the background to the varied pictures of family relationships in Homer and elsewhere, to the discussion in Aeschylus and Euripides, Aristophanes and Plato, of the relative importance of men and women.

Whereas parallels with our own time, however interesting,

explain nothing in ancient history or literature, study of survivals from the past can bring much light to the many dark places in our knowledge of the Greeks. But the field needs careful exploration. There are traps into which it is all too easy to fall.

The prominence of survivals is not merely determined by the passage of time. Their influence varies in different places, among different states and classes, with different individuals. Their effect upon Greek literature is a more complicated story than domination at the beginning, fading in the middle and extinction at the end. Still more important is a distinction that must be drawn among survivals themselves. Some are no more than meaningless relics, empty forms. Others—and it is these that matter—continue to exist because they still answer a need in the life of society. Their character may change. They may be adapted to new purposes. But as long as they have a function to fulfil they do not atrophy and die away.

Consider for a moment one example—the question of kinship. The subject as a whole is extremely complex, but this particular point about it can be briefly made. The fact or belief that all members of the community are bound together by ties of blood is common to all primitive societies. Although the concept is remote from the organisation of society today, Nazism has shown how it can be adapted to modern purposes. What was its role in ancient Greece?

There can be no doubt that the peoples from whom the Greeks were descended were at one time organised on a kinship basis. Tribe (*phylē*), brotherhood (*phratria*), clan (*genos*)—surely conceptions handed down from early times rather than artificial creations of later days—survived not only as words but as institutions into the classical and even the Hellenistic age. In the more backward areas tribal divisions and customs seem to have been maintained with little change throughout the most brilliant

periods of Hellenic culture. Yet to base interpretation of any
author on the supposition that the Greeks had a tribal outlook is
a dangerous—and not uncommon—mistake. To ransack Greek
literature for evidence of tribalism *in its original form and fulfilling
its original purpose* yields few results, and to look for it at the
beginning of the story is particularly fruitless: there is far less
of such primitive ideas in Homeric epic than in some later works.
What we do find in literature is new versions of the old institutions and sentiments connected with kinship, often transformed
into something far different from what they must once have been.
When we first meet the 'clans' in the historical period they are
no longer subdivisions of the whole people: by a development
which we can no longer trace they have become exclusive bodies
to which only the rich landowning families belong, strongholds
of aristocracy whose power had to be broken before Athenian
democracy could come into being. Fifth-century Athens itself
revived the outlook of tribal democracy in a new form, with its
Assembly, its use of lot in the choice of officials, its belief in a common bond of kinship and exclusion of those with alien blood in
their veins, its cult of a common ancestry and a common hearth.
We shall see that the aristocratic clans played an important part
in the evolution of choral song, that the almost tribal solidarity of
Athens had much to do with the development of drama.

This question of survivals from the past is one that arises in
many forms in literature. But the key to the problems of tradition there is the same as in the sphere of social organisation: the
past survives not as it was, but as it is, reshaped by the needs and
circumstances of the present. The primitive elements are rarely
mere relics of bygone times: most of them have been transmuted
by the alchemy of history into metal of contemporary stamp.

The importance of tradition and traditional survivals leads to
an obvious further question.

What part does religion play in Greek literature?

> My children, sons of Cadmus and his care,
> Why thus, in suppliant session, with the boughs
> Enwreathed for prayer, throng you about my feet,
> While Thebes is filled with incense, filled with hymns
> To the Healer, Phoebus, and with lamentation?

Prayer ... incense ... hymns ... Phoebus Apollo ... These opening lines of Sophocles' *Oedipus the King* are typical in one way of nearly all Greek poetry. Turn at random to drama, epic, or choral song, and within a few sentences you are confronted with the gods or plunged into mythology. Even in most prose works they make their appearance after a page or two.

Why? The reason is not merely that ancient poets and writers were exceptionally religious men. This feature of Greek literature, like others, reflects the general nature of Greek life.

The modern landscape may show a church tower in the distance. But here is the geographer Strabo's description of the countryside round a river-mouth in the Peloponnese: 'The whole country is full of temples of Artemis, Aphrodite, and the Nymphs, being situated in sacred precincts that are generally full of flowers because of the abundance of water. And there are also numerous shrines of Hermes on the road-sides, and temples of Poseidon on the capes.'[1] The scene puts into visible form something which pervaded every aspect of existence in the ancient world. Modern man's attitude to religion has been profoundly affected by the spread of scientific thought and by the same habit of specialisation which has conditioned his approach to literature. For most people today religion, like poetry, is a thing apart: if it enters their lives at all, it is at specific times and for specific objects—in connection with particular ceremonies, particular emergencies. Even the few for whom religion spreads over the whole of life are aware of it as a conscious process. But for the

[1] VIII, 3, 12. Tr. H. L. Jones (Heinemann, Ltd.).

39

Greek—there were, of course, exceptions—religion and life were inextricably interfused. The supernatural was a part of all his thinking, though not through any conscious effort. In his personal life religion had its role at every turn, reached into the humblest corner of his home. As the philosopher Heraclitus said when visitors found him in the kitchen, 'there also there were gods'.[1] For the Greek the community could not exist without religion, without its deities and ceremonies. When he looked at the wider world around him, the same habit of mind coloured all he saw. Where modern man normally turns to science for an answer, for the Greek the ordinary and expected explanation was a supernatural one. When lightning flashed, nothing so rational as the formulae of physics lay behind it: it was—of course—the thunderbolt of angry Zeus.

As in life, so in literature. Greek literature is rarely 'religious' in the modern sense, just as it is rarely 'topical' or 'propagandist'. Before the Stoic Cleanthes' *Hymn to Zeus* in the third century B.C., few surviving writings show a conscious religious fervour or missionary spirit. The gods and mythology are there because through them lay the normal approach to life, because before the rise of rationalism, and for the majority even after it, mythology was the mould from which thought took its shape, the gods were the symbols in terms of which every problem must be solved. All poetry employs concrete imagery in preference to abstract thought: the Greek poets used the imagery of legend and religion as their natural medium. The telling of a story about individual beings (*mythos* is the Greek word for 'story') was for them the obvious way of accounting for all experience. To the modern reader the unfamiliar ancient deities and their adventures are often a tiresome obstacle to the appreciation of Greek literature: to the public for whom it was written, they seemed as normal and necessary as the use of the alphabet.

[1] Quoted in Aristotle, *Parts of Animals* I, 5, 645 a.

It is in this sense that Greek literature is permeated by religion. But it is not dominated by religious dogma. Greek writers were not under the control of any heresy-hunting priesthood. There was no sacred book to the letter of which all must conform. On this point a distinction must be made between two aspects: ritual and belief.

Ritual had a place in Greek life difficult for us to realise today. Each turning-point in the cycle of human existence was an occasion for ritual: birth, initiation, marriage, death. So also was each turning-point in the cycle of the seasons, which the Greeks saw as analogous to human life: the sowing of the seed, the ripening of the crops, reaping, threshing, gathering into barns—all had their ceremonies. Even warfare must be interrupted or delayed for the correct sacrificial acts. Sickness, plague, pollution, disaster of any kind must be averted by ritual. There was ritual to regulate the relationship between living and dead. Ritual makes its appearance again and again in literature.

Ritual—the thing done—tended to remain stereotyped and fixed. Its influence on literature is a factor making for conservatism. Some ancient ritual survives almost unchanged in Greece today. But belief—the thing thought, the thing said—had no such rigidity. Belief associated with the same ritual changed from generation to generation, varied from place to place and from class to class, grew and developed with the growth and development of society. The religious thinking of the Greeks was never transformed from a living growth into a dead dogma by the domination of a hereditary priesthood or an unchanging ruling class. Some attempts were made to bring order into the chaos of mythology, like the *Theogony* attributed to Hesiod. The Delphic Oracle came nearer than any other institution to being accepted as a central religious authority. But there was no orthodoxy in the modern sense. If ritual remained the same, new content and meaning were continually put into

it. Religion as it appears in literature is not single or homo-
geneous, consistent or systematic. It is a medley of many
elements, which themselves constantly change and so alter the
complexion of the whole.

What were the origins and development of religion and mythology?

The distinction between the various elements can never be
clearly drawn, nor their source clearly traced. But something
can be said of the sources and evolution of the main components
of the mixture.

Somewhere in the dim background of Greek religious ideas
must lie some equivalent of the belief in *mana*—the impersonal
supernatural power which the primitive mind finds everywhere
in nature, and in some persons, animals and objects to a special
degree. Though such primitive conceptions have left comparatively little mark on literature, there is ample evidence that they
remained alive everywhere in the popular mind, and were
dominant in those areas where civilisation made least progress—
just as the ritual of human sacrifice continued in the mountains of
Arcadia till the second century A.D. Magic and taboo were
practices familiar among the countryfolk. So were animal-gods
and countless minor spirits in which *mana* locally or temporarily
took a half-personified form. Natural objects of importance to
man were seen as themselves divine. It was some kind of *mana*
that distinguished certain individuals from ordinary mortals:
among them, the poet, whose 'inspiration' was a living reality, a
state of madness, of becoming 'outside' or 'beside' himself, of
being 'full of the god'—*ekstasis, enthousiasmos*—later regarded
as the gift of the Muses or Graces or Apollo, the god of song.
For the Greeks, genius was much more than an infinite capacity
for taking pains.

It is easy to understand how from such origins the lesser
deities evolved which peopled the Greek world: the nymphs

who haunted the streams, the satyrs and pans that inhabited woods and pastures, the spirits that brought good or bad luck in the potter's workshop or the smith's forge. Ultimately even the most developed forms of Greek religion must have come from an equally primitive source, but their evolution took place long before the beginnings of literature, even before the period known to us through archaeology. Like other aspects of Hellenic civilisation, the upper strata of Greek religion resulted from the fusion of two traditional elements: one from the culture of Crete and Mycenae, the other contributed by invaders from the North.

The finds of archaeologists show that the religion of Minoan and Mycenaean days was dominated by female divinities. Supreme above all was the great mother-goddess of nature, with an armed male deity as her subordinate partner. Hence perhaps came Hera, Artemis, Athena, Aphrodite, whose names do not appear to be Indo-European. The tombs discovered at Mycenae and elsewhere with their rich treasure are proof of the importance in these early times of the cult of the dead. Very different were the conceptions brought down into the Aegean area by the immigrants from the North—a patriarchal, pastoral people who burned their dead. Their gods took their name from Olympus, perhaps the name they gave to any high mountain, and certainly that of the great peak in Northern Greece near which they may have temporarily settled during their trek to the South. Lord over the Olympians was Father Zeus, god of the sky that stretched far and wide over the plains from which the invaders came. Among them was probably Apollo, and Poseidon, god of waters. In contrast with them was Demeter, goddess of corn, who like several other deities dwelt below the earth, and whose presence indicates that even before their arrival in Greece these pastoralists had developed agriculture. As the years passed the newcomers joined with the divinities of the old Aegean civilisation—by

43

what steps, we do not know—to form the Olympian pantheon familiar to us from literature. But they were not an exclusive community. Because there was no fixed or 'orthodox' list of the inhabitants of Olympus, room could still be made for foreigners like Dionysus, who presently rivalled in importance any of the rest, or even for personified abstractions like Love, Friendship or Peace.

From these different beginnings the gods and goddesses came together. Equally remote are the origins of the stories told about them—tales which place no emphasis on the creation of man and assume that the universe existed before the gods, but tell of countless relationships of the deities to each other or to humanity. Most of Greek mythology—along with heroic legend, from which it cannot be clearly distinguished, the constant material of literature—was fully developed before the time of the Homeric poems. Much of it probably dates back to Mycenaean and Minoan days. The sources and motives behind it have been the subject of endless analysis, endless speculation. Many legends are clearly aetiological—stories created to explain some feature of human experience, from the practices of ritual to the existence of sun, moon and stars. Some have as their core the dim and distorted memory of actual events, actual travels and expeditions in the distant past. Others are typical folk-stories—tales of heroes who fight wild and fabulous beasts, or perform superhuman tasks as the price of freedom; of miraculous birth from dragon's teeth or drops of blood or the forehead or thigh of a god; of dismemberment and rejuvenation and change of shape and a dozen other topics which recur in the folk-lore of many lands. Others again reproduce in imaginative form the stock themes which are repeated again and again in Greek literature—stories of bloodshed or incest within the family, illustrations of the certainty that excess will bring disaster, that pride will have a fall. As Malinowski puts it, 'the function of myth . . . is to strengthen tradition and endow it with a greater value and prestige by tracing it back to a higher, better, more supernatural reality of initial events'.[1]

Survivals of primitive customs and ideas, deities and cults from the early Aegean culture, from the North, and elsewhere, a tangle of myth—these are the components which made up the ever-changing medley of Greek religious practice and belief. The character of this medley, its principal features as they appear in literature, varied from place to place and changed with the changes in the nature of society. Worship of the Olympians was by no means confined to one stratum of the community. Hesiod treats them as the small farmer's gods as well as the prince's. The poor man as well as the rich looked to Zeus to protect his home. Athenian democracy reverenced Athena as its queen. Yet in the Homeric poems (and, by imitation, in much later literature) we shall find the Olympians reflecting all the qualities of the class for which epic was composed—its organisation, its manners, its sophistication. These literary products of Ionia were dominated by the memory of the heroic past and its national religion, but even while they were taking final shape the isolation of Greek communities that followed the Dorian invasion was shifting the emphasis from the Olympians to local cults; above all, to the cult of the dead, ignored in Homer but maintained among the people since pre-Homeric days. Out of the cult of the dead evolved the cult of heroes, the 'saints' of pagan Greece, whom their worshippers regarded as men once alive on earth, but who actually included a motley variety among their company—fictitious ancestors, figures from epic saga, faded gods, spirits called into being by ritual, beings who were beneficent if correctly venerated, but malicious and harmful if not given their due. From the eighth century B.C. onwards hero-worship spread all over Greece, and here again political

[1] *Myth in Primitive Psychology*, p. 125.

and religious development went hand in hand. In this period of aristocracy the countless hero-cults were controlled—often even owned—by the great landowning families, and provided one of the foundations on which their political supremacy was built. Encouragement for the cults and 'canonisation' of the heroes came from conservative Delphi, which changed its political colour in chameleon fashion to suit the temper of the time. But while Delphi called for 'moderation', for 'nothing too much', for proper appeasement of the divine powers which control the short span of human life before it is ended by inevitable death, others who had no vested interest in the religious heritage of the past were turning in a direction far more important for the future history of human thought—towards belief that through mystic faith and ritual there is an escape from death's inevitability for the individual soul, that life on earth is only a prelude to life hereafter. In the increasing popularity of the worship of Dionysus and the mysteries of Eleusis in Attica, and still more in the cult of Orpheus, tendencies which we shall find growing in literature had their religious counterpart.

The decisive political change in the history of the Greek city-states was the rise of the 'tyrants'. It was the 'tyrants' also who broke the nobles' grip on religion. They strengthened the worship of Dionysus and the Eleusinian Mysteries at the expense of the hero-cults. They turned the Olympian religion into a weapon against aristocracy. They set the stage for the part which religion was to play in the fifth-century democratic state and its literature, when city-god and city were identical in the mind of the citizen and war between cities was war between their gods, when Athena became the symbol and focal point of Athenian patriotism, when huge festivals and fine temples proclaimed the people's wealth and power, when dramatisation of the common myths acted as a social cement to bind the community together, when there was an uneasy equilibrium between the particular cults of the separate city-states and the Panhellenism of the Olympians, of Delphi and the great Games. That religion was no mere formality in democratic Athens is shown by the trials of Anaxagoras and Socrates, the nearest approach to religious persecution in ancient Greece. But the very existence of such 'heresy' is evidence of a development to which literature bears ample testimony—the disintegration of tradition alongside the break-up of the unity of the state, the growth of scepticism and individualism paving the way towards the individualist and cosmopolitan philosophies and religions of the Hellenistic world. Of all the varied religious ideas of the Greeks the Olympian gods ultimately proved least able to stand the test of time. The Orphic and Eleusinian conception of salvation for the individual soul lasted till Graeco-Roman days and merged into Christianity. Some of the beliefs and practices of the common people, rarely mentioned in ancient literature, have survived in Greece until the twentieth century.

One question raised at the beginning of this chapter remains still unanswered.

Why is Greek literature often so cold, so reserved?

The modern reader finds many Greek authors frigid, stilted, remote not only from the twentieth century but from any warmth of flesh and blood. Most Greek poetry and prose seems far removed from the supposed excitability of the Mediterranean peoples. Yet the ancient Greeks as we see them through their literature were not unemotional. From the wrathful Achilles onwards, they burst into tears on many occasions when the hero of a modern novel would maintain a stolid calm. What is the explanation of the paradox?

Several points go some distance towards providing an answer. Translation is partly to blame, because it cannot reproduce the full life and vigour inherent in the original words. So is the taste of those mainly responsible for the selection of the literature which has come down to us, thanks to whom it is largely the more sober stuff that exists now. So also is the comparative absence of individualism in the periods from which the chief literary masterpieces have survived: the reader of today often finds himself more at home in the individualistic Alexandrian age than in fifth-century Athens. A still more important reason is the religious background; and together with religion, the conservatism which restrained the form and sometimes the content of literature within conventional bonds. Like the fashions of twenty years ago, like the silent film, any technique once accepted seems 'stilted' to those who have passed on to new and (as they think) better things. When a writer of Attic tragedy describes a murder or suicide through the mouth of a messenger instead of putting it on the stage, a modern critic may condemn his coldness or praise his good taste, but the playwright's real motive was a convention which had little to do with either. If we now find his play 'stiff' or 'stilted', it is largely due to conventions of technique, to traditional limitations of theme, the strangeness of which inhibits our emotional reaction but did not affect the reaction of the original audience. Just as those who watched a silent film a generation ago were not prevented from admiring the hero or hating the villain because no sound came when they moved their lips, so the Greek audience was not 'put off' because the chorus repeatedly interrupted (as we should express it) the action of the play.

These are partial answers to the problem, but the principal explanation lies elsewhere, in another difference between the ancient Greeks and ourselves. The seeming 'coldness' of Greek literature must not lead to the belief that those among whom it was produced lacked emotional warmth. On the contrary, all the available evidence places the Greek man-in-the-street on a

par with the weeping Achilles: far from being 'reserved' or
'frigid', he was more sensitive, more easily moved, than we are
His palate for literature and art was not dulled by newspaper or
cinema sensationalism. The Greek audience was more ready to
surrender to illusion, to allow itself to be carried away by a
speaker. It found emotional excitement where we find little.
Aristotle's statement that tragedy purges the spectator by pity
and fear, Plato's decision to ban poets from his ideal community
because of their corrupting influence on the young, have as their
background the dynamic effect of drama and other forms of
poetry on the emotions of those before whom they were performed. We shall see that when Aeschylus' chorus of Furies first
appeared in the theatre, the sight of these dreaded creatures is
said to have started a panic; and that when another playwright
portrayed an incident of which the Athenians were ashamed, the
audience (according to Herodotus) 'burst into tears'. In one of
Plato's dialogues a professional reciter of the *Iliad* and *Odyssey*
tells of the effect of his performances on himself and his audience:

'When I speak of something pitiful', he says, 'my eyes are filled with
tears; and when I tell of something fearful or strange, my hair stands on
end through fear and my heart throbs'.
    'And do you realise that you have the same effect on most of the audience?'
asks Socrates.
    'I certainly do', replies the reciter; 'for whenever I look down at them
from the platform I see them weeping, gazing wildly at me, marvelling at
what they hear'.[1]

Oratory could arouse the Athenian assembly to decide that all
the adult inhabitants of rebellious Mytilene should be put to
death and their women and children enslaved—and move them
to revoke the decision the following day. Clearly the Athenian
crowd was not cold or unemotional. To readers accustomed to
the spectacular events of the beginning of the atomic era, those

[1] *Ion*, 535 c-e. Cf. Gorgias, *Encomium on Helen*, 9.

whose mental sustenance is the mystery story and the horror film, Homer and Sophocles and Theocritus may well seem flat and dull. But the fault does not lie with the Greeks: it is in ourselves and the conditions of our modern age.

CHAPTER III

'HOMER' AND THE EPIC TRADITION

GREEK literature as we have it starts with its greatest achievement: the *Iliad* and *Odyssey*, the earliest epics we possess. Each
is the size of a longish modern novel. Each is divided into
twenty-four books to fit the twenty-four letters of the Greek
alphabet, but the division—pointless except for reference purposes—was made centuries after the creation of the poems
themselves. Both are narratives of the lives and deaths of the
buccaneering warrior chieftains who were masters of Greece
in the 'heroic age'. Both are connected with the most famous
warring and plundering expedition known to Greek tradition—
the Trojan War, the siege of Ilion.

The *Iliad*—the name means simply 'the poetry about Troy'—
is a tale of blood and slaughter, glory and sorrow. The core of
its story is a single episode during the war itself. Achilles, greatest
fighter among the Greeks, is insulted when a captive girl is taken
from him by Agamemnon, and withdraws himself and his forces
from the struggle and sulks in his tent. In the great battle that
follows the Trojans press the Greeks hard, till the fall of Achilles'
comrade Patroclus brings him back into the fight. He kills the
Trojan leader Hector and maltreats his body, but is persuaded
by Priam to hand it over for burial. All this fills only a few weeks
of the tenth year of the war; but incidentally the whole background of the siege is introduced—the armies assembled, the
leaders on either side and some of their exploits, scenes within
the beleaguered city, the quarrels and machinations of the gods.

The *Odyssey* tells of another aspect of the 'heroic age'—

51

wanderings across the sea, adventurous and romantic but less bloody and less intense than the fighting around Troy. Here we are concerned with a sequel to the war: how one Greek chieftain, Odysseus (Ulysses is his Latin name), travelled home to the island of Ithaca and his wife Penelope. The poem begins with Ithaca in the tenth year after Troy's fall: many suitors have been vainly wooing Penelope and eating up the riches of the kingdom, till now Odysseus' young son Telemachus goes to look for his father. Presently the story turns to Odysseus himself in the midst of his travels and brings him to the land of Phaeacia, where he describes his experiences since the war ended —his escapes from lotus-land, the Cyclops, the Sirens, Circe, Scylla and Charybdis; Aeolus and the bag of winds; his visit to the land of the dead; his seven-years' stay as lover and prisoner of the goddess Calypso. From Phaeacia he reaches Ithaca, meets Telemachus, kills the suitors, and is reunited with Penelope. It is the world's first and most dramatic story of an ex-serviceman's return.

Open the *Odyssey*—most modern readers find it easier to appreciate than the *Iliad*—and this is what we read. The scene is Phaeacia, on the morning after Odysseus has been cast up on the shore. His divine helpmate the goddess Athena has appeared in a dream to the princess Nausicaa in the form of one of her companions, and suggested that her marriage-day is near and they should wash her clothes:

> At once came Dawn of the bright throne, and woke
> The fair-robed maid Nausicaa. Now she
> Was lost in wonder at her dream and went
> From room to room to tell it to her mother
> And father dear. She found them both indoors:
> Beside the hearth amid her handmaids sate
> Her mother spinning yarn of deep sea-blue;
> Her sire she met as he was going forth
> To meet the high kings in the council-room

Where the Phaeacian chiefs had bidden him.
So coming close she said to her dear father:
  'Couldst thou not, Daddy, order me a cart,
A big one, with strong wheels, that I may take
My nice clothes which are lying dirty by
To wash them in the river? And besides
'Tis right that going to council with the kings
Thou shouldst be clad in spotless robes thyself:
And thou hast five sons living in thy halls—
Two married, and three lusty bachelors—
And they are always wanting new-washed clothes
For dances: I must think of all these things.'
  So said she; for she was ashamed to speak
Of happy marriage to her father; but
He fully understood, and answered her:
  'Nor mules I grudge thee, child, nor aught beside;
Go, and the slaves shall have thy waggon ready,
High and strong-wheeled, and fitted with a hood.'
  Then to the slaves he called, and they obeyed;
Outside, they made the light mule-waggon ready,
And led the mules close up, and yoked them to it;
Meantime the maiden brought out from her room
The shining robes, and on the polished cart
She laid them. And her mother filled a basket
With food of all sorts to the heart's content,
And dainties too: and in a goat-skin bottle
She poured some wine. Then the maid stepped up on
The cart; and in a flask of gold her mother
Gave her soft olive oil, that having bathed
She and her maids might rub themselves therewith.
Then the girl took the whip and shining reins
And flicked the mules to start: there was a clatter,
And on they sped unflagging with their load,
The raiment and the princess—not alone,
For with her also her attendants went.
  Now when they came to the bright running river,
Where there were troughs unfailing, into which
The strong clear water welled and then poured over,
Enough to wash the dirtiest garments clean,

The girls unharnessed from the cart the mules,
And shooed them off beside the eddying river
To browse on honeyed clover. In their arms
They took the raiment from the cart and bore it
To the dark pool and briskly trod it down
Inside the cisterns, racing one another.
Now having washed and cleansed the robes of stain
They spread them out in rows upon the shore,
Where most the breakers washed the pebbles clean.
Then the girls bathed and rubbed them well with oil,
And took their meal upon the river banks,
And waited for the clothes to dry in the sun.
Then when the princess and her maids had had
Their joy of food, they cast their veils away
And fell to playing ball, and to her mates
White-armed Nausicaa began the song.[1]

Even in a translation which—like all translations of Homer
—loses many of the qualities of the original, every reader can
get some pleasure from this. However much our twentieth-
century palate has been dulled for such simple stuff, we feel the
freshness of that early world, yet know that we are reading a
polished work of literature. We can see why critics throughout
the ages have marvelled at Homer, why Matthew Arnold finds
in these epics the four great merits of rapidity, plainness of
speech, plainness of thought, nobility. Read the poems as a
whole, and though some passages seem boring, there are other
features which no sensitive reader can miss: the tragedy of
Achilles, the comedy of life among the gods, the romance of
Odysseus' story; the characterisation—Hector, gentle father and
husband though a lion on the battlefield; Agamemnon, proud,
impulsive, overburdened with the task of managing his own
forces; Ajax, renowned for brawn but not for brain; Diomedes,
full of the dash and optimism of youth; old Nestor, wise but

[1] *Od.* vi, ll. 48-101. This and all other quotations from Homer are from
the translation by Sir William Marris (Oxford University Press).

incapable of giving brief expression to his wisdom; patient Penelope; Helen, beautiful, unhappy, a lonely stranger among the Trojans.

Unlike many works of ancient literature, the *Iliad* and *Odyssey* can be enjoyed without study, appreciated without penetrating analysis or critical dissection. For centuries the Greeks approached them in this uncritical way, assuming that Homer existed and that his characters and events were part of history. On similar assumptions—or no assumptions at all— millions of others have read the poems and enjoyed them. But look at them more critically, examine them in the probing light of modern knowledge, and works at first glance so simple become full of mystery. We are faced with all the complex problems of the 'Homeric question'.

Both *Iliad* and *Odyssey* are ascribed by tradition to a single poet, Homer, and each reads like a unity; yet they contain inconsistencies and contradictions almost incredible in the pro- duct of a single brain. A chieftain at one point killed by Menelaus later mourns his own son's death. The Greek camp sometimes has a wall and a moat, sometimes neither. The same incident happens to different characters, or even twice to the same character. There are differences of language between the *Iliad* and the *Odyssey*, and even in different sections of each poem. Homer himself is a shadowy figure about whom no certain facts have come down to us. The eight existing 'lives' of him all belong to the Christian era and are full of obvious fiction. Many cities claimed the distinction of being his birthplace. The poems themselves bear no stamp of any local patriotism, nor of any individual personality or individual style. It is the individuality of the translator, not of the Greek poet, that is reflected in each of the many translations.

Is all this compatible with individual authorship? Did Homer exist, or was he only the imaginary ancestor of the so-called

'Sons of Homer' who later recited the poems? Are the difficulties merely proof that even Homer nodded, or are *Iliad* and *Odyssey* compilations of ballads, the accumulated achievement of many hands?

Turn to another aspect of the problem. Since Schliemann over seventy years ago hewed his way down through the hill of Hissarlik and found the remains of Troy, archaeology has lifted these epics out of the realm of myth into that of fact. There can be no doubt now that a city of Troy existed—or rather, a number of cities. The sixth of the nine towns piled on the famous site bears the marks of sudden destruction and is probably the Ilion which the Greeks sacked. Not only have particular objects been unearthed like those the poems describe—a golden cup, boar's tusks from a helmet, a blue glass frieze, bronze spearheads of a particular type. Not only have some Homeric phrases—descriptions of armour and fighting, for example—gained new meaning through the discoveries which the archaeologist's spade has brought to light. Many of the main characteristics of the Homeric scene—the riches of Mycenae, for instance, or the importance of Crete—are now confirmed. Yet the equation does not work out. There is no complete correspondence between the picture of life in the *Iliad* and the *Odyssey* and any one phase of Greek culture. The picture itself is inconsistent, a mixture of features that belonged to different periods or places—if they ever existed at all. There is much that is clearly unhistorical. Many things are physically impossible, others out of place: episodes are set in the tenth year of the Trojan War which would obviously suit its beginning or early stages. Some of the stories of the *Odyssey* are found in the folk-lore of many lands.

Whether by one author or many, at what time and place were the poems brought into being? How are they related to history? How much of them is fact, how much fiction?

These two closely linked questions of authorship and relation to reality became a battleground of scholars 150 years ago. Increased knowledge has not stopped the academic conflict, and the dust it has raised has all too often obscured the merits of the *Iliad* and *Odyssey* themselves. But this is not a case where ignorance is bliss. Although we can sail with Odysseus or watch Achilles in the fight without identifying their creator or classifying them as history or fairy-tale, understanding and enjoyment of the poems are heightened, not lowered, by the insight into their origins which discussion has gradually brought.

First things first. The first thing about the Homeric poems is not the existence or non-existence of Homer, but the tradition out of which they grew. Even the most diehard champions of single authorship now admit that the material from which the *Iliad* and *Odyssey* are formed is the creation of many hands and many generations, that the general character of the poems has its roots in a convention—the first of the many conventions in Greek literature. The convention in turn was the product of the economic and social and political circumstances in which it arose. It is the convention, not the individual poet, that must be studied first.

The *Odyssey* itself gives us a picture of the epic convention in the making. Odysseus is being entertained by the Phaeacians and a feast has been prepared:

> Now drew the herald near and with him brought
> The loyal minstrel, whom the Muse loved dear,
> And good and evil gave him, of his sight
> She reft him, but she granted him sweet song.
> For him Pontonous the herald set
> A silver-studded chair amid the guests,
> By a tall pillar leaning it, and hung
> His clear-toned lyre upon a peg close by
> Above his head, and showed him how to lay
> His hands upon it. And at his side he placed

> A basket, a good table, and a cup
> Of wine to drink when so his heart inclined.
> So they put out their hands to the good fare
> That lay before them; but when they had had
> Their fill of food and drink, the Muse impelled
> The bard to sing the deeds of mighty men.[1]

This minstrel, Demodocus, is not unique. In Odysseus' own Ithaca there is Phemius, who is forced to entertain the suitors. Clearly it was the custom of Achaean chieftains, like soldier-chieftains in other ages, to maintain a 'singer', honoured for his divine inspiration but guided in his use of it by dependence on the prince's patronage. To a lyre accompaniment these minstrels tell the stories which will please their patrons best—short lays on contemporary or recent events.

> Men praise the most
> That song which comes the newest to their ears,

says Odysseus' son to his mother.[2] The minstrel, like more modern forms of entertainment such as the radio, must always be up-to-date.

The court minstrel is not the beginning of the story. In the *Iliad* Achilles sits in his tent and accompanies himself on the lyre while he sings of the glorious deeds of heroes. Once in the *Odyssey* a narrative lay of Demodocus is accompanied by the dancing of young men. Behind the professional singer and his conventionalised art scholars have placed the impromptu singing of the amateur, the warrior entertaining himself. Earlier still, narrative song may have evolved out of the primitive ritual combination of music, song and dance—a court offshoot from an original popular stock. But even if we venture no further back than Demodocus and Phemius, if we only consider the effect of a succession of generations of such bards, the sources

[1] VIII, ll. 62-73.   [2] *Od.* I, ll. 351-2.

of many features of Homeric poetry are clear. Some of them are shared by ballad poetry everywhere.

The minstrels did not write their songs. In the Homeric poems writing is mentioned only once, and then as something mysterious and abnormal. They improvised and memorised. The technique of improvisation was their 'gift from the Muses', the key to their art. But improvisation did not mean the creation of something completely new: on the contrary, it was only made possible by the use of what was already old. Invention and memory worked together. For impromptu construction of the 'newest song' the singer must have his materials ready to hand—his metre, his language adapted to the metre, his stock phrases, his stock descriptions of familiar things and events. Ordinary impromptu conversation in all languages is full of accepted and familiar turns of speech. So, of necessity, was the minstrel's song.

Here are the main items of the singer's technique as we find them in the *Iliad* and *Odyssey*:

The metre. The Homeric hexameter is a long line—a combination, some scholars say, of two short lines of choral song. Like blank verse in English, it has the two qualities most needed in narrative poetry: continuity and speed. Some of its features can be traced to the lyre accompaniment—evidently a simple affair, to which the verses were chanted rather than sung. As used in the *Iliad* and *Odyssey*, the hexameter is far beyond the experimental stage. It is a conventionalised, highly polished instrument of recitative.

The language of the poems is also neither primitive nor experimental. It is nearest to the Ionic dialect, but contains many Aeolic forms and some from other sources. Attempts have been made to find a place where such a mixture was in normal use, or to explain it as the result of translation from one dialect into another, but the whole character of the language is proof that they cannot succeed. Nor can a date be allotted to it: its mixture of several stages in the development of vocabulary and syntax shows that it belonged to no one time, as to no one place. What we have in the *Iliad* and *Odyssey* is no ordinary, everyday speech, but the heightened language of poetry—an artificial creation, with vocabulary and spelling shaped by generations of singers to suit their needs: above all, to suit the hexameter. Improvisation was an easier task when words themselves were moulded to meet the demands of verse.

Stock epithets. Like most ballad poetry, the *Iliad* and *Odyssey* have a list of conventionalised adjectives and phrases which are applied again and again to people and things, sometimes when far from appropriate. Achilles is usually 'swift-footed', Odysseus 'of many wiles', Zeus 'the cloud-gatherer'. Dawn is 'rosy-fingered', the sea 'loud-resounding' or 'wine-dark'. Here is another element which assisted the minstrel's memory and aided improvisation. Noun and epithet together formed a unit adapted to fill part of the hexameter line.

Repeated lines. The same function is fulfilled by other verbal repetitions on a larger scale. Stock lines recur whenever a familiar event takes place. The coming of the morning light:

> But when rosy-fingered Morning, daughter of Dawn, appeared . . .

An answer:

> So said he, and I answered him and said . . .

Death in battle:

> He fell with a crash and his armour clanged upon him . . .

Exhortation before a fight:

> Be men, my friends,
> Lay on with all your might!

Often whole sets of lines are repeated. A message stated once is reproduced in full by the messenger in the same words, and a common process like the donning of armour is described twice in the same terms. About one third of the twenty-seven thousand lines of the *Iliad* and *Odyssey* are repeated or contain repeated phrases. The reader of today is troubled by these repetitions. The critics of ancient Alexandria held that some of them must be interpolations. Some modern scholars have seen them as signs of multiple authorship. But all are wrong. For the minstrel, repeated phrases, lines, passages were an essential part of his technique. To his audience they brought satisfaction, not annoyance. New stories might be the most welcome, but they must be told in the old and familiar ways, established by tradition and worthy of repetition again and again.

Similes. Metaphor is far less common in Homeric epic than in some later Greek poetry: it would be out of keeping with the clarity, the 'plainness', of the conventional style. But similes are used some two hundred and twenty times in the course of the *Iliad* and the *Odyssey* to describe characters or events. They contain some of the best things in the poems—the description, for example, of two comrades standing side by side in battle:

> As in fallow land
> Two wine-dark oxen in complete accord
> Strain at the jointed plough, and round their horns
> Oozes much sweat: only the polished yoke
> Divides them as they struggle down the furrow
> Until the share cuts to the ploughing's end:
> So stood those two beside each other close.[1]

Or of a warrior's fall:

> Like a thriving shoot
> Of olive which a farmer cultivates
> In some lone place with ample water moistened,

[1] *Il.* XIII, ll. 703-8.

A fine and well-grown shoot; the breaths of all
The breezes toss it, and in blossom white
It bursts; but suddenly there comes the wind
In a great hurricane and wrenches it
Out of its pit and lays it low on earth;
E'en so did Menelaus son of Atreus
Slay Panthous' son of the good ashen spear.[1]

Similes on this scale are not common in early narrative verse. When we ask the source of them in Homeric epic, whether they are an 'early' or a 'late' element, we step on to violently disputed ground. But it seems likely that here again we are dealing with a conventional device, the origin of which probably lies in primitive habits of mind, while the reason for its survival is to be found in the technique of improvisation. In Greece as elsewhere, analogy came before logic in the development of thought. Before the growth of logical reasoning it was in comparison of the strange with the familiar, of the new with the old, that man found his easiest means of understanding and describing both his own experience and the external world. For the minstrel who wanted to add ornament to his song, to relieve a dull passage or intensify a dramatic one, what device was more natural than to develop the simple habit of analogy into a regular practice of his craft? On the lips of a Demodocus or a Phemius similes may have lacked the elaboration characteristic of them in the *Iliad* and *Odyssey*, but that in some form they used them there can be little doubt. Some of the Homeric similes closely resemble scenes in the art of Mycenaean times, and sometimes they fit none too well in the passages where they are introduced.

Hexameter, artificial language, stock epithets, repeated lines and similes were weapons in the professional minstrel's technical armoury, and when improvisation ceased to be a normal feature of the poet's art, these products of it still survived. The same

[1] *Il.* XVII, ll. 53-60.

background of improvised song accounts for other more general characteristics of the Homeric style: simplicity of expression, omission of unnecessary detail, clarity and straightforwardness of description and narrative. Three at any rate of the qualities praised by Matthew Arnold—rapidity, plainness of thought, plainness of diction—find their beginning here. Last but not least, the convention built up by the minstrels was a court product. As far back as we can trace it, story-telling in hexameters was an entertainment of that minority among the population to whom property and the use of serfs and slaves gave the means of being patrons of song and the leisure to listen to it. Though class division was less acute in the communities of these early days than in later times, epic poetry by tradition reflected the outlook and interests of the chieftain, not the peasant, the rulers of society, not the ruled.

The existence of an epic convention not only explains many particular features of the *Iliad* and *Odyssey*. It also puts the entire Homeric question in a different perspective. The twin problems of the authorship of the poems and their relation to history must now be seen in a new form: *if there was this background of the growth of a convention, in what way and at what stage did the Iliad and Odyssey emerge out of it in something like their present shape?* It is here that the conflict of opinion among scholars grows violent.

The easiest course is to trace the story backwards from the point at which we can be fairly sure the poems existed as we have them now. In all but minor details our text of the *Iliad* and *Odyssey* is probably the handiwork of the scholars of Alexandria in the third and second centuries B.C., who used new methods of collation and correction to produce a standard edition. Before their time, differences in different writers' quotations of the same Homeric passages show that many versions existed: possibly each man of letters made his own. But there was a limit to the variation. From the sixth century onwards, any tendency to change the poems was kept in check by the fact of public performance. They were presented amid scenes very different from either the library at Alexandria or Alcinous' court—at great public gatherings associated with festivals of the gods. The performers were 'rhapsodes', professional artists not attached to any one state, but moving from place to place. The musical accompaniment had gone, and the rhapsode had a staff instead of a lyre. Probably these 'Sons of Homer', as they called themselves, had their own written version of the epics, the treasured stock-in-trade of their craft. Tradition places the beginning of such performances before a mass audience in the time of the 'tyrants'. They took place in various states—Delos and Sicyon and Sparta, for example; possibly as far afield as Cyprus and Syracuse. At the Panathenaea, the great Athenian festival celebrated every four years, a competition was held between rhapsodes in which they took over from each other in relays till the poems had been performed complete—a practice scarcely possible without a more or less stable text. The bringing of 'Homer' to Athens was variously ascribed by later writers to Solon or Pisistratus or his younger son, Hipparchus. Whoever instituted the performances, it was probably the 'tyrants' who built them up into great spectacular occasions, attracting travellers to Athens and strengthening her claim to be foremost city of all Greece.

When we first meet the *Iliad* and *Odyssey* in history, then, the background amid which the epic convention developed has largely disappeared. Aristocracy is dead or dying. The *presentation* of epic poetry is already adapted to the new environment, the court minstrel has given place to the rhapsode, the select audience of banqueters to a mass meeting. Did the change of circumstances cause a change in the poems themselves as well as in the manner of their performance? Was the rhapsodes' text the first version of the *Iliad* and *Odyssey* in anything like their present form?

Yes, say some scholars. They accept the tradition mentioned by some late ancient writers, that it was Pisistratus who first brought about the creation of both epics by causing shorter lays to be put together and written down. Professor Murray names the genius who did it for him—the rhapsode Cynaethus of Chios.[1] Although the evidence is thin, the theory is tempting because it effectively explains the poems' great length, suited to the magnificence of the Panathenaea but not to the banqueting hall. But if it was at Athens and to glorify Athens that the dish was concocted, it is strange that it has not a more Athenian flavour. If a poet as late as the end of the sixth century was known to be the author, it is odd that nobody but an obscure chronicler of Alexandrian times mentions the fact. Strongest objection of all, the general character of the poems themselves is foreign to the age of the growth of commerce and the beginnings of democracy.

The general belief is that the two great epics were already moulded to something like their present form when they were recited at Athens or Delos or Sicyon. Their arrival at maturity must be placed earlier than Pisistratus or the sixth century B.C. A few commentators among both ancients and moderns have put it almost as early as the siege of Troy itself, postulating a Homer at the close of the Mycenaean age, contemporary or nearly contemporary with Agamemnon and Hector and Achilles. A less romantic course, but one more in accord with the evidence of ancient writers and the poems themselves, is to accept the testimony of Thucydides, who states that 'Homer existed long after the Trojan War',[2] and Herodotus, who says Homer and Hesiod lived 'four hundred years and no more' before himself.[3]

---

[1] *Rise of the Greek Epic*, ed. 4, p. 308.

[2] I, 3.   [3] II, 53.

For a date this gives us the ninth century B.C., two or three hundred years after the 'heroic age'. As to the place, the language of the poems and the extent of their geographical knowledge combine with ancient tradition in pointing to the Eastern coast of the Aegean, to Ionia. In the passing of those centuries, in the Ionian environment and its remoteness from the times and circumstances of the Trojan War, lies the explanation of much that is puzzling in the *Iliad* and *Odyssey*, the answer to several aspects of the 'Homeric question'. Many different constituents are combined in these epics. Cheek by jowl with more sophisticated stuff they contain primitive elements like the Catalogue of Ships (*Iliad* II) or lists of casualties—useful records when first drawn up, interesting to the scholar, but dreary to the reader of today. Poems whose components came into being at various times during two or three hundred years or more naturally vary in style, naturally reflect different and sometimes inconsistent material circumstances and ways of life. In the broadest sense the creation of the *Iliad* and *Odyssey* was the work of many generations. But it was round about 900 or 800 B.C. in Ionia that they received their more or less final form.

Recall for a moment the change which had come over the face of Greece during those intervening centuries. The new tide of invaders from the North—principally, the Dorians—had disintegrated Agamemnon's loose-knit military confederacy and thrown the whole Eastern Mediterranean into turmoil. Many wealthy Achaeans, fleeing before the storm, had migrated eastward across the Aegean taking with them their social organisation, their habits of life—and their songs. In Ionia among largely alien peoples they established new settlements which gradually became stable city-states. The old life went on, but in a minor key—more settled, more isolated, more peaceful, less glorious. Within society itself changes gradually took place. The chieftain was brought down to the level of his fellow-nobles, monarchy gave way to aristocracy. Between nobles and common people the gap increased. This background of a declining ruling class, looking not to the future but back over the years to a more glorious past, is the key to reconstruction of the way in which our *Iliad* and *Odyssey* grew out of earlier minstrelsy. If there was an individual Homer, we can give meaning and content to the empty name only by seeing him as a product, even a personification, of the qualities which this environment produced.

Let us see what these qualities were—how this version of the poems' relation to history explains their subject-matter, their length, the nature of their heroes, their outlook on society, their attitude towards the primitive, even the character of their gods.

In Ionia, doubtless, the nobles still had their singers, their court minstrels. Those who like such speculations can imagine Homer as one of them. They must still have used—and developed—the conventional methods and devices of their craft. But their subject had changed. Neither they nor their hearers could now be content with songs of the present or the recent past. Petty squabbles with neighbouring communities, the struggle to extract subsistence from the land, cattle-raids and tussles with local tribes—these offered no theme comparable with the glories of which Demodocus and Phemius had sung. The custom of the 'newest song' was replaced by repetition and enhancement of the old. The topics demanded now by the minstrels' patrons were the greatest exploits of the days when their adventurous Achaean ancestors were united and masters of their world. Improvisation gave way to tradition. As the art was handed down from generation to generation a whole collection of short lays of heroic times was created, in which the singer could begin his tale at any point. But there were two closely connected themes which had a special appeal to the audience and were treasured and developed beyond all the rest: first, the supreme example of their ancestors' united strength—the siege of Troy itself; second, the wanderings oversea which eventually had brought *émigrés* to Ionia —wanderings symbolised in the 'returns' of the heroes, and above all in the journey of Odysseus. Round the Trojan War and its sequel developed a saga familiar to any Ionian aristocrat. The Homeric epics do not explain the outlines of their story or introduce their main characters at length: it is assumed that they are already known. But saga in the form of short lays was not enough. These were topics for something grander than brief tales which in ballad fashion gave a bald account of events. The splendour of the subject, the increased leisure of the ruling class, the growing skill and rivalry of the minstrels called into being narrative verse which used the traditional saga as its material, but was constructed on more epic dimensions. In the course of the process both themes were enlarged and magnified far beyond historical reality. The *émigrés* looked back to the Trojan War as a crowded hour of glorious life, and made it more crowded than it could ever have been in fact. Events which must have belonged to different times and places were transformed into incidents of this one great campaign. The length of the siege was placed at ten years. The armies involved were swollen to an impossible size: although the remains of the sixth city of Troy cover only five acres, the *Iliad* numbers the defenders at 50,000 men. The nucleus of history behind the romance of the *Odyssey* seems even smaller than for the *Iliad*. Odysseus' travels also take ten years, and folk-lore and fiction have a bigger place than fact in his adventures on his way home.

Was there one outstanding poet who brought this development to a climax by selecting the material which makes up the *Iliad* and the *Odyssey* and producing them in something like their present form? In all probability there was, and his name may well have been Homer. The unity of each of the two epics points strongly to an individual author. But if he was outstanding in talent, he was not different in aims or method from others among

68

his contemporaries. He was not the one and only epic poet among a multitude of balladists, the unique genius who alone transformed brief ballads into works on a different scale. By the time of the *Iliad* and *Odyssey* the whole style of narrative verse had moved away from the ballad and acquired new dimensions, a new tone. The old simplicity and rapidity were not lost, but generosity of treatment was added to them. Both audience and minstrel—now a more conscious and sensitive artist—had the time and the inclination to dwell on the details of an important incident or speech. On a small scale the same trend was illustrated by the evolution of the simile. Surely it was in these more peaceful days that the epic simile acquired its leisurely tendency to dwell on details irrelevant to the comparison drawn, and developed into a work of art in its own right, a superb though not always pertinent vignette (no, the creator or creators of the *Iliad* and the *Odyssey* cannot have been blind) of the ploughing oxen, the shepherd by the fold, the smith at work in the forge.

Not only the minstrel's theme developed on lines that suited his aristocratic *émigré* audience, while the dimensions of his song were magnified to match. The same glorification of the remote past on which his hearers' imaginations loved to dwell affected also the characters of his story. It is true that no artificial glamour of the Hollywood brand surrounds the warrior heroes of the *Iliad* and *Odyssey*. Achilles and Hector have none of the romantic aura which hangs over the latest Hollywood star and stirs a frenzy of hero-worship in the film-fan's heart. Helen herself has no sex-appeal for the reader, though when they look at her the old men of Troy understand well why Trojans and Achaeans suffer years of hardship for her. The characters of these epics are real men and women, not figments of sentiment. But theirs is no ordinary stature. In the minds of lesser men who claimed descent from them, who as they listened to the singer must have identified themselves with Ajax or Odysseus or Diomede just as the modern cinema-goer momentarily endows himself with the voice of a Sinatra or the muscles of Tarzan of the Apes, the warriors of the Trojan War were transformed into supermen. Here are two of them in action:

> Then down Aeneas leapt with his long spear
> And shield, foreboding that the Achaeans might
> Drag off the dead from him, and o'er the corpse
> Strode lion-like, confiding in his strength.
> In front he held his spear and rounded shield,
> Eager to kill whoever came against him,
> And shouting terribly. But Tydeus' son
> Took in his hand a stone (a feat of strength)
> A stone which not two men, as men are now,
> Could carry, and yet he swung it easily
> Unaided; and he smote Aeneas with it
> Upon the hip . . .[1]

'Which not two men, *as men are now*, could carry.' The same thought reappears again and again. The Mycenaean gold cup found by archaeologists which closely resembles the cup of Nestor is of no great weight. But in the *Iliad*:

> That cup, when it was full, another man
> Could scarce have raised from table, but old Nestor
> Would lightly lift it.[2]

Ajax's shield of seven ox-hides and a layer of metal must have weighed over twenty stone.

By thus magnifying the heroes, the rulers of the Homeric world, the creators of the saga heightened the prestige of the heroes' supposed descendants, the rulers of Ionia. But with rare exceptions it was only on the rulers that they shed their splendour. Although society in the ninth century B.C., as in the 'heroic age', was not so divided against itself that noble was

[1] *Il.* v, ll. 297-305.   [2] xi, ll. 636-7.

entirely remote from peasant, although to some extent both lived
the same life and shared the same activities and interests, although
the similes are often glimpses of simple folk and everyday
processes, not only of princely pursuits, elsewhere the aristocratic
outlook of the singers' patrons is everywhere in evidence. When
the doings of common folk enter into the picture, they are seen
and described from outside: there is no talk here of motives or
attitudes, as with Achilles or Agamemnon. The one notable
exception is the loyal swineherd Eumaeus, so essential to the
story of the *Odyssey*, but even he turns out to have been a king's
son carried off by slave-raiders in years gone by. In battle the
armies are mentioned, advancing 'like waves on the sea', but it
is the champions who count. In counsel the chieftains are everything, the common people nowhere. When at an assembly of
the Achaean army one of 'the common sort' does raise his voice
above his station and oppose his betters, he is caricatured as
violently as any 'agitator' of today:

> The most ill-favoured man who had come to Troy;
> Bow-legged, with one foot lame and shoulders hunched
> Round on his chest; his head with its thin crop
> Was pinched on top: he was abominated
> By both Achilles and Odysseus, whom
> He used to rail at. But he turned his taunts
> And screamed at noble Agamemnon now.[1]

Thersites—'the impudent one' is the meaning of his name—is
doing no more than Achilles, who also objects to continuing the
fight and to the conduct of Agamemnon. But Odysseus strides
up to the 'trouble-maker' and gives him a lesson just as the
Ionian landowner might put any upstart peasant in his place:

> 'If ever again I find thee
> Playing the fool like this, let not my head
> Sit on my shoulders, and no more let me

[1] *Il.* ii, ll. 216-22.

Be called the father of Telemachus,
Unless I take and strip thy garments off,
Mantle and cloak, that hide thy nakedness,
And beat thee like a dog and send thee forth
Out of the meeting, yelping to the ships.'
Then with the staff he beat him on the back
And shoulders. And Thersites cowered down
And dropped big tears, and on his back rose up
A bloody wale beneath the staff of gold.[1]

Preservation of the glorious past, even in an idealised form, meant exclusion of the present, an effort to keep true to traditional ideas of the 'heroic age'. Though in some spheres—dress and methods of burial, for example—archaeology has proved the Homeric picture wrong, there can be no doubt that the epic poet, like the modern writer of historical novels, consciously practised archaism. The *Iliad* and *Odyssey* make no reference to Greek settlements east of the Aegean. There is one mention of the Dorians, but in a passage likely to have been added at a late date.[2] The similes, it is true, often reflect customs of the ninth century B.C. or thereabouts: the eating of fish and birds, milk and cheese; the use of the trumpet, and of iron as the normal hard metal; the riding of horses or use of four-horsed chariots. But in the narrative the heroes eat roast meat and drink wine, drive two-horsed chariots, fight with bronze weapons. The old days are brought back again—except for what would give offence to the Ionian aristocrats, more sophisticated than the Achaean warrior-chiefs. One of the most striking features of these poems is the comparative absence of the primitive—an absence more marked in the *Iliad* and *Odyssey* than in many later works of Greek literature. The reason for it lies partly in the outlook of the Ionian *émigrés*, partly in the character of the 'heroic age' itself.

As the Achaeans developed from comparatively primitive

[1] *Il.* II, ll. 258-68.   [2] *Od.* XIX, l. 177.

immigrant tribes into the masters of Mycenaean civilisation, their ruling class acquired other loyalties which superseded the tribal ties of kinship. In their own communities, their position depended mainly on wealth, and on the military leadership which brought them the lion's share of booty and increased their wealth. Together they formed an international princely caste, bound to each other by their military confederacy, by obligations of hospitality, sometimes by marriage, and ignoring or defying the traditions and prejudices of tribalism. Their descendants three centuries later had lost this international outlook, but had other reasons for keeping aloof from all that seemed primitive and uncivilised. To them the Dorians who drove their ancestors from the mainland were uncultured savages, though in fact their distant cousins. Their new settlements in the East were hemmed in by alien peoples, islands of Hellenic culture on the edge of a sea of barbarism. Among the 'common sort' the old primitive strains doubtless lived on, to emerge once more in literature in more democratic days. But unlike their own peasantry, still more in contrast to the peoples around them, the nobles cultivated a refinement and sophistication which are reflected in the *Iliad* and *Odyssey*. Although the patriarchal family and its great household are a commonplace of the poems—King Priam of Troy and his fifty sons and twelve daughters and their wives and husbands all live under the same roof—references to 'tribes' and 'clans' are rare and vague, and no religious rites are attached to them. At one point the aged Nestor advises Agamemnon to 'marshal his men by clans and tribes',[1] but it is not clear whether this reveals the actual organisation of the Achaean army or is a reminiscence—one of many from Nestor's lips—of the customs of earlier days.

Even the accounts of warfare which fill so many pages of the poems were modified by the same tendency. For the modern

[1] *Il.* ii, l. 362.

reader, despite or perhaps because of modern wars, the *Iliad* is
too full of blood and the stripping of corpses, there are too many
matter-of-fact descriptions of wounds and violent death. He is
inclined to skip the battle-scenes, or turn to the *Odyssey*. For
the ancient audience, it was in fighting that the heroes were most
glorious. Diomedes, Patroclus, Ajax, Achilles reached their
greatest moments in battle. It was to heighten portrayals of
battle that similes were most used—sometimes, whole series of
similes. Yet the Ionians shared something of the same squeamish-
ness as ourselves. Though the martial deeds of their warrior
ancestors were meat and drink to their descendants' self-respect,
an unmixed and unseasoned diet of battle and slaughter was too
much for the fastidious palates of more peaceful days. The poets
lifted the fighting on to a higher and more chivalrous plane.
Some of the crudities and brutalities of the traditional story were
toned down or quickly passed over or described only to be
condemned. Digressions relieved the monotony of the fighting.
The long and bloody struggle which fills the early books of the
Iliad is interrupted by diversions like the meeting of Glaucus and
Diomedes or Hector's visit to his family, and interwoven with
the semi-comic activities of the gods. The *Odyssey* deserts the
battlefield for travel and romance.

Nowhere is the absence of the primitive outlook more
remarkable than in the sphere where we might most expect to
find it present—Homeric religion, the most puzzling side of the
poems to the reader of today. In one aspect of religion these
epics follow the general rule of Greek literature: ritual is respected and meticulously observed. The boldest Homeric warrior
is careful in making the correct sacrifices and drink-offerings to
the gods. Before a great event, at times of crisis or rejoicing,
the customary ceremonies are the heroes' first concern. Hector,
who on one occasion expresses contempt for divination, will not
pour a libation to Zeus with unwashed hands. By Patroclus' great

74

funeral pyre—'a hundred feet this way and that'—and as prelude to the funeral games in his honour, Achilles slaughters
not only sheep and oxen, but four horses, two of the dead man's
dogs, and twelve Trojan prisoners. The original motive of the
burial rite—the dead man's use of the animals and slaves after
death—was forgotten in an age of cremation, but the ritual
remained.

On this point the *Iliad* and *Odyssey* are in line with Pindar or
Aeschylus or Sophocles, with a characteristic which (as far as
we can judge) also marked religion before the 'heroic age'. But
turn to the sphere of belief, and the picture is different. Ritual
apart, the religion of the Homeric poems is distinct from what
preceded and what followed: it lacks the primitive strains which
occur in both. There is little reference to magic in Homer, little
talk of local spirits or deities. Except for Achilles' slaughter of
the twelve Trojans (and even this is condemned) there is no
mention of human sacrifice. Except for Odysseus' tale of the
monstrous Cyclops, stories of celestial or mortal cannibalism or
gruesome mutilations of the gods, common elsewhere in Greek
mythology, make no appearance here. Rites of purification or
expiation play a small part compared with later days. Most
striking contrast of all, there is little sign of ancestor-worship,
religious counterpart of the primitive emphasis on kinship. There
is no worship of the dead, great or humble: in these epics of the
deeds of heroes there is no hero-cult. The *Iliad* and *Odyssey* are
inconsistent in their view of existence after death. On this as on
more material topics, conflicting views stand side by side. In the
dark 'house of Hades' which Odysseus visits beyond the edge of
our world, the seer Tiresias still retains his wits and powers of
prophecy: though Heracles' ghost is there, he himself, we are
told, feasts among the immortal gods. But these are the exceptions. For the most part the great warriors, supermen in life,
are feeble creatures once they have left it—mere shadows of their

former selves, which flit like dreams or squeak like bats. The
shade of Achilles rates their existence lower than the life of the
most oppressed class on earth:

> 'Speak not to me of death, renowned Odysseus,
> In comfortable words! Fain would I choose,
> So might I live on earth, to serve as hireling
> Some other man—a landless man, a poor man—
> Than be a king o'er all the dead and perished.'[1]

Such 'strengthless heads' have no power over the living, no
claim to worship. Odysseus is afraid at their 'wondrous clamour',
but as a living man he is clearly superior to them all. The burning
of Patroclus is followed by funeral games which fill most of a
book of the *Iliad*, but when his ghost appears to Achilles it, too,
vanishes 'like smoke with a shrill cry'.

Much that is commonplace elsewhere in Greek literature,
therefore, is lacking here. What remains? A theology more
simple, more systematised, more sophisticated: the gods of
Olympus—Zeus, Hera, Athena, Apollo, Artemis, Poseidon,
and the rest. True, at times we read of other powers nearer to the
primitive conception of *mana*—'fate', 'blind folly', a 'god' or
'spirit' without name. On occasion, 'fate' is stronger than Zeus.
But for the most part it is the Olympians who dominate the scene.
Their origins, as we have seen, are various and debatable. Only
Zeus can with certainty claim Aryan descent—the sky-god of
immigrants from the Northern plains, whose weapon is the
lightning and whose gift the rain. His consort, Hera, may be
Minoan, and their marriage symbolise the fusion of the patriarchal
culture from the North with the matrilineal society of pre-
Hellenic days. Others also may have their roots in Minoan-
Mycenaean times. But however remote and even primitive their
beginnings, they have travelled far before their appearance in
Homeric epic. Out of this miscellany of theological material

[1] *Od.* xi, ll. 488-91.

evolved the most anthropomorphic deities in the history of mankind. In stock epithets applied to them—'cow-eyed' Hera, 'owl-eyed' Athena, 'wolf-born' Apollo—in their frequent transformations into bird or beast, some of the Olympians carry traces of a former existence in animal form, but no gods could be more modelled in the image of man than these as we meet them in the pages of the *Iliad* and the *Odyssey*. They feel human emotions—pleasure and pain, jealousy, partisanship. Their life and social organisation mirror those of the upper strata of heroic society. They are not creators but conquerors, who have taken over the world from the defeated Kronos. Each has his kingdom, but Zeus has the greatest and is lord of the rest. On Olympus—their acropolis—his palace is loftier and bigger than the others. They meet in council, but there and in all their relations they are more quarrelsome and unruly than the chieftains in the Greek camp: even between Zeus and Hera there is continual bickering. The gods ride in chariots. They fight and are hurt, but they have *ichor* for blood and their wounds are easily healed. They feast on ambrosia and drink nectar 'all day till the setting of the sun', while Apollo holds the lyre and the Muses sing. Some among them act as servants—Iris or Hermes as messenger, Hebe as cup-bearer—but there is no place for the lower classes, the peasant or the serf, among this divine aristocracy. Even Hephaestus the smith, lame since Zeus threw him from heaven to earth, is a figure of fun, of 'Homeric laughter'.

Whether something like this Homeric picture of divine society existed in the days of the siege of Troy or whether it came to maturity in Ionia we cannot tell, but clearly it was long established by the time the *Iliad* and *Odyssey* reached their present form. The Olympians have become gods of literature. Like metre, language, similes, they are part of the epic technique. Their life has become inextricably interwoven with the story of the Trojan War. Except for Zeus, they are divided by the struggle into two hostile camps, and their fighting on one side or the other culminates in a battle among the gods themselves. 'Who of the gods set on those two to strife?' asks the first page of the *Iliad* in beginning the story of Achilles and Agamemnon: from then on events are constantly open to Olympian intervention and control. Time after time a fatal climax in battle is avoided and the story is prolonged because a god or goddess turns aside the spear or throws a protecting cloud round a threatened favourite. But it is only the chieftains who are thus befriended. The gods, themselves members of a community with upper classes and no peasantry, mix almost exclusively with the upper layers of human society. For the Ionian singer and his aristocratic audience the effect of all this mythological machinery is to heighten still more the glory of the heroes, to raise them still further above the 'common sort' by mingling them with the immortals and making them objects of divine love or hate. Achilles' mother is a goddess and his armour is the work of Hephaestus. So is Agamemnon's sceptre, a gift to his forebears from Zeus.

In many ways, of course, the gods and goddesses are superior to the human warriors and their women. They can move faster, become invisible, change their shape. The shout of Poseidon or Ares is as loud as that of nine or ten thousand men. They do 'easily' things which for men are difficult or impossible. Above all, they are deathless. But there is one region to which this superiority does not extend: the sphere of morality. The morality of the Homeric heroes is not ours. They are plunderers, pirates, stealers of women and cattle. In a civilised and settled society they would sooner or later have ended up in gaol. But Diomedes and Achilles and even Odysseus have a moral code of their own, and they live up to it far better than the gods. Although to some extent, particularly in the *Odyssey*, the gods are guardians of right and wrong, punishers of injustice or insolence, even benefactors of mankind, their main function in relation to the human race is to fulfil their favourite's desires and frustrate his enemies, not to uphold morality. They themselves are often cunning and deceitful, fickle and treacherous, cruel and cowardly. Here is the most puzzling aspect of Homer's gods for the reader of today. Behind it lies an inconsistency which only later literature tried to solve: the antithesis between the Olympian deities' developed form and their primitive origins.

While the creators of epic made their gods like men, tradition gave them attributes more acceptable in natural forces than in human beings. Lightning may be expected to strike both the righteous and the unrighteous, but an anthropomorphic hurler of such lightning will be accused of injustice and cruelty. Local fertility rites call forth no condemnation, but the reader may be shocked when they are collected together to become the innumerable love-affairs of a vigorously masculine and prolific Zeus. Writers of more earnest days—Pindar, Aeschylus, Euripides—sought various solutions to this puzzle of the 'immorality' of the gods. The *Iliad* and *Odyssey* make no attempt at a solution. They avoid the difficulty: first, by ignoring the most primitive tales of the deities; second, by humour. Divine attributes and stories which troubled the mind of fifth-century Athens are used among the sophisticated Ionian aristocracy as material for comic relief. Homer does not laugh at his heroes, except perhaps Nestor with his senile flow of words. Although the ancient commentator's description of the *Odyssey* as a 'comedy of manners' is often not far off the mark, there is little of the mock-heroic in the poems. It is chiefly among the gods that we find comedy—in their squabbles and tears, in their ludicrous battle, in the list of Zeus' amours or his challenge to his fellow-deities to a celestial tug-of-war. Ancient traditions about the gods are transformed into tales of fun. For the modern historian the mystic marriage of

Zeus and Hera may symbolise a union of peoples, but in the *Iliad* it becomes a vamping scene in which the lord of the gods is seduced into sleep and forgetfulness to distract his attention from the war. How different from the relations between Hector and Andromache! The dignity of the *émigrés'* heroic ancestors is raised all the higher by the antics of Olympus.

I have said something of the technique of the *Iliad* and *Odyssey*, their metre, language, tricks of style: something also of the effect of time and circumstance on the length of the poems, their subject-matter and their treatment of it, their characters, human and divine. All these are elements which go to make the poems what they are, yet in none lies the quality which above all distinguishes them from other early epics and gives them greatness. We still lack the keystone of the arch. To find it, we must turn yet again to the all-important contrast between the origins of the material of the poems and the time and place in which they reached their maturity. In the sphere of mythology and in parts of the *Odyssey* that contrast produced comedy. But elsewhere the same cause led to another result, a quality which rouses tears rather than a smile: pathos, tragedy, call it what you will. No single term can describe it, but it is there. Because the *Iliad* has more of it than the *Odyssey*, the *Iliad* is the greater poem of the two.

Singer and aristocratic audience in ninth- or eighth-century Ionia looked back to heroic days, conjured up the exaggerated glories of a distant past. But deep in their consciousness was the knowledge that these things *were* past, that such times were gone never to return. The Trojan War and its sequel are seen from a distance, and although some figures in the picture are magnified far beyond any possible historical reality, although the proportions are distorted to suit aristocratic prejudice, the perspective has a depth which no contemporary document could achieve.

Homer does not take sides. The heat of battle is over, the partisanship of the moment forgotten, and the poets of later and more
peaceful years see not only the glory, but the pity of it all. All
the sorrow of war is summed up in the brief glimpse we catch
of the Trojan washing-troughs past which Achilles pursues
Hector to his death:

> There by the springs are roomy washing-troughs,
> Fine troughs of stone, where in old days of peace
> Or ever the sons of the Achaeans came,
> The ladies and fair daughters of the Trojans
> Would wash their shining robes. Thereby they ran,
> One fleeing, one pursuing.[1]

No moment of struggle or adventure is so intense but that we
may pause to watch its wider consequences—the spreading
ripples after the stone is dropped. When Diomedes is tearing like
a lion through the minor warriors of the Trojan army—

> Then he went in chase of Xanthus
> And Thoön, sons of Phaenops, both well-loved.
> And Phaenops was worn out with sad old age
> And had no other son who should inherit
> The wealth he left. There Diomedes slew
> Them both and took their lives, and left their father
> Laments and melancholy memories, since
> They did not live for him to welcome them
> Home from the war: but cousins shared his wealth.[2]

No villain is so evil but that in some way he can stir our sympathy—not even the monstrous Polyphemus, who devours
Odysseus' men. The blinded giant speaks to his favourite ram
as it leaves his cave with Odysseus—'Noman', as he has called
himself to trick the Cyclops—clinging beneath its belly:

> 'Old ram, why is it, pray, thou art the last
> Of all the flock to leave the cave? Of old
> Thou wert not wont to lag behind the sheep,

[1] *Il.* xxii, ll. 153-7. [2] *Il.* v, ll. 152-8.

> But with thy bounding stride wert far the first
> To hurry home to fold at eventide;
> But now art last of all! Thou mournest surely
> For thy lord's eye, which a bad man put out,
> He and his scurvy fellows.[1]

No hero is so great but that he is doomed, and the prospect or fact of inevitable death, emphasised by the deathlessness of the gods, gives even these supermen a humanity loftier and more memorable than all their prowess in the fight. Achilles, whose early fate—repeatedly forecast in the *Iliad*—typifies the destiny hanging over them all, never touches us more nearly than when in Hades Odysseus has brought him good news of his son:

> 'So said I, and the ghost of swift Achilles
> Departed o'er the field of asphodel
> With mighty strides, rejoicing in that I
> Had told him of his son's pre-eminence.'[2]

Never in the *Iliad* do we remember Hector better than when he leaves the battle to visit his infant son and his wife. He foresees death for himself, slavery for Andromache, and then—

> So glorious Hector said, and stretched his arms
> To take his son: but the child cried and huddled
> Close to the breast of his neat-girdled nurse,
> Feared at his father's looks, scared by the bronze
> And plume of horse's hair which in his eyes
> Wagged from above the helmet horribly.
> At that his father and his mother laughed,
> And glorious Hector snatched his helmet off
> And laid the glowing thing on earth, and then
> Kissed his dear son and danced him on his arm
> And spoke a prayer to Zeus and all the gods:
> 'Zeus, and ye other gods, ordain that this
> My son may be as I am, excellent
> Among the Trojans, and as great of strength
> And be a mighty king of Ilios;

[1] *Od.* IX, ll. 447-54.   [2] *Od.* XI, ll. 538-40.

82

> So people, when he comes from war, may say:
> "He is far better than his father was":
> And slay his man and carry home the spoils
> Blood-red, and make his mother's heart rejoice.'
>   So saying, in his wife's arms Hector laid
> His son. She took him to her fragrant breast
> Smiling through tears.[1]

This, perhaps, is pathos. But give the same approach different material, let it work on a larger scale, and it creates tragedy. The tragedy of Achilles, central theme of the *Iliad*, is as dramatic as any play of the fifth-century Athenian theatre. Achilles is not only—as his contemporaries might have portrayed him—the greatest fighter of the Trojan War, the pillager of cities and ravisher of women. The eyes of a later and more sophisticated age endow him with superhuman bravery and strength, it is true; but they see him also as a human being, whose character brings his own moral downfall—and his redemption. The insulted pride which makes him withdraw from the struggle leads him from sin to sin, disaster to disaster. He rejects the overtures of the Greeks when they come to repair the wrong done to him. He lets his friend Patroclus go in his own place to the battle, and so sends him to his death. Mad for revenge, he kills Hector and outrages his corpse. All this is degradation on degradation. Only at the last does he save himself by allowing Priam to move him to pity and letting the old man take the body of his son. This individual drama develops against the background of the larger tragedy of Troy itself, foredoomed to destruction by the crime of Paris—a tragedy continually heightened by pictures of the city's women and children and old men.

It is this aspect of the *Iliad* and (to a lesser degree) of the *Odyssey* which more than any other brings the poems into the forefront of great literature. Some see in it the strongest ground

[1] *Il.* vi, ll. 466-84.

for belief in a single author. Only the finer sensitiveness of an exceptional individual, they argue, could have seen the drama latent in the traditional tale. The claim may well seem reasonable to the modern mind, but here again the individual poet can only be seen as a product of his times. Critics who take for granted the concepts of an individualist civilisation are no proper judges of the possibilities of collective production of literature or art. The main source of the greatness of the *Iliad* and the *Odyssey* does not lie in the genius of a single individual. It lies in the tradition built up by generations of singers, in the changing environment amid which they worked. The growth of the convention of narrative poetry gave Homeric verse its freshness, its simplicity, its speed. The Ionian aristocracy among which it reached its maturity, looking back on the times of the Trojan War as a more splendid past, sophisticated in its attitude towards the gods, glorifying the heroes yet deeply conscious of their humanity and their feebleness in the face of death, added still greater qualities to the material inherited from earlier days: epic dimensions, magnificence and subtlety of character, laughter and pathos, comedy and tragedy. The old and the new might have clashed, as we shall see later in the work of Euripides. But in moulding the epic they worked together to produce two of the greatest poems the world possesses.

The *Iliad* and *Odyssey*, of course, were not the only products of the verse convention brought into being by Demodocus, Phemius and their like. These two great epics outlasted all others because they alone were recited at the Panathenaea, and because in any case they were the fittest to survive. But generations of court singers had built up a vast mass of further material—short lays on other incidents of heroic times, other tales of mythology. Some time after the creation of the *Iliad* and *Odyssey*, when the environment in which they grew to greatness had changed and the art of narrative poetry was already past its best, this material was collected into epics modelled on the two masterpieces, but shorter, more mechanical, less generous in treatment of characters or theme. The topics covered were the whole range of legend, the minstrels' entire repertoire: the mythical origins of the universe, the conflicts of gods and giants, the saga centring on Thebes, the rest of the Trojan War and the return of the other heroes—everything except the ground covered by the *Iliad* and *Odyssey* themselves. These first great achievements were to be supplemented, not repeated. The scholars of Alexandria introduced order into this chaos, arranging all these works to form a kind of epic history of the world down to the death of Odysseus —the official close, as they saw it, of the heroic age. Later still the series became known as the *Epic Cycle*. The names and themes of the Trojan section of the *Cycle* are known to us through a commentator of the time of the Roman Empire, but of the poems themselves—apart from the *Iliad* and *Odyssey*—only a few pages of fragments still survive. Time has been kinder—in some cases, deservedly so—to thirty-four *Homeric Hymns* which we still have more or less complete today: hexameter pieces in honour of one or other of the Olympian gods. The shorter of them are clearly preludes for use by rhapsodes at the beginning of their epic recitations. In the longer ones, some of which come near to the true Homeric standard, the prelude has developed into a separate art form: the 'hymn' has become a short mythological epic in its own right.

Late Greek writers attributed these poems to various authors of whom we otherwise know little. In earlier times all were regarded as the work of Homer himself or his disciples. But several poems of the epic type still extant were never associated with the name of Homer: earliest and most interesting, the *Works and Days*. In metre and language this thirty-page medley of verse is close to the *Iliad* and *Odyssey*. Stock epithets and

7

phrases and even whole lines are repeated. Though the movement is often rough instead of smooth, sluggish instead of flowing, clearly we have here a product of the same convention which was followed by the singers of the glories of the Trojan War. But turn from technique to content, and we are far from the Ionian banqueting hall. Main topics of the *Works and Days* are those from which the poem gets its name—advice to the farmer on the need for work and how work should be done, precepts for lucky and unlucky days. Prefixed to this are mythical explanations of why work is necessary—the story of Pandora and of the Five Ages of Man. Other ingredients complete the mixture, but it is no Homeric dish. This is no half-imaginary tale for the entertainment of aristocrats. 'I would tell of true things', says the author (assuming for the moment that there was a single author). His object is not to please or to amuse, but to teach, in the narrow sense of the word—to impart useful information and advice. Like the Catalogue of Ships in the *Iliad*, the *Works and Days* is near to the primitive utilitarian use of verse. It was composed not for leisured nobles living largely in bygone times, but for farming folk concerned with the needs of the moment—an audience troubled less by the thought of death, but much more by the problem of subsistence. The heroic age—fourth among the Five—is past and gone, and sheds no glamour over the present:

> For now is a race of iron; they win no respite by day
> From labour and sorrow; each night out of life death
>   plucks them away.[1]

Life is grim, life is earnest. When we pick up the *Works and Days* after reading the story of Nausicaa, obviously we turn to metal of a different stamp.

[1] Ll. 176-7. This and all other quotations from the *Works and Days* are from the translation by A. S. Way (Macmillan and Co., Ltd.).

What was the origin of this strange work? Again we are
confronted with a problem and a controversy. Much of the
Works and Days reads like a scrap-book of verse. It has far less
unity than the *Iliad* or the *Odyssey*. Yet there is far more circum-
stantial evidence of individual authorship. According to Greek
tradition, the poem was the creation of Hesiod, of the mainland
territory of Boeotia. Herodotus, as we have seen, makes him
contemporary with Homer. Other versions of his date place him
in the tenth, ninth, or eighth century B.C. The poem itself gives
us some details of his life and origins. His father was a native
of Aeolis on the Eastern side of the Aegean, whither his ancestors
must once have fled as refugees. Forced by poverty to return
across the sea, he settled as a farmer in Boeotia in a 'wretched
hamlet', Ascra,

Which in winter is bleak, is in summer oppressive, is never kind.[1]

On the father's death his two sons, Hesiod and Perses, quarrelled
over the division of his farm, and by bribing the local nobles who
acted as judges Perses (to whom the poem is addressed) gained
the larger share—only to waste it until he was forced to beg from
Hesiod himself.

Some scholars question the existence of Hesiod. The personal
reminiscences, it is said, are fictions, Perses 'a lay figure for the
didactic epos to preach at'.[2] The poem is disjointed, a mere
collection of elements from different sources. But if disjointed-
ness is to disprove individual authorship, many modern as well
as ancient writers must be convicted of fraud. It is true that the
Works and Days as we have it is likely to be the work of more
than one hand—a written collection of material handed down
orally before it reached this form. Here there was no ceremonial
public recitation to crystallise and stabilise the text. But in the

[1] Ll. 639-40.
[2] Murray, *Ancient Greek Literature*, p. 53.

supposition that the core of the material came from an individual with the background ascribed to Hesiod lies the easiest explanation of the poem. Although some kind of primitive hexameter may have survived independently on the mainland of Greece, the chief characteristics of the manner of the *Works and Days* are imported from the home of the epic convention: the technique of the tale chanted in the banqueting-hall has been applied to a very different message addressed to a very different audience. The matter of the poem is the product of the Boeotian environment and of the author's personal difficulties, and doubtless includes local folk-lore and folk-wisdom. Certainly the whole tone of the work, its entire outlook on life, fit an author with such a background and in such an environment. If his biography was invented to suit the poem, the job was done extraordinarily well. Not only are the descriptions of nature and the seasons what we should expect from such a source—June 'when the artichoke flowers, and the chirping grasshopper sits in a tree', winter days 'fit to skin an ox', when the north wind blows over the earth. The whole political, social, economic atmosphere is that of the 'Age of Iron' after the Dorian invasion. The local background is small and isolated. For those below the rank of the nobles life is a continual struggle to wrest a living from the land, and competition is keen. They turn reluctantly to seafaring and trade as a means of supplementing their meagre income. The author himself is evidently a farmer. He makes no mention of horses—they belong to the sphere of the *Iliad*, the existence of the wealthy aristocrat—but he possesses his own piece of land, pays hired labourers, owns slaves. Though he grumbles at his hardships, he is a conservative, not a revolutionary. He puts forward no alternative to the prevailing way of life. His ideal state is one in which 'women bear children like their parents'.[1] For him the sole solution to the problems of existence, the sole

[1] L. 235.

escape from its woes, is to 'fill his barns' by thrift and, above all, by work:

> Who addeth to that which he hath, keeps wolf-eyed hunger at bay:
> And though to a little thou add but a little, yet never cease
> Doing this, full soon to a goodly pile will thy little increase . . .
> So then if thine heart in thy breast desireth wealth's increase,
> Thus do, and with labour on labour toil without surcease.[1]

Against the local aristocracy—perhaps descendants of invading Dorians—the author has bitter complaints, but he makes no suggestion that they should not be there. His one cry for change is not revolutionary, although it could lead towards revolution. It is the denunciation of 'crooked judgements', the call for 'justice'—the middle-class demand which in one community after another led to the codification of law. The creator of the *Works and Days* has not got justice from men, but he is confident that sooner or later he will get it from heaven. Though his verse, like its Ionian prototype, is full of the Olympian gods, they have none of the playfulness of the Homeric deities. He needs them too deeply to use them as comic relief. From the first lines onwards, Zeus is the guardian of the right. And alongside the inhabitants of Olympus there is not only emphasis on ritual, but primitive superstitions such as we do not find in Homer but would expect in the countryside, from oddly-phrased warnings about paring the nails to the list of lucky and unlucky days. When we turn from the *Iliad* and *Odyssey* to the *Works and Days* we not only find ourselves in a different part of the Greek world—the dull and backward mainland instead of sophisticated Ionia. We are in the midst of a different class from Achilles or Odysseus or Nausicaa or the aristocrats who claimed to be their descendants. We are seeing a side of life which the Homeric epics ignore.

To Hesiod, as to Homer, tradition ascribed many poems

[1] Ll. 361-3, 381-2.

which cannot have been one and the same author's work—probably selections from material handed down orally, the ultimate origin of which is unknown. Some dealt with the same kind of subject-matter as the *Works and Days*. Others were of the 'list' type—catalogues of women and their offspring, for example, useful for genealogical purposes though doubtless wearisome to hear. Of this class the sole survivor is the *Theogony*, a dreary account of the origins and history of the gods from Chaos down to the reign of Zeus. Mutilation, cannibalism, all the mythological crudities avoided by Homer are included here. The *Theogony*, or parts of it, may conceivably be by the same author as the *Works and Days*, though if so his attitude towards the nobles has changed: now, princes are 'of Zeus'. At any rate, the poem was probably in existence by 700 B.C. Much later, and certainly not by Hesiod, but less like a scrap-book and more like a single poem, is the *Shield of Heracles*, a brief 'heroic' epic which brings us back to close imitation of the *Iliad*—subject-matter, divine machinery, even the accumulation of similes to heighten the tension of a battle scene.

The mass of verse from which these specimens have reached us is often described as the work of the 'Boeotian School', as opposed to the 'Ionian School'. Antiquity symbolised the contrast by developing a reference to a poetical competition in the *Works and Days* into an obviously apocryphal story of a contest in song between Hesiod and Homer themselves. Boeotian epic, the special product of the mainland of Greece, had an influence which reappears in many places in later poetry. But on the mainland as well as in Ionia, indeed throughout the Greek-speaking world, the brilliant Homer tradition rather than the gloomy sobriety of Hesiod was the inheritance that most affected life and literature. In its origins narrative song had been the amusement of the leisure hours of aristocrats—hours which came rarely, as Hesiod's picture shows, to those of lesser means.

The disintegration of aristocracy and the rise in Ionia of tyrants dependent on support from the East, unlikely to favour anything so national and Panhellenic as a heroic story of the Trojan War, brought the decline of epic in the region where it was born. But they did not end its importance to Greece as a whole: on the contrary, the sequel was popularisation of epic recitation, the spread of the knowledge and appreciation of Homer to all other parts of Greece and all classes of citizens. The prime movers in the change, as we have seen, were also 'tyrants'; above all, Pisistratus, who doubtless hoped to revive under Athenian leadership the Panhellenism of heroic days, and was as eager to strengthen the epic tradition as the tyrants of Ionia were to suppress it. The rhapsode declaiming before the crowd replaced the singer at the banquet, and as time went on the increase of slavery brought to thousands of free men the leisure to enjoy what had once been the privilege of the few. The fruits of the change were many: the legends which grew up round the name of Homer, the almost magical significance given to his works, the place of the *Iliad* and *Odyssey* in Greek education, their commanding influence on later literature and thought.

To the creation of epic poetry itself this process did not and could not bring new life. On the contrary, the existence of these great models, sanctified by ceremonial performance, hastened the atrophy of an art which had lost the power of growth. With the decline and fall of aristocracy, the environment was gone in which the epic convention had reached maturity: the convention itself was continued, in the form to which the *Iliad* and *Odyssey* had brought it. Mechanical imitation replaced creative development. We have already seen this trend in the other works of the Homeric Cycle. Presently, as the *Shield of Heracles* shows, it invaded the territory of the 'Boeotian School'. All through the great centuries of the city-state we hear of imitators, the disappearance of whose work is evidently no great loss. Only in

Alexandrian times is there a fresh offshoot from the old stock—the literary epic, a pale, anaemic child compared with its lusty ancestor, but with a certain charm and beauty of its own. Our earliest extant example, the *Argonautica* of Apollonius, was produced five or six centuries after the *Iliad*, but still has the same features of technique—hexameter, artificial language, stock epithets, similes, mythological apparatus. On all later exponents of the same craft—Virgil, for example, in Latin, and Milton in English—the convention created by the early minstrels has left its mark.

While later epic received from the Homeric poems the dubious gift of a fixed tradition and technique, to other branches of Greek literature they brought a very different and far more handsome legacy. The *Iliad* and *Odyssey* and the rest of the Epic Cycle were the memory of Greece, the storehouse in which were preserved all the half-recollected glories of pre-Hellenic days—the splendours of Mycenae and Crete, the adventures of the heroes, the legends of the gods. From this great treasury later centuries drew wealth which enriched literature and thought just as the discovery of Greek culture later enriched Rome, or the rediscovery of the Classics the Renaissance. We shall see that choral poetry blossomed into new brilliance and elaboration from the time when it began to treat heroic themes, weaving into a new texture the threads already used in epic verse. Drama reached its full stature only by turning to the same realm of myth and saga for its plots: Aeschylus himself is said to have called his plays 'slices from the great banquets of Homer'.[1] Sustenance from the same source helped to build every type of literature which could thrive on such a diet. But the epic tradition gave later authors more than subject-matter. Along with the material of the Epic Cycle something of the Homeric manner and outlook was also handed down. Lyric, drama, even prose caught some

[1] Athenaeus VIII, 347e.

of the atmosphere of the heroic age which, softened by the milder climate of Ionian aristocracy, breathes through the pages of the *Iliad* and *Odyssey*. I do not mean only the epic grandeur of the work of Aeschylus or Herodotus. There are more specific qualities which in no small degree look back to Homer as their source. First, Panhellenism. Homeric epic became one of the few *national* possessions of all Hellenes. It was recited at festivals to which men came from every quarter of Greece. It told of the days of Achaean unity. Many a later author, writing amid the conflicts and wars of quarrelling city-states, took from Homer some of this wider outlook and, with it, freedom from the bonds of local prejudice. Alongside Panhellenism was that emphasis on the hero, the great man, which not only pervades Athenian tragedy but colours the outlook of the historians, distorting our whole picture of Greek history and leaving us woefully ignorant of the life and thoughts of the 'common sort'.

The wealth which the Homeric poems bequeathed to the Greeks became the mental currency into which they converted their ideas and experience. The epic saga of gods and heroes not only gave definite form to the legend and mythology in terms of which later poets thought and expressed themselves: it moulded the Hellenic mind and determined the pattern of its thinking, perhaps even prolonged that mode of thinking and delayed the rise of rationalism. When logic eventually began to replace mythology, it was inevitable that thinkers should sympathise with Heraclitus' declaration that 'Homer should be turned out of the lists and whipped'.[1] Yet compared with some other civilisations, Greece was fortunate in inheriting a tradition which carried with it so little fettering of the mind. Homeric poetry has often been called the Greek Bible, but it laid down no dogma,

---

[1] *Fr.* 119. Tr. Burnet, *Early Greek Philosophy* (A. & C. Black, Ltd.). Except where otherwise stated, fragments from all authors are numbered as in the Loeb edition.

drew no sharp dividing line between orthodox and heretic. The legends it handed down were flexible, could be remoulded to suit later taste and ideas. Its healthy scepticism towards the gods was echoed in Aristophanes' caricatures of them and Euripides' censure, the criticisms of Xenophanes and the theories of Plato. When more rational thought developed, the Homeric legacy helped to give it that wider outlook, that objectivity, universalism, call it what you will, which is one of Greek literature's least tangible but highest qualities. Herodotus and Thucydides, writing of the conflicts of their own time, are almost as free from partisanship as the *Iliad*'s picture of the Trojan War. Like the creators of the *Iliad*, they see the tragedy which transcends the heat of the battle-field. Again and again in our journey through Greek literature we hear the weeping of Andromache.

CHAPTER IV

DANCE, MUSIC AND SONG

To the modern mind dancing seems to have little to do with literature. The conjunction of dance, music and song is familiar in the musical comedy chorus or the jazz lyric, but apart from these means of entertainment or pleasure it has no part in our lives. But it is well known that among less sophisticated peoples the dance, especially the choral dance, has played and still plays a far more vital role It is perhaps the commonest means of expressing the emotion, the desire, the hope felt by the group. Usually it has been bound up with ritual and religion. It was common among the early Christians, and continued in English cathedrals down to the fourteenth century. Among the ancient Greeks choral dancing was an essential feature of life, one of the foremost among the arts. Pindar describes Hellas as 'the land of lovely dancing'. Vase-paintings constantly depict dancing groups. That poetry and music and dancing should be combined was as natural then as it is unusual today, and the combination must have had a long and continuous history. All we now know of that history is concerned with two of its phases—one for which our chief source is the Homeric poems, and the other the sixth and fifth centuries B.C., the great period of choral song as a mature and independent art. Let us look at these two periods before attempting to fill the gaps.[1]

When Nausicaa and her maids had spread out the family

[1] Here and in the next chapter I have avoided the ambiguous term 'lyric' poetry, which can only mislead the modern reader. For the history of the term, see Bowra, *Greek Lyric Poetry*, p. 1.

washing to dry and eaten the food her mother provided,

> they cast their veils away
> And fell to playing ball, and to her mates
> White-armed Nausicaa began the song.[1]

The game is a sort of dance, accompanied by singing. To the twentieth-century reader, the picture is strange. To the reciters of the *Odyssey* and their hearers, it was a commonplace. The simple scene by the Phaeacian riverside has many parallels in both Homeric epics—brief glimpses of the place of combined dance, music and song in those early times. Sometimes the occasion is solemn ritual—a sacrifice to propitiate Apollo and remove pestilence, or mourning for Patroclus or Hector or Achilles. Sometimes it is a marriage feast. Sometimes, an exhibition of skill detached from any religious rite. When Hephaestus makes a great shield for Achilles and portrays on it the life of the day, he includes three pictures of music and dance and song. One is a marriage procession. Another, a display on a special dancing-place. Another, a vintage scene. While girls and boys carry the grapes in baskets,

> in their midst a boy
> Made lovely music with his ringing lyre,
> And sang to it the pretty Linos song
> In his clear treble, while the rest kept time
> With shouts and song, and followed up behind
> On dancing feet.[2]

Elsewhere in the *Iliad* Menelaus names 'sweet song and perfect dance' alongside love and sleep as familiar things of which 'sooner than war a man would take his fill'.[3] Like other normal human activities, this has its divine counterpart—the chorus of the nine Muses, who at Achilles' funeral 'one to the other replying with sweet voices began the dirge'.[4]

[1] *Od.* vi, ll. 100-1.   [2] *Il.* xviii, ll. 569-72.
[3] xiii, ll. 636-9.   [4] *Od.* xxiv, ll. 60-1.

Generation after generation must have carried on this tradition of dance and song. What did they sing? The *Iliad* and *Odyssey* cannot answer the tantalising question, nor can the *Homeric Hymns* or the *Theogony* or the *Shield of Heracles*, which also describe such scenes. Any version of chant or lament that the epic poets give us must be in hexameters. Of all the mass of traditional choral song which must once have existed only the most meagre remnants still survive—brief fragments of verse quoted by scholars and antiquaries writing many centuries later. We cannot date them with any certainty, nor be sure that they are still in their original form, but such as they are they confirm the Homeric picture. Some are obviously part of religious ritual—the Elean women's hymn to Dionysus, for example:

> Come, hero Dionysus,
> Come to the Eleans' shrine,
> To our holy shrine with the Graces,
> Raging hither with ox's hoof,
> O goodly bull,
> O goodly bull.[1]

Or an Athenian prayer for rain:

> Rain, dear Zeus, send rain
> Over the fields of Athens
> And over the fields of the Plain.[2]

A few from work-songs, such as the line:

> A sheaf, a sheaf, send, send a great sheaf.[3]

Others are part of children's games. An ancient version, for example, of 'Here we come gathering nuts and may':

[1] Plutarch, *Greek Questions* 36, 7.
[2] Marcus Aurelius v, 7. Tr. Edmonds (Heinemann, Ltd.).
[3] Athenaeus xiv, 618 c. Tr. Edmonds (*Oxford Book of Greek Verse in Translation*, no. 125).

> Where are my roses, where are my violets,
> And where is my fine parsley?
> Here are your roses, here are your violets,
> And here is your fine parsley.[1]

Or there is the spring begging-song sung in Rhodes by children dressed as swallows, which ends:

> Will you give us? Or shall we go?
> If you will,—why, rest you so;
> But and if you shall say us nay,
> Then we will carry the door away,
> Or the lintel above it, or, easiest of all,
> Your wife within, for she is but small.
> Give us our need
> And take God speed.
> Open the door to the swallow, then,
> For we are children and not old men.[2]

These are the merest rags and tatters, but enough to show the cut of the cloth as a whole. Clearly choral song and the music and dance that accompanied it were not confined to Nausicaa and her class, not a product only of the chieftains' banqueting-hall. They were popular and they were simple. Yet out of these beginnings developed perhaps the most elaborate type of Greek literature—the choral song of the sixth and fifth centuries B.C., a performance which only professionals could produce. The 'choral lyrics' of Pindar or Aeschylus are the would-be Greek scholar's worst headache, the worst puzzle for the reader of translations. Both are tempted to abandon them as unintelligible. But they are the most magnificent—and perhaps the most typical —of all Greek poetry. To ignore them would be to neglect what the Greeks themselves regarded as one of the highest forms of art.

Time has shown little more kindness to these mature creations of dance, music and song than to their simpler predecessors,

[1] Athenaeus XIV, 629e. Tr. Edmonds (*O.B.G.V.* 126, i).
[2] Athenaeus VIII, 360b. Tr. Beeching (*O.B.G.V.* 130).

though the sands of Egypt may still bring more of both to light. All that we possess today is the words of forty-five songs by Pindar and a few pages, much mutilated, of the work of Bacchylides. All these were composed in the fifth century B.C. The thousands of lines of fragments that remain from other choral poems are mainly from these two and from the work of Alcman (late seventh century), Stesichorus (a generation or two later), Ibycus (sixth century), Simonides (556-467), Timotheus (about 477-357). Not many of the fragments are more than a dozen lines. Even so, there is enough to show that all these examples are variations on one and the same type—a type which developed from simplicity to elaboration, and changed in tone and outlook as it was affected by different circumstances or the personalities of different individuals, yet was uniform enough for it to be said that here again out of traditional beginnings there has emerged a single literary convention. Let us look at the convention first, then consider how it arose.

Most of these poems were composed to be part of a ritual ceremony, and in some ways the convention they follow is as fixed and rigid as ritual itself. Yet one feature of choral song in this final form—unlike its traditional prototypes—is novelty: each occasion must be celebrated with a fresh product; within the limits allowed by the convention each poem must be unique. The bottle is old, the wine continually new.

Every aspect is affected by this paradox. First, the form of the songs, which confronts us with not one convention, but many. The genus now usually called the 'choral ode' had no one name of its own among the Greeks. It was known by the names of its species, which were differentiated in various ways—according to the type of occasion celebrated, the make-up of the choir, the kind of movement with which it accompanied the song. In Homer we can already distinguish four or perhaps five brands.

Others were called into being later by new phases of religion or social life—the 'dithyramb' in honour of Dionysus, the 'epinikian' to celebrate victories at the games, the 'encomium' as a secular song of personal praise. Alexandrian scholars classified the works of Pindar alone into eight different types. Each of the many kinds had its own movement or posture and gestures, each its own variety of musical accompaniment on lyre or flute (actually an instrument more like a primitive clarinet) or both, probably a slight affair to an audience of today—no harmony in the modern sense, but a melody repeated again and again. To fit music and dance each species had its own stock rhythms and metrical phrases. Common to all was the practice of dividing the song into stanzas, grouped in pairs to which the movements of the dance gave the name *strophe* and *antistrophe*, and usually capped by an *epode* to form a *triad*. Throughout the series of such *triads* which made up an ode (Pindar's longest has thirteen), *strophe* and *antistrophe* repeated the same metrical pattern, while *epode* exactly corresponded to *epode*. Though the music and dance parts of the performance are now quite unknown, and scholars have to disentangle the metrical intricacies of each poem by study of the written word, there can be no doubt about the extreme formality of the whole design. Yet within these limits to their realm, novelty and invention reigned supreme. Each ode combined the traditional rhythms in new ways, each was a new experiment in metre, a new rhythmical creation, often—as their complexity increased to a climax—reaching a variety and elaboration which have few equals in the songs of more modern times.

Turn to the language of the poems. Like epic verse, they use an artificial 'dialect' which no Greek normally spoke—a varying mixture of Doric, Aeolic and Homeric forms. But here the parallel with epic ends. The choral poet was a painstaking deviser of new things, an expert who took time to complete his work. Neither aids to memory nor tricks of improvisation affected his mode of composition. His repertoire was not filled with stock phrases treasured because they would fill up half a line. He even avoided making sense correspond to metrical form: the end of a stanza often finds us in the middle of a sentence. Far from repeating what was familiar and old, most of the later choral poets constantly produced novel effects by words and phrases of their own coining; above all, by metaphor, by carrying the use of analogy as a means of thought and expression to sublime heights of poetry. Here is Pindar on the effect of the music of the lyre:

> On God's sceptre the Eagle sleeps,
> Drooping his swift wings on either side,
> The King of Birds.
> You have poured a cloud on his beak and head,
>   and darkened his face:
> His eyelids are shut with a sweet seal.
> He sleeps, his lithe back heaves:
> Your quivering song has conquered him.[1]

In choral song at the climax to which Pindar brought it we have 'heightened language' at its richest and most vivid—the greatest glory of the Greek original, but the translator's despair.

Turn from language and form to content. Every choral song, of course, was constructed to fit the particular occasion at which it was performed. But this was the foundation on which the architect built rather than his main concern. The chief constituent of most odes was the familiar subject-matter of most Greek poetry—legend or myth. Our earliest specimen—part of a song by Alcman for a chorus of Spartan girls—makes use of a local myth. It was Stesichorus, we are told, who imported into this form of literature all the rich heritage of the past, the legends which 'Homer' and 'Hesiod' had made known throughout Greece. Stesichorus told his mythical tales at length, and through

---

[1] *Pythian* i, ll. 6-10. Tr. Wade-Gery, Bowra (*O.B.G.V.* 278).

the mouth of his chorus came near to being an epic poet himself. Pindar nearly follows his example in one ode, but not elsewhere. The tales of gods and heroes which the minstrel and rhapsode narrated had become part of the mental equipment of the choral poet and his audience—an equipment as familiar to those who heard Pindar's songs as the elements of scientific knowledge are to modern man. The poet could assume that his public knew the story: nothing more than allusion—though sometimes the allusion is lengthy—was necessary to set up a whole chain of associations in the hearer's mind. It is this use of myth and saga as a *common language* that causes most difficulty to the modern reader of these poems, especially to those who have only a nodding acquaintance with ancient legend. But here again one point is noteworthy: the tradition was no dogma. The choral poets one and all considered themselves free to change the myths —to decorate them with picturesque detail, to remove crudities, to introduce new twists and turns in which the writers of tragedy later saw better dramatic material than in the original versions. Once again the desire for novelty was at work. The ritual it could not affect. The myth could be repeatedly moulded into new shape.

Demodocus and Phemius and their successors told their stories with little or no comment. Not so the choral poet. He was prophet and preacher as well as narrator, regarded by both his audience and himself as the mouthpiece of the gods, the inspired interpreter of the ceremony at which his ode was sung. He was expected to use the legends as cautionary tales, to repeat the traditional maxims in new form. Here is Simonides' version of an old theme—the fickleness of fortune:

> Being but man, forbear to say
> Beyond tonight what thing shall be,
> And date no man's felicity.
>> For know, all things

> Make briefer stay
> Than dragonflies, whose slender wings
> Hover, and whip away.[1]

In this sphere there might seem to be little scope for originality
or novelty, but here too they have their effects. Despite the
traditional background of choral song, despite its association
with ritual, in this final form of the art the poet's individual
character and thoughts are by no means suppressed. Again and
again he speaks in the first person. Although we possess only
fragments from the work of Simonides, we can sharply distinguish his rationalism from the mysticism of Pindar. Ibycus
seems even to have made choral song a vehicle for love poetry.
In our long fragment of Alcman it is not the poet's personality
that comes to the fore, but the rival halves of the girl-chorus and
their leaders, whose beauty and skill in song are described in
comparisons charming but quaint to the modern ear:

> Of radiant Agido my lay
> shall be—her radiance as clear
> as the sun, whose morning ray
> she conjures to appear.
> I hear,
> but any praise or any blame of her
> is silenced by our fair chief-chorister
> whose beauty seems as high and rare
> as if with brutes one should compare
> a sturdy thundering horse, a champion,
> of wingéd dreams the son.
> There's the likeness, plain to see:
> steed of proud Enetic race,
> and my cousin—fair is she
> and her tresses have the grace
> of a golden filigree . . .[2]

[1] *Fr.* 22. Tr. Higham (*O.B.G.V.* 205).
[2] *Fr.* 1, ll. 39-54. Tr. Higham (*O.B.G.V.* 114).

In this poem the three conventional constituents — myth, moral comment, personalities—followed each other as separate elements, but as choral poetry developed they became more and more fused into one composite whole, woven together to form an elaborate texture of song unparalleled in ancient or modern literature. The transition from one topic to another is both sudden and subtle.

> Naught that gods do, methinks, is past belief
> Wondrous. Lay by the oar, and in firm ground
> Fast let the anchor bite, from rocky reef
> To keep the shallop sound;
> For all the charm of my triumphal lays
> Flits, like a honey bee, from praise to praise,

says Pindar at the end of a digression, with a typically swift and violent change of metaphor.[1] It is hardly surprising if the bewildered modern reader sometimes gets lost in the garden while pursuing such a restless insect and finds himself mentally on the rocks.

From this brief description it will be clear that the 'choral ode' of Pindar or Bacchylides is far removed from the scenes on Achilles' shield or the Athenian prayer to Zeus for rain. Simplicity has been replaced by elaboration, repetition of traditional material by novelty. Yet equally clearly both Homeric picture and mature 'ode' spring from the same root. The story of which only these two phases are known to us must go back far beyond Homer to the ritual magic of the primitive tribe. It is significant that it was among the Dorians, who clung most closely to tribal custom, that choral song flourished and found its chief spiritual home. The beginnings of the story are guesswork; at best, inference from our knowledge of primitive society elsewhere. But if we are prepared to venture into this conjectural realm we can

[1] *Pythian* x, ll. 48-54. Tr. Billson (Basil Blackwell).

see a possible origin for various features of both the Homeric descriptions and the Pindaric ode. With the distinction between ritual songs and work songs and play songs we cease to be concerned: as the vintage scene on the shield of Achilles suggests, all have a ritual quality to the primitive mind.

The primitive combination of music, dance and song has a leader. Amid the hysteria of the rite he becomes the god. If he speaks, it is with the god's voice. In many of Homer's brief pictures such a leader appears. Nausicaa 'leads the song' while she and her maids play ball. The sea-nymphs mourn the dead Patroclus and Thetis 'leads the lament'. Where singing and dancing were done by separate groups (as often in Homer, though later they were combined) each had its separate leader. Out of the chief singer emerged the poet—no longer identified with the god, but still his mouthpiece and interpreter.

The ritual itself in its earliest form probably consisted of rhythmical movement and a repeated cry—an inarticulate ejaculation of which we may see survivals in the refrains which gave some types of choral song their names. The refrain in turn may have been the origin of the *epode*. When the chorus and its leader were clearly distinguished from the god, when the magic rite became an act of worship, the repeated cry developed into a song which explained the ritual, told the story of the god, conveyed to the bystanders the significance of the occasion and the lesson they must learn. This, perhaps, was the evolution which culminated in the myth and moral comment of the Pindaric ode.

Such conjectures may help to fill in the beginning of the story, but there is still another mystery—the reason for the great outburst of choral song in the sixth and fifth centuries, the striving after new effects, the splendour and complexity which they attained. Part answer to the problem lies in the sphere of music. The first half-legendary names in the traditional history of choral song are those of musicians, and it is with the musical reforms

attributed to them that the elaboration of choral song begins—
first and foremost, the institution of a musical scale and its
adaptation to the lyre and flute. These advances in musical technique opened up vast possibilities of development towards more
elaborate metre and rhythm, but new avenues are not always
explored, new inventions not always used. The motive force
behind the growth of the choral ode must still be sought elsewhere. It is to be found in the changing complexion of Greek
life and Greek society. Though choral poetry was popular in its
beginnings, the background of its most glorious days was the
time of wealthy aristocracy and 'tyranny'. The minstrel and his
hexameter lays were products of the chieftain's banqueting-hall:
choral song owed its rise to greatness to the patronage of rich
landowning families and wealthy merchant princes who had a
use for poet and chorus and could afford to pay. The noble
houses which were in the ascendant in the political and social life
of the Greek states were even more dominant in the religious
sphere—above all, in the worship of Zeus and Apollo and in the
local hero cults. It was natural that they should appropriate to
themselves a form of art closely bound up with religious ritual,
should exploit it as a means of enhancing their own prestige and
the glories of their ancestors. It was equally natural that the
'tyrants' who ousted aristocracy—often themselves of noble
birth—should continue the same practice amid the more secular
atmosphere of their courts, using choral poetry, like new temples
or religious festivals, as an instrument for magnifying the splendour of their regime and of the cities over which they ruled.

Sublime literature has often had a close connection with hard
cash, and so it was here. To meet the demand for choral song the
professional song-writer came into being. The status of Alcman
and Stesichorus we cannot judge, but there is no doubt that their
successors in the list of choral poets wrote to order and for fees.
Our sole long fragment of Ibycus seems to be part of a secular

'encomium' elaborately flattering the son of his patron, Polycrates
of Samos. 'You too shall have glory for ever, Polycrates,' says
the poet, 'just as is my glory in song'.[1] Simonides, whom Lessing
called the Greek Voltaire, was notorious for readiness to change
masters and to let him who paid the piper call the tune. Flattery
is not always the keynote. With Pindar the customer is by no
means always right: from time to time he turns to advice, even
to admonition. But the influence of material motives on the
whole nature of choral poetry cannot be ignored. In the professional poets' desire to please their patrons and ensure that one
commission should lead to others we must see one of the main
reasons both for the striving after novelty in their work, for its
elaboration and magnificence, and also for another of the outstanding features of choral song—its Panhellenism. By the sixth
century the noble families in the various states were breaking free
from the isolation which followed the great migrations. They
were brought together by a common class outlook which in later
days crystallised into the co-operation of oligarchic parties everywhere. The same trend was still stronger among the 'tyrants',
the basis of whose power lay in the growth of commerce. Choral
poets reflected this 'internationalism' and promoted it. From
their various original homes they travelled wherever they were
invited among the many settlements to which colonisation had
carried the Greek tongue. They sent songs across the seas, sure
of finding a highly-trained professional chorus capable of performing them. Though they wrote for local occasions, they lifted
them on to a different plane by linking them not only with local
legend and tradition but with the heroic saga and Olympian
religion, the common traditional heritage of all Greece.

Nowhere are the motives and outlook of the choral poets more
clearly exemplified than in the greatest of them all, the only one
from whose work a substantial part still survives: Pindar, born

[1] *Fr.* 67, ll. 47-8.

near Thebes in 522 or 518 B.C. Pindar was himself an aristocrat, a member of the ancient family of the Aegidae, which had branches in Sparta, Thera and Cyrene as well as Thebes. Among its privileges were hereditary priesthoods, and the poet himself was probably a priest of Apollo. At Thebes the young Pindar learned to play the flute; during a stay at Athens he acquired the technique of choral song. The first years of the new century found him already a professional poet fulfilling a commission from the rich aristocratic rulers of Larissa in Thessaly. During the Persian Wars the oligarchy which ruled Thebes was pro-Persian, but Pindar's failure to oppose this 'medising' did not ruin his professional career. He received commissions from every quarter of the Greek world—not only from the mainland of Greece, but North Africa, Macedonia, Sicily, whose wealthy tyrants were his most generous patrons. He catered for all types of ceremonial occasion. When Xenophon of Corinth fulfilled a vow to devote a hundred slave prostitutes to the service of the temple of Aphrodite, Pindar celebrated the event in a song which the women accompanied with a dance. The sixteen lines which survive combine metaphor, religion and moral comment to form one of the worst pieces of bathos in Greek poetry:

> Young girls of many guests, ye servants all
>   Of Suasion at rich Corinth,
> Who burn gold tears of frankincense as oft
> In thought ye fly to Aphrodite fair,
>   Heavenly mother of Loves;
> To you, my children, hath she without blame,
> Granted the culling of the fruit of youth
> On lovely couches. Everything is good
>   Where force is lord . . .[1]

Pindar has no reticence about his fees. The good old days when the Muse sang free of charge are past, he tells us:

[1] *Fr.* 122.

For then was the Muse not yet a lover of gain, nor a hireling was she.
Nor then honey-throated Terpsichore sold the melting melody
  Of her lays, nor with faces silver-masked did they tread the stage.
  But now she biddeth us heed the word of the Argive sage
  Which cometh all too near to the truth in this our age:
' 'Tis money, 'tis money that maketh the man!' he said,
When his friends forsook him so soon as his wealth had fled.[1]

The poet heeded the saying well. When he died at the age of
eighty he was a wealthy man.

Pindar's many songs, like so much of Greek literature, were
collected and edited by the scholars of Alexandria in the third
century B.C. Only those have survived which had most appeal
to later antiquity—his *Epinikian* or *Victory Odes*, probably
about one fifth of what he wrote. Nothing in Greek literature
illustrates better how on an apparently trivial basis and with
motives far from lofty an artist can build a magnificent structure
of verse.

The four books of *Victory Odes*—*Olympian, Pythian, Nemean,
Isthmian*—are songs composed to celebrate successes scored at
the four great athletic festivals of Greece, held at Olympia,
Delphi, Nemea, Corinth. They honour the victor in a Boys'
Wrestling Match or a Mule Chariot Race or perhaps a Foot Race
in Full Armour. The idea is strange to us. A Don Bradman or
Babe Ruth or Joe Louis may have a leading place among the
popular heroes of their time and share newspaper headlines with
the greatest events of war and peace, but no choir sings their
exploits, no poet compares their prowess with the deeds of their
great ancestors or the legendary feats of gods. The difference lies
in the fact that the great Panhellenic games, unlike Test Matches
or the Wimbledon Championships, were religious festivals.
With the much-debated problem of their origin and the place of
the victor within the picture we are not here concerned, but there

[1] *Isthmian* II, ll. 6-12. Tr. Way (Macmillan and Co., Ltd.).

can be no doubt that he was regarded as the favourite of the gods as well as the winner of secular success. The games at Olympia began as early as the eighth century B.C. The others were started early in the sixth century. It was in the latter days of aristocracy and 'tyranny' that all attained their greatest significance and splendour, which was intensified during the threat to Greece from Persia. To the nobles and 'tyrants' victory in the games meant prestige for themselves and their families, glory and respect for the cities over which they ruled. The victor's triumph proved the strength and courage of all his kith and kin. His homecoming was an occasion for public rejoicing and religious ceremony: a breach was made in the city walls, we are told, to welcome him.

How was choral song connected with the games? The story is typical of the evolution of the complex ode from simple traditional beginnings. In the early days of the competitions at Olympia the victor and his friends on the way to get the prize from the temple of Zeus are said to have sung a short song (attributed to Archilochus) with a thrice-repeated two-word refrain. But this was not enough for the sons of the rich. They needed something more elaborate, something strikingly new; above all, something that could be performed at their homecoming, in their own state, to impress the prestige of their family on the local population, the greatness of their city on the whole Greek world. Here was work for a professional poet and chorus, and *Victory Odes* were composed first by Simonides, then by Pindar. For the honouring of boxer or charioteer Pindar employs all the technique at his command, all the conventional constituents of choral song, all the pictorial powers which enable him to soar—as he himself claims—like an eagle above all other choral poets. The language of these songs has a splendour unequalled elsewhere in Greek, if in any, poetry. One vivid picture merges into another, metaphor is piled on metaphor. Such magnificent fare, Pindar tells us, is for those that understand, not for the common herd:

> Many swift shafts lie in my quiver;
> To the wise is their meaning plain;
> For the common herd need they interpreters.[1]

The *Victory Odes* give us no details of the triumphs they celebrate. Reports of sporting events are common enough lsewheere in Greek poetry—in the *Iliad*, for example—but they are not Pindar's business. Chief item in the make-up of these odes, as of all developed choral poetry, is myth—the element which seems strangest to us, but must have brought the greatest pleasure to Pindar's patrons. When the chorus turns to legendary themes the victorious young scion of the noble house is raised to the level of his great ancestors and all the heroes of the past. For Pindar the athletic victor of today is no weakling compared with the mighty men of old. There is no hint that he could not lift the same stone as they or use the same drinking-cup. His triumph shows that his kindred are still made of heroic stuff. In the last *Isthmian* ode young Cleander, who has won the all-in boxing-plus-wrestling match, is seen as a worthy successor to his dead boxer-cousin Nicocles, who in turn recalls Achilles whom even the Muses mourned:

> Him even in death forsook not minstrelsy;
> For at his pyre and place of burial
> The Heliconian Maidens gathered all,
> Out-pouring their full-throated threnody.
> So to this precept gods themselves gave warranty—
> *The valiant man, though cold his clay,*
> *As ever-living theme to lay*
> *In keeping of the choir celestial.*
> Still is that saw in high account,
> For lo, the Muses mount

[1] *Olympian* ii, ll. 83-6. Tr. Way.

Their car, and hither speed to memorize
The tomb where Nicocles the boxer lies.
Honour to him, whom Dorian parsley crowned
In the Isthmian vale; for in his day and land,
He also with inevitable hand,
Achilles-like, his foemen did confound.
Yet this our athlete shames not kinsmen so renowned.[1]

Over the whole occasion of the victor's return is shed not only the glamour of the heroic past, but the sanctity of religion. Pindar has none of the scepticism of Ionia. His Olympian gods are not the gay, irresponsible deities of the *Iliad* and *Odyssey*. They never lose their dignity. If legend makes them repulsive or ridiculous, then legend must be reformed.

What was Pindar's own point of view, his own philosophy? No details or systematic answer can be given—not merely because the poet who composes to order must write what pleases his patron, but because the ideas of an author who thinks and speaks in terms of metaphor and mythology cannot be reduced to a philosophic system or expounded in rational form. Look for a definite creed in Pindar's odes, and often you find little more than the theme which was preached by Delphi and beloved of the aristocracy: nothing too much; the mean is best; be content with what you have. 'Seek not to be as Zeus', he warns us, 'for mortal bounds must mortal men confine.'[2] Occasionally he explicitly states his belief in the divine right of the nobly born. For example:

Yea, best in the hands of high-born men doth the piloting lie
Of cities wherein their fathers have ruled in the years gone by.[3]

But for the most part Pindar has no theories. His work has a tone, an atmosphere, an attitude—the attitude of the aristocrat

---

[1] *Isthmian* VIII, ll. 56-65. Tr. Miss W. M. L. Hutchinson.
[2] *Isthmian* V, ll. 14-6. Tr. Way.
[3] *Isthmian* X, ll. 71-2. Tr. Way.

who despises the common herd, who in the age of rising democracy longs for an existence like his own vision of the young
noblemen's paradise:

> For them the sun shines ever in full might
> Throughout our earthly night;
> There, reddening with the rose, their paradise,
> A fair green plaisance, lies,
> Cool beneath shade of incense-bearing trees,
> And rich with golden fruit:
> And there they take their pleasure as they will,
> In chariot-race, or young-limbed exercise
> In wrestling, at the game of tables these,
> And those with harp or lute:
> And blissful where they dwell, beside them still
> Dwells at full bloom perfect felicity:
> And spreading delicately
> Over the lovely region everywhere
> Fragrance in the air
> Floats from high altars where the fire is dense
> With perfumed frankincense
> Burned for the glory of Heaven continually.[1]

Pindar produced most of his *Victory Odes* after the Persian
Wars. Even while he wrote, history was passing him by. He
composed nearly all his songs for aristocrats and tyrants, for
those who held sway in the by-ways of Greek civilisation; but
its centre was now democratic Athens. His mind was filled with
legend and mythology; but the last decades of his life saw the
beginning of the spread of rationalism. In politics, in intellectual
make-up Pindar was behind the times. It is not surprising that
within a few years of his death a writer of comedy at Athens[2]
complained that his work, for all its beauty, was already ignored.
But not only Pindar was out of date: the trend of the age meant
the end of the greatest days of choral song itself. Bacchylides

---

[1] *Fr.* 129. Tr. Headlam (*O.B.G.V.* 295).
[2] Eupolis. See Athenaeus 1, 3a.

still composed odes which had charm, grace, polish, if no higher quality. Simonides, friend of Themistocles and 'adopted laureate of Athens', as he has been called, handled choral poetry with a rationalism and a simple directness of style which (as far as can be judged from the scanty fragments) were a marked contrast to Pindar's obscurity and magnificence. But Simonides had no successor. Rationalism found its natural vehicle in prose. As the century went on only the dithyramb—of which more later— was popular at Athens, where contests between dithyrambic poets were held at the festival of Dionysus. By the time of Timotheus the lofty art of Pindar had degenerated into bathos and musical virtuosity. It was an offshoot of the choral ode that brought it new life, a new function, a new audience: the drama. Among Pindar's contemporaries was one called Aeschylus.

CHAPTER V

THE INDIVIDUAL SPEAKS

Epic developed from the lays of the minstrel in the nobles' banqueting-hall. Choral poetry, in its heyday the brilliant accompaniment of aristocratic pomp and religious ceremonial, had its origins in the simple popular ritual of dance, music and song. Beside these two types the early centuries of Greek history also present us with a third: poetry expressing what the individual had to say. Here the poet spoke not as entertainer of chieftains, nor as mouthpiece of a god, but as man (or occasionally, woman) voicing the outlook which birth or environment had given him. His subject was not the glorious past, but the immediate present. Whether he wanted to teach or to ridicule, to persuade others or to state his own feelings, whether his theme was 'poetical' in the modern sense or not, he used verse because verse was the only medium he knew.

Much of this topical personal poetry is the nearest thing in Greek literature to the poetry of modern times. But there was one all-important limitation which now no longer exists. Even the most individual of Greek verse was still as a rule the product of occasions, expressing the poet's reaction to a particular situation or his ideas on an occasion when song was expected of him—his feelings in a national crisis or his thoughts among the winecups. There is no deep soul-searching here, no self-expression for its own sake, no creation born of the time

> when on my couch I lie
> In vacant or in pensive mood,

no vision seen by

> that inward eye
> Which is the bliss of solitude.

For the same reason there is little poetry of nature as such. From the Homeric simile onwards there is no lack of evidence that the Greeks were alive to natural beauty, but at any rate till late in their literature reference to it was incidental to human events.

When did this personal and topical poetry begin? Some say it must be as old as human speech, and doubtless in an age of individualism it is natural to assume that language has always been used to express individual thoughts and emotions. But there is no proof that this was so among the Greeks. There is no mention of anything of the kind in the *Iliad* or the *Odyssey*, even though Achilles in his tent sings alone of the 'glorious deeds of men'. According to our scanty evidence it was epic and choral poetry that had the longest history, perhaps both reaching back ultimately to one and the same source. The first poet who puts his own thoughts and feelings into verse is Hesiod, whose reaction to the situation created by his brother Perses is the motive behind the *Works and Days*. It is in the seventh and sixth centuries that poetry with such a purpose becomes a commonplace. Partly, no doubt, its growth into a recognised form of literature was due to the spread of writing, without which such ephemera would hardly have survived. Partly it was made possible by the development of music, which set choral song also on its feet. But its main stimulus lay in the political and mental ferment of the time. The adventurous period of sea-raids and migrations had produced the material for heroic saga, but in the make-up of society itself it had brought no drastic break with tradition, no fundamental change. It was decay within the comparatively settled society which followed—decay whose beginnings are reflected in Homer—that led the individual to break away and speak for himself. Personal poetry came into its own when conflicts developed within the community, when aristocracy found its position challenged and began to lose its nerve. The individual spoke out first and most boldly in the states where these changes started and went furthest: Ionia was the chief home of personal poetry, as the Dorian communities were the home of choral song.

The forms which this type of verse took were many and various. All had their beginnings in Ionia. All were originally chanted or sung to music. All tended to be direct and simple, without the elaborate splendour and lavish imagery of the Pindaric ode. In translation all are too often bald, arid, ineffective.

The earliest was the elegiac couplet, developed from the hexameter by the addition of a shorter line, and sung to the accompaniment of a flute. Its original use may have been in ritual lamentation, but when we first know it both elegiac metre and flute music are linked with feasting and war. Along with its metrical basis elegiac also took from epic the same artificial language which we find in the *Iliad* and *Odyssey*—language convenient for the couplet, as it had been for the hexameter. No verse form has lived longer: elegiac couplets were still written in the tenth century A.D.

More obscure is the source of iambic and trochaic metres, but their origin must have lain among the common people. Of all types of Greek verse this was the nearest in both rhythm and language to everyday speech. One suggested parentage for it is a magic curse; certainly it later became the instrument of invective and satire, till it found its most lasting home in the dialogue of drama.

To fit lyre music another form came into being, nearer in everything except complexity to choral verse. Its elements were short stanzas, often four lines each. Its rhythm, a combination of common and triple time. Some see its roots in folk-song, others regard it as an offshoot of choral song itself. The one genus included many species: in our fragments of Sappho alone there are fifty different metres.

Some poets used one of these forms, some two, some all three. Of all their work a mere remnant survives—a small number of

9   117

complete poems, a few hundred fragments long enough to show their worth, several thousand lines or phrases or words preserved for various reasons, but rarely for their merit. Theognis is the only composer of such poetry under whose name we possess medieval manuscripts, and amid the collection of poems they contain we cannot be sure which are really his. Even so, there is enough to give us not only gems of exquisite poetry, but vivid glimpses of seventh- and sixth-century Greece. The very fact that these songs arise from particular occasions makes them revealing documents of the life of the time. They catch and crystallise brief moments of history. Through them we can see the spirit of the period when the aristocracy was not yet challenged, but already uncertain of itself. We can see a little of the struggles of settlers against 'barbarians', the conflicts between cities, the class war within the community itself—nobles against 'tyrants', the 'good' against the 'base'. We can read the individual poets' advice or exhortations, gain some inkling of their likes and dislikes, their desire to plunge into the fight or to escape from it. If anyone imagines that all Greek literature is 'impersonal' or 'abstract', these poets contradict him.

Some of them wrote also on more conventional themes—on mythology or history. But it is their revelations of their own personalities and problems and emotions that still have significance. Let us glance at the most important of them in the surroundings amid which they lived.

Our first glimpse is of a wanderer—Archilochus, born on the mid-Aegean island of Paros probably late in the eighth century B.C. Archilochus was an aristocrat, yet an outcast from aristocracy—stuff from which even so early in Greek history an individualist might well be made. The key to his character was an accident of birth, the results of which dogged him all his days. His mother was a slave, and he shared the lot of many a bastard son of a noble house. Unable to inherit land or wealth at home, he joined 'poor wretches from all Greece' in an attempt to colonise Thasos off the coast of Thrace—an island 'like the backbone of an ass, covered with savage wood'. Perhaps it was in fighting and plundering the Thracians of the mainland that he began the soldier's life which seems to have been his till he was killed in battle:

> My spear wins bread, my spear wins Thracian wine:
> To drink it, on my spear-head I recline.[1]

For Archilochus there is no place in society. The wealth of golden Gyges and lofty tyranny are 'far from his eyes', but he scorns the common people. At one point he came near to marriage with a well-born Parian girl, but her father withdrew the promise when he discovered her suitor's origins. Thereafter father and daughter were lashed with poetical invective which eventually (said legend) drove both to suicide.

Archilochus composed all types of personal poetry, and must have done much towards perfecting them. Most famous were his iambics, which in antiquity earned him the name of the Scorpion. A Roman critic, who could read more of him than we, found in him 'the greatest force of expression, a phrasing not only telling but terse and vigorous, and abundance of blood and muscle'.[2] The martial elegiac metre was used by Archilochus to tell of soldiering, but not on conventional lines. He calls for wine to stave off the boredom of guard-duty. He scoffs at foppish generals. He tells how he threw his shield away and ran:

> A perfect shield bedecks some Thracian now;
> I had no choice: I left it in a wood.
> Ah, well, I saved my skin, so let it go!
> A new one's just as good.[3]

[1] Fr. 2. Tr. Bowra (O.B.G.V. 103).
[2] Quintilian x, 1, 60. Tr. Edmonds (Heinemann, Ltd.).
[3] Fr. 6. Tr. Marris (O.B.G.V. 104).

Unlike his more correctly-born relatives, Archilochus claims no affinity with the heroes of old. He is no Achilles. Yet his rough camp cynicism has its positive side. In hexameters which come as near to introspection as anything in Greek literature he uses the imagery of war to express his philosophy of life:

> Heart, my heart, with griefs confounded whence you no deliv'rance find,
> Up against them! guard yourself and show the foe a gallant breast;
> Take your stand among the foremost where the spears of battle fly
> Gallantly. Nor when you conquer make your pleasure manifest,
> Nor in turn, if you are conquered, lie down in your home and cry.
> Take your joy when life is joyful, and in sorrow do not mind
> Overmuch, but know what ups and downs belong to humankind.[1]

About the time of Archilochus' death an elegiac fragment of a very different spirit turns us to the city of Ephesus in Ionia. The town is under attack by the wild Cimmerians, barbarians from beyond the Black Sea who have ravaged cities and kingdoms on their westward trek. But the young nobles have lost the fighting spirit of their forefathers, and the poet Callinus inveighs against them as they lie idling at a banquet with the enemy at the gate:

> How long, young men, unsoldiered, disregarding,
>   laze you, scorned by neighbours round about?
> Slack to the bone, on peace resolved, supinely
>   careless in a land where all is war?[2]

Twenty-one lines of this poem and a few odd phrases are all we have of Callinus' work.

From Ephesus we move a generation later to Colophon, less than twenty miles further north. The Cimmerian threat has passed, and another poet, Mimnermus, while praising the fighters of earlier days, skilfully uses the elegiac couplet in charming

---

[1] *Fr.* 66. Tr. Bowra (*O.B.G.V.* 110).
[2] *Fr.* 1, ll. 1-4. Tr. Higham (*O.B.G.V.* 102).

songs of feasting and love. But though peace has come he sees
no prospect of permanent well-being ahead. Both youth and
love are for him brief preludes to the horrors of old age—we have
come far from Homer's Nestor—and the inevitable end. For
the first time in Greek literature, the keynote is 'Gather ye roses
while ye may'. An early death is the best escape from an existence
where there is no lasting happiness:

> We are as leaves in jewelled springtime growing
>   That open to the sunlight's quickening rays;
> So joy we in our span of youth, unknowing
>   If God shall bring us good or evil days.
>
> Two fates beside thee stand; the one hath sorrow,
>   Dull age's fruit, that other gives the boon
> Of Death, for youth's fair flower hath no to-morrow,
>   And lives but as a sunlit afternoon.[1]

After Ionian Colophon, Dorian Sparta, menaced in these last
decades of the seventh century by a conflict known to historians
as the Second Messenian War. The native inhabitants of Messenia
in the Southern Peloponnese had been conquered by the Dorian
invaders a hundred years or more earlier, and many of them had
been reduced to serfdom. Now they rose in revolt. Tyrtaeus,
probably a Spartan by birth in spite of stories to the contrary,
came forward as military leader and spokesman of the Spartan
ruling class in this struggle to hold 'Messene, so good to plough
and so good to plant'. Spartan troops went into battle to the
sound of the flute, and Tyrtaeus put into elegiac flute-songs,
perhaps sung over the camp fire or on the march, not only descriptions of battle but exhortations to fight, attempts to rally his
countrymen in defeat, even instruction on the tactics of war. The
three we still possess in complete form stress again and again the
honour of death on the field and the shame of wounds in the

[1] *Fr.* 2, ll. 1-8. Tr. Pott (*O.B.G.V.* 119).

back, the need for the young to fight instead of leaving it to the old:

> Young men, stand firm and fight, stand one by other;
> base retreat and rout let none begin.
> Be high of heart, be strong in pride of combat;
> grapple, self-forgetting, man to man.
> Forbear to fly, deserting men grown older—
> stiff about the knees, in honour old.[1]

Heroism is the theme, but the poet's ideal warrior is not the Homeric hero. Though Tyrtaeus speaks as an individual, he is no individualist. The warfare for which he calls is that of infantrymen massed in close ranks, fighting not to seek adventure but as a grim duty, not for themselves but for the state. The Spartans must fight for their land or wander in poverty abroad.

While the Messenians brought Sparta into danger from outside, another danger was beginning to threaten her aristocracy from within—the demand, common to many Greek states at this time, for a fairer distribution of land. To quell the rising discontent Tyrtaeus wrote a poem on Law and Order, and in one fragment he lectures his fellow-citizens on the superior wisdom of the Elders and the divine right of the Spartan kings. Eventually both crises passed. Thanks partly to Tyrtaeus' military strategy, if not his verse, the revolt was crushed. The land-hunger of the Spartans was satisfied by the conquest of all Messenia, and easier days followed, to which Alcman's girl-songs must belong. But Tyrtaeus had anticipated the future. In later times when Sparta was once more an armed camp continually on guard against its discontented serfs—the nearest parallel in the ancient world to Europe under the Nazis—the Spartans looked back to him as their spiritual guide.

Tyrtaeus' Sparta is the first of these scenes from the poets in

[1] *Fr.* 10, ll. 15-20. Tr. Higham (*O.B.G.V.* 97).

which class strife has any considerable part to play. In the next, it occupies the centre of the stage. The place is Athens. The time, the first years of the sixth century B.C. The poet, none other than the statesman Solon himself, who put what would now be the contents of political pamphlets into elegiac, iambic and trochaic verse. Called on by his fellow-aristocrats to deal with the growing agitation against serfdom and debt without seriously damaging the landowners' own position or opening the way to tyranny, Solon based his counsel on the familiar theme of moderation. Both rich and poor are guilty of greed. Neither must go too far in their desires. Law and order must take the place of civil strife. He boasts:

> I gave the commons their sufficient meed
> of strength, nor let them lack nor yet exceed.
> Those who were mighty and magnificent,
> I bade them have their due and be content.
> My strong shield guarded both sides equally
> and gave to neither unjust victory.[1]

For support for his policy Solon (like many statesmen after him) turns to conventional beliefs—divine retribution, for example:

> God-given riches come to man to stay
>   From the beginning till the very end.
> The wealth that insolent ambition seeks
>   Comes wrongfully, impelled by evil deeds
> Against its will—and ruin follows soon.[2]

Or to the inevitability of death, which makes all the riches of the noble house no better than the mere possession of food, clothes and shoes:

> One man has silver, gold, and fields of wheat,
> Horses and mules; another, nought but this—
> Comfort enough for belly, sides and feet;
> Yet this one's wealth than t'other's is no less.

[1] *Fr.* 5. Tr. Higham (*O.B.G.V.* 159).   [2] *Fr.* 13, ll. 9-13.

This little is abundance: none may bear
Great riches with him when he goes below,
Nor for a price escape our evils here—
Death, sickness, old age that comes creeping slow.[1]

Although Solon claims that his compromise has the sanction of religion, it could not stem the tide of history. He lived long enough to see the 'tyranny' of Pisistratus.

The origins of our next poet take us back to Colophon in Ionia, but a hundred years later than when we saw Mimnermus there. In the middle of the sixth century another threat came from the East—the westward surge of Persian imperialism which was to reach its climax at Marathon and Salamis. When Colophon, like other Ionian towns, fell an easy prey to the invaders, one of its citizens, Xenophanes, left home and began a life of wandering which lasted till after the Persians had been defeated and driven back from Greece. We cannot judge Xenophanes' rank in society. Unlike Tyrtaeus and Solon, he writes for no one community, no one class. Yet his is not the earthy cynicism of the earlier wanderer, Archilochus. Xenophanes is a thinker, a radical at large, prototype of the Cynic philosophers who roamed the Greek world in later times. In hexameters and elegiac couplets probably recited before gatherings of friends he expressed a spirit which others, as we shall see, had already begun to express in prose. Because he placed himself outside the traditions and conventions of the day he could criticise them with startling objectivity. He attacked the glorification of victors in the games. Most of all he assailed the epic picture of the gods:

Stealing, adultery, and base deceit,
All that among men brings rebuke and blame,
Homer and Hesiod to the gods ascribe.[2]

[1] *Fr.* 24.   [2] *Fr.* 11.

He ridicules anthropomorphism itself:

> Could horses, oxen, lions hold
> The tools to paint and carve like men,
> They'd make the gods in their own mould.
> Gods would be horses and oxen then.[1]
>
> The Aethiop's gods are black, snub-nosed;
> Blue-eyed, red-haired the Thracian's.[2]

Xenophanes' travels, it is said, took him to the Greek settlements in Italy. In some of his hexameters he put forward a positive philosophy. For these reasons he was regarded by tradition as the forerunner of other Western thinkers who stated their views in hexameter verse—Parmenides and Empedocles. Their work belongs more to the history of philosophy than to that of literature.

Tyrtaeus and Solon had tried in their different ways to deal with the land question. For Theognis, citizen of Dorian Megara late in the sixth century B.C., what they had feared and tried to prevent came all too true. Theognis is the landowner at bay and finally dispossessed. At Megara, like Sparta, the Achilles-Patroclus relationship was a part of military tradition, and the young soldier looked for training—among other things—to his older comrade-in-arms. Theognis' bitter elegiacs are addressed to such a 'squire', Cyrnus, whom he instructs on the state of society and the whole art of life. If out of all the 1,400 lines attributed to him in the collection handed down under his name we take as authentic only those passages which mention Cyrnus, we catch many striking glimpses of the class conflict of the day at its most acute pitch.

Theognis has a simple political philosophy. He divides men into 'good' and 'bad'—the 'best people', as a modern Theognis

[1] *Fr.* 15.   [2] *Fr.* 16.

might call them, and the rest. He complains that the 'bad' are now usurping the place of the 'good':

> Cyrnus, our city is a city still.
> Its folk are changed. Who once outside our walls
> Pastured like deer, with goatskins round their sides,
> And knew not laws or judgments, these today
> Are good men, Cyrnus; and those high before
> Are now sunk low. Who can endure the sight?[1]

Even stronger than Theognis' dislike for the serfs who are gaining land and citizenship is his hatred for the new rich, for those among the 'bad' whose wealth—from commerce, we may guess—enables them to mix with the 'good' and spoil their noble stock:

> Ram, ass, and horse, my Cyrnus, we look over
> With care, and seek good stock for good to cover;
> And yet the best men make no argument,
> But wed, for money, runts of poor descent.
> So too a woman will demean her state
> And spurn the better for the richer mate.
> Money's the cry. Good stock to bad is wed
> And bad to good, till all the world's cross-bred.
> No wonder if the country's breed declines—
> Mixed metal, Cyrnus, that but dimly shines.[2]

Worst danger of all from this source is tyranny. To kill a tyrant is a righteous deed:

> Honour the Gods, and fear them; that will stay
>   Impiety in all you speak or do.
> Strike down the ravenous despot in what way
>   You will, the Gods will not be wroth with you.[3]

Theognis' positive advice to Cyrnus is to do what is right and follow the golden mean. A significant couplet shows how the

---

[1] Ll. 53-8.   [2] Ll. 183-92. Tr. Higham (*O.B.G.V.* 188).
[3] Ll. 1179-82. Tr. Bowra, *Early Greek Elegists* (Harvard University Press).

traditional theme was adapted to the aristocrat's point of view:

> Walk quietly in the middle path, as I do
> And give not one man's goods to other men.[1]

It was easy for the owner of many goods to keep to such a rule, but the 'bad' folk of Megara did not follow it. They took away Theognis' land. Perhaps it was after this that he wrote so bitterly on the curse of poverty:

> Poverty, Cyrnus, breaks a gallant man
> More than white hairs or shivering fevers can.
> To flee it, Cyrnus, in the deep sea drown,
> Or from a towering precipice leap down;
> Broken by poverty, a man's denied
> All power of speech and act: his tongue is tied.[2]

Later in exile, perhaps far away in Sicily, the crane's cry in November reminded him of what he had lost:

> I heard the crane cry unto men his greeting,
>   To tell them it was time to drive the plough;
> Ah, friend! he set my sorry heart a-beating,
>   For others have my fertile acres now.[3]

With Theognis we have moved too far ahead in our chronological list of poets. We must go back half a century or more, and once again cross the Aegean—this time to Lesbos, one of the most fertile and charming of all Greek islands. Lesbos was no exception to the general trend of history. Her capital, Mytilene, became a centre of trade, and was one of the earliest scenes of the rise of merchant princes to power. In the closing years of the seventh century the 'tyrant' was Myrsilus, against whom the diehard aristocratic families fought bitterly first in Mytilene itself, then from a town nearby. Eventually Myrsilus was killed and

[1] Ll. 331-2.　　　　　　[2] Ll. 173-8. Tr. Higham (*O.B.G.V.* 187).
[3] Ll. 1197-200. Tr. Marris (*O.B.G.V.* 199).

the nobles returned to the capital, but what followed was as little to their liking as 'tyranny' itself. Pittacus, who also at one time had fought against the 'tyrants', was elected to a position recalling Solon's status at Athens—temporary dictator by popular consent. Though posterity regarded Pittacus as one of the Seven Wise Men, to the aristocrats he was one more despot like the rest, and he showed his wisdom by exiling them again till his position was secure. After ten years he voluntarily laid down his power. But for Mytilene, as for Solon's Athens, there was more 'tyranny' to come.

Long before this the name of Lesbos had been linked with choral music and song. The island was said to be the birthplace of Terpander and of Arion, creator of the dithyramb. But amid the struggles of the late seventh century and the disintegration of tradition which must have accompanied them poets of the aristocracy turned to a slighter and more personal medium of self-expression than choral poetry. Their model was probably folk-song, of which we may possess an example—adapted to the days of Pittacus—in a ditty men sang while they ground the corn:

> Grind, mill, grind,
> Even as Pittacus grinds,
> Master of great Mytilene.[1]

From such simple stuff as this poets developed many forms of short stanza to be chanted by one singer to the music of the lyre. Their diction, though not the language of everyday speech, was close to the local vernacular. How many writers of such verses Lesbos produced we do not know, but from the work of two of them—Alcaeus and Sappho—we possess fragments which are among the best things in Greek literature, and incidentally show us two different facets of life among the hard-pressed aristocracy.

[1] Plutarch, *Seven Wise Men*, 14. Tr. Syme (*O.B.G.V.* 125, ii).

Alcaeus, like Theognis, is a bitter spokesman of his class. But the cultured aristocrat of Lesbos is more light-hearted, more sophisticated, than the Dorian landowner. Like Archilochus, he tells how he dropped his shield in battle and fled. Alcaeus does not instruct. He puts his emotions into song for the entertainment of his friends. For 'base-born' Pittacus and the rabble who support him he has hatred and contempt:

> This upstart Pittacus, this base-born fool,
>   They greet with joy, and acclamations great,
> And set the willing tyrant up to rule
>   The strife-torn city, most unfortunate.[1]

The list of personal epithets he is said to have applied to Pittacus far outdoes Homer's description of Thersites. But in the intervals of the struggle he turns readily to wine and love—and to writing charming hymns to the gods—as a means of relief. 'Tis time for wine and time for women', he cries, 'now that Myrsilus is dead.'[2] A number of our fragments are from his drinking-songs, and praise the best remedy for the cares of troubled times:

> Drink! Why wait for lamps? The day
> Has not another inch to fall.
> Fetch the biggest beakers—they
> Hang on pegs along the wall.
>
> Bacchus, son of Semele
> And of Zeus, discovered wine,
> Giving it to man to be
> Care's oblivious anodyne.[3]

Sappho, a few years younger than Alcaeus, was the first and greatest poetess of Greece. The thought of a woman writing love-songs, especially to members of her own sex, has had

---

[1] *Fr.* 160. Tr. Easby-Smith.
[2] *Fr.* 42. Tr. Edmonds (Heinemann, Ltd.).
[3] *Fr.* 163. Tr. Bowra (*O.B.G.V.* 135, iii).

strange effects on the imagination of both ancient and modern times, and it is doubtful whether scandal (which turned her into a prostitute) or romance (which made her leap to her death, heartbroken, from a cliff) or ideas and prejudices on the subject of 'Lesbianism' have done more to obscure the historical reality. The facts as far as we can piece them together are simple enough. Like Alcaeus she was a member of the aristocracy, and with them went into exile as a young girl. Back in Lesbos, she married and had a daughter. But her life was not limited to the normal sheltered existence of a woman of her class. The key to her personality and her poetry is another aspect, difficult for the modern mind to understand. In most states of ancient Greece there was no education for young women beyond the domestic crafts they learned in the home. Among the Lesbian aristocracy several rival schools—for want of a better word—sprang up where the daughters of the well-to-do could learn such higher arts as music and song. One of them was Sappho's. But this description in secular terms distorts the truth. Sappho's 'school', like the rest, centred on a religious cult, yet it was no nunnery. The cult was that of Aphrodite, goddess of beauty and of love. The girls who took part in it were taught not to ignore physical loveliness but to admire and seek after it, not to renounce marriage but to prepare for it in heart and mind. Isolated by custom from men till the time of marriage came, they inevitably turned their emotions towards each other—above all, towards Sappho herself.

This and her family are all-in-all to Sappho. She cares nothing for the things that roused Alcaeus and the other male members of her class. She would rather see her beloved Anactoria once more than all the chariots of the Lydians or armies on the battle-ground. And again:

> I have a child; so fair
> As golden flowers is she,

My Cleïs, all my care.
I'd not give her away
For Lydia's wide sway
Nor lands men long to see.[1]

As far as we can judge from the miserable remnants time has left us—her works were publicly burned at Rome and Constantinople in A.D. 1073—most of the occasions for which Sappho wrote her songs were connected with the cult of Aphrodite and the girls who took part in it: festivals of the goddess herself or the Graces and Muses, marriage ceremonies which ended the girls' stay at the 'school'. Some were for choral performance, but they too seem to have expressed intimate personal emotion. The one complete poem we possess is a prayer to Aphrodite which is close to ritual and the original purpose of ritual—magic. Through all her work run qualities which the background I have described helps to explain: craftsmanship such as could best be developed in a school of song; radiance shed by the worship of physical beauty and all things beautiful. Yet no one could be further than Sappho from Swinburnian romanticism. To the simplicity of folk-song she adds the restraint of ritual. She is as untranslatable as Pindar, though for a very different reason. Poetry brilliantly direct in the original becomes bald and mediocre in translation. Perhaps Rossetti's version of two of her similes still comes nearest to success. The first certainly, and the second possibly, refers to a young bride:

Like the sweet apple which reddens upon the topmost bough,
A-top on the topmost twig—which the pluckers forgot somehow—
Forgot it not, nay, but got it not, for none could get it till now.

Like the wild hyacinth flower, which on the hills is found,
Which the passing feet of the shepherds for ever tear and wound,
Until the purple blossom is trodden into the ground.[2]

[1] Fr. 130. Tr. Bowra (O.B.G.V. 153).
[2] Frs. 150, 151. (O.B.G.V. 148).

Sappho and Alcaeus stand alone. Second to them—but a poor second—was a poet born two generations later at Teos on the Ionian mainland: Anacreon, who wrote elegiacs and iambics but was most famous for his lyre-songs. Whether Anacreon owed more to local tradition or to the poets of Lesbos, we cannot tell: his metres are not close to theirs; his language is Ionic, often Homeric. More striking than the difference of form is the change of spirit. Although Anacreon was probably an older contemporary of Theognis, he is not concerned with the fight against the tyrants. That struggle is over. The poet is not tyranny's antagonist, but its servant. 'He that will fight may fight if he will', he says.[1] Like the later choral poets, Anacreon exists on the patronage of the wealthy and great, and allows that fact to limit his mental horizon.

When Teos, like Colophon, was attacked by the Persians, the Teans migrated to Abdera on the coast of Thrace. Like Archilochus, Anacreon had his fill of fighting against the wild Thracians. He seized the opportunity of exchanging a hard life for an easy one by accepting an invitation from Polycrates of Samos to come to his court as music and poetry teacher for his son—the same princeling whom Ibycus flattered in choral song. When the Persians put Polycrates to death Anacreon found a new patron in Athens. When Hippias was driven out, he went to the princes of Thessaly, returning to Athens to entertain her noble families till at the age of eighty-five—says legend—he was choked by a grape-pip sticking in his throat. Pindar glorified the grander side of the life of princes and aristocrats. Anacreon is the poet of their lighter hours. Most choral odes were written for public ceremonies. His simple songs were sung over the wine-cups. He is rarely completely serious. His main qualities are charm and wit. Sappho worshipped Aphrodite; Anacreon, like Alexandrian poets centuries later,

[1] *Fr.* 106. Tr. Edmonds (Heinemann, Ltd.).

ANACREON

talks of the goddess' pretty son Eros—the Greek Cupid:

> Water bring, and bring me wine,
> Bring the wreaths where flowers entwine;
> Hasten, lad; our fists we try,
> Matched together, Love and I.[1]

Or when he is old:

> When Love beholds my beard that flows
> White as the ocean's snowy spray,
> He flies me swift as the eagle's flight
> On rustling wings of golden light,
> And seems to murmur as he goes,
> 'Old fellow, you have had your day.'[2]

Even death is anticipated with a touch of gaiety:

> Sweet Youth no more will tarry,
> My friend a while ago;
> Now white's the head I carry,
> And grey my temples grow,
> My teeth—a ragged row.

> To taste the joy of living
> But little space have I,
> And torn with sick misgiving
> I can but sob and sigh,
> So deep the dead men lie.

> So deep their place and dismal,
> All means, be sure, they lack
> Down in the murk abysmal
> To scale the upward track
> And win their journey back.[3]

Several times Persian imperialism has intruded into this story

[1] *Fr.* 75. Tr. Higham (*O.B.G.V.* 176).
[2] *Fr.* 25. Tr. Davidson (J. M. Dent and Sons, Ltd.).
[3] *Fr.* 69. Tr. Higham (*O.B.G.V.* 175 b).

of the rise of individual poetry. At the end of the sixth century
B.C. the same force caused the eclipse of the Ionian civilisation
which had brought individualism into being. Amid the unified
democracy of Athens, the new centre of Greek culture, there was
at first no place for individualism: when it emerged, its main
medium was prose. Yet the forms of verse with which this
chapter has been concerned did not die. Imitation of Anacreon
in later years produced the collection of pretty trivialities known
as the *Anacreontea*, containing more complete poems than survive from all the earlier writers here described. The iambic and
trochaic metres found a new function well suited to their
conversational tone; they became the normal vehicle for dramatic
dialogue, in both the Greek and the Roman theatre. Most long-
lived of all was the elegiac couplet, which lasted till far into the
Christian Era as the accepted form for the epitaph and the
epigram. But throughout the centuries no writer of elegiacs
excelled Simonides. Here, to close the chapter, are three of his
epitaphs. On a merchant:

> Here Brotachus from Cretan Gortyn lies:
> He did not come for this, but merchandise.[1]

On an enemy:

> After much eating, drinking, speaking ill
> Of others, here Timocreon lies still.[2]

On the Spartans who fell at Thermopylae:

> Go tell the Spartans, thou who passest by,
> That here obedient to their laws we lie.[3]

---

[1] *Fr.* 156. Tr. Bowra (*O.B.G.V.* 220).
[2] *Fr.* 110. Tr. Bowra (*O.B.G.V.* 222).
[3] *Fr.* 119. Tr. Bowles.

CHAPTER VI

DRAMA AND DEMOCRACY

THE place: the theatre of Dionysus—Bacchus was another of his names—on the southern slope beneath the Acropolis at Athens.

The time: the dawn of a fine spring day late in March, 458 B.C. —one of the days of the Great Dionysia, greatest of Athens' four festivals in honour of Dionysus. The whole city is on holiday.

This is not the beginning of the festival. On the day on which it began there was a great procession—the symbol of the god's first coming to this spot from Eleutherae further North. The image of Dionysus was carried in state from his temple a few yards away from the theatre to a point on the road from Eleutherae, and gaily brought back by torchlight and placed in the theatre. The next day was taken up with choral song and dance in his honour. Five choruses of men and five of boys, each drawn from one of the ten Attic tribes, competed. There were fifty in each chorus—no fewer than five hundred in all. This morning the citizens are gathered together again in the theatre to see another spectacle—*drama*, 'performance', is their word for it. They sit on wooden benches on the curving hillside, a natural ampitheatre, facing the sun, and here they will stay till late afternoon. They have breakfasted well, for there will be no interval for refreshments. Although they have each paid two obols—a third of a day's wage—to come in, more than fifteen thousand are here. Besides citizens there are *metics*, women— sitting separate from the men—boys, even a few slaves. Since it is spring and the sailing season has begun, many people are here from other states, especially from the lesser members of the

Confederacy of which Athens is now head. A few of these visitors are in the front rows in places of honour along with Athenians specially privileged on this state occasion—priests, generals, state officials, public benefactors or their descendants, the sons of men killed in battle, and the ten judges chosen by a combination of lot and selection to judge the competition. In the middle of the front row sits the priest of Dionysus himself. The audience is noisy, but less unruly than might be expected of these excitable Athenians. The 'staff-bearers' who are here to keep order will have little to do. This is a religious ceremony, and we are on holy ground.

This hillside is the *theatron*—the 'watching place'. From it the vast crowd looks down on to a circle of level ground rimmed with stone, separated by only a few feet from the front row of seats. The circle, more than twenty yards across, is the dancing-ground—the *orchēstra*. In the centre stands a simple altar of Dionysus; at the back, a structure of wood and canvas. Some members of the audience can remember when there was nothing more than a tent—*skēnē*—in which actors could change, but now the structure is substantial enough to represent a palace with three doors. A few broad steps lead up to the doors, and on them altars stand. When the audience raise their eyes beyond this setting for the play, they see to the right a small temple of Dionysus, and look over part of the town, the harbour, and open country.

It is time for the performance to begin, but there are pre-liminaries first. A sacrifice is made at the altar of Dionysus, an offering of wine is poured on the ground in front of his statue. Various proclamations are made. While this is going on the great throng think—and talk—of what they are going to see. On the main points their curiosity has already been satisfied. At a cere-mony several days before the festival they have learnt the names of the three tragic poets chosen to compete, and the plays they are to present. Lots have been drawn for the order of presentation, and today has fallen to an old favourite—Aeschylus. The titles of the series of three tragedies, or 'trilogy', of his which is to start the day—*Agamemnon, Libation-Bearers, Furies*—are enough to tell the audience that they will deal with a familiar theme: how Agamemnon, returning to Argos in triumph from Troy, was murdered by his cousin Aegisthus and his queen, Clytemnestra, who had taken Aegisthus as her lover during the king's ten-year absence; how his son Orestes, absent from Argos as a child when his father was killed, returned to avenge him by murdering Aegisthus and Clytemnestra; how for this matricide Orestes was pursued and driven mad by the Furies, savage goddesses who punished any unnatural act. This is a well-worn tale. But what will Aeschylus make of it?

The moment has come. A herald calls upon Aeschylus to present his play. Then a ripple of surprise runs over the closely packed benches. An actor has appeared, but not where the audience expected him—in front of the 'palace' building. Instead he stands on its roof. He is an imposing figure, though tiny for those in the furthest rows. His face is hidden by a mask with huge mouth and elongated forehead. Boots with soles several inches thick raise him above the floor. Long, sweeping robes cover his body, which is evidently padded to match his extra height. He carries a spear, otherwise there is nothing to show the spectators whom he represents: all the characters in the play will wear more or less this costume. But when he speaks he soon tells them all they need to know: he is a watchman on the roof of the palace of Agamemnon, Atreus' son, at Argos; it is night, and he is watching, as he has watched for a year, for the beacon of fire that will bring news of the fall of Troy. In ringing tones that reach the back rows of the audience he slowly declaims magnificent iambics—such language as no ordinary Greek watchman ever spoke:

> I've prayed God to deliver me from evil
> Throughout a long year's vigil, couched like a dog
> On the roof of the House of Atreus, where I scan
> The pageant of Night's starry populace,
> And in their midst, illustrious potentates,
> The shining constellations that bring men
> Summer and winter, as they rise and set.
> And still I keep watch for the beacon-sign,
> That radiant flame that shall flash out of Troy
> The message of her capture.[1]

A moment later he hints that all is not well within the palace, but presently shouts a welcome: he has seen the beacon-fire in the distance, and disappears into the palace to tell the news. Cries of triumph are heard, and a throng dressed as women come through the palace doors. Among them is an actor evidently representing Clytemnestra, but he does not speak. Both Queen and handmaids busy themselves with ritual at the altars on the steps, while from the side a flute-player enters followed by twelve men dressed alike. This, as the audience knows, is the chorus of the play, and will stay on the *orchēstra* to the end. Their masks and the sticks they carry show that they represent old men. As they march on to their dancing-ground, the flute-player accompanies them in a chant, and in magnificent language rich with metaphor they recall Agamemnon's departure for Troy ten years before, then turn to the Queen and ask the reason for this ritual in the night. But Clytemnestra returns into the palace still silent and the chorus begin their first 'ode', moving across the dancing-circle and using different postures and gestures to suit music and words. They start with a 'triad'—two long stanzas with the same metre and dance-movement, followed by an 'epode'. All three parts end with the same one-line refrain. Then come five pairs of corresponding stanzas, each pair different from the last. The language of the song is picturesque,

[1] *Agamemnon*, ll. 1-10. Tr. Thomson (Cambridge University Press).

difficult, mysterious. Its theme: the beginning of the expedition against Troy, interrupted by a digression on the wisdom of Zeus. The climax of its story is Agamemnon's sacrifice of his daughter Iphigenia to gain a fair wind for the ships—the killing which Clytemnestra (the audience knows) will avenge today. As the chorus ends its song and the music stops, the Queen and her attendants come out again from the palace, and one of the chorus—their leader—repeats in iambic verse their question about the news. This time she replies:

> Good news! So charged, as the old proverb says,
> May Morning rise out of the womb of night!
> 'Tis yours to hear of joy surpassing hope.
> My news is this: the Greeks have taken Troy.[1]

In rapid question and answer, line for line, Queen and leader move from the first revelation of the victory to the topic of the bringer of the news. Then Clytemnestra plunges into a long speech, and in over fifty lines of superb poetry (interrupted once by the leader) tells how a chain of beacons brought the glad tidings from Troy. The applause is deafening. Even from Aeschylus the Athenian audience has never heard more stirring stuff than this.

When the noise has died down the chorus begins another lengthy song and dance—and so odes and dialogue alternate to the end of the play. This is no place to describe in detail the other scenes that follow: the triumphant but war-weary herald who reports that Agamemnon has landed (the speed of his arrival does not trouble the audience) and will presently reach the town; the coming of the King himself with his prize of war—the princess Cassandra—and his entry into the palace over the carpets of royal red on which Clytemnestra persuades him to walk; the long prophecy of murder by Cassandra, fated not to be believed,

[1] Ll. 276-9. Tr. Thomson.

before she follows him; the shrieks from inside the building while the chorus debate what to do; the revelation in the palace doorway of the bloody scene within—the Queen standing, axe in hand, over the bodies of the dead; the triumphant entry of Aegisthus and the quelling of opposition. When this play is done and the chorus has marched off headed by the flute-player, only a few minutes elapse before the second part of Aeschylus' trilogy shows Orestes' revenge, beginning with solemn ritual at his father's tomb and ending with the young prince fleeing from the Furies. In the third play the building behind the *orchēstra* represents two temples in turn—first, Apollo's at Delphi, then Athena's at Athens, where in a great trial scene Orestes is acquitted and the chain of murder and revenge brought to a close. The chorus is the Furies themselves, and when these dreaded creatures first rush on robed in black, with savage masks and snakes in their hair, there is panic among the audience. But as the play ends with the relenting of the Furies and a representation of the great Panathenaic procession the hearts of the Athenians who make up the mass of the audience swell with pride.

The trilogy is finished, but the great throng does not leave the benches. They know the three tragedies must be followed by another very different performance—a 'satyr-play'. From the name announced beforehand—*Proteus*—they can guess that the theme is to be another tale of a return from Troy, for in the *Odyssey* Agamemnon's brother, Menelaus, tells how on his journey home he met Proteus, the Egyptian old-man-of-the-sea who could change his shape. In this story there is plenty of scope for fun, and the crowd is not disappointed. The dialogue raises roars of laughter with jokes and situations that would have brought the shocked spectators angrily to their feet if they had occurred in the tragedies. But it is the chorus that sets the pace. Each member wears a grotesque mask and a loincloth to which a tail and an erect phallus are attached. Their dances are fast and furious. Their leader, drunken old Silenus, mingles with the actors. After the tension of the tragedies this frolic is a welcome relief.

This finale, shorter than any of the first three plays, brings the morning's spectacle and Aeschylus' part in the festival to a close. Comedy—of which more later—will follow in the afternoon. After three such days of drama the ten judges will write their verdicts on tablets, and five of them will be picked at random to decide the contest. The first prize for tragedies and satyr-play—a crown of ivy and a sum of money from the public treasury—will fall to Aeschylus. When a special assembly of the citizens meets in the theatre two days later to review the conduct of the festival, no one is likely to say the judges were wrong.

I have described one example of fifth-century tragic drama at Athens, but the main features of the description apply to all. Every one of the thirty-two tragedies we still possess and the hundreds now lost was presented in this theatre under these conditions. The Great Dionysia and (after about 433 B.C.) the winter festival of Dionysus called the Lenaea were the only occasions when plays were performed in the city, though similar contests came to be held in other Attic towns. Two facts, I think, stand out from the whole picture: first, drama was part of the life of the entire citizen-body, a product of Athenian democracy—a point still more obvious later in the century, when the entrance money was paid by the state; second, the performance was a religious ceremony rather than a mere entertainment, a spectacle which must have originated in religious ritual. The great size of the theatre was due to the fact that this was a religious occasion to which all the citizens must be able to come.

How did this form of drama arise? What was the original ritual, and how was it connected with democracy? The evidence is slight, inconsistent, open to various interpretations. Like the 'Homeric question', this problem is a jungle where many scholars have lost their way, and many attempts have been made to discover the right path. Amid all the tangle of controversy one guide has been too often forgotten: the relation of the history of drama to the development of society itself.

Instances from many times and places show that religious ritual can easily take on a dramatic form. Various rites in ancient Greece may have had something of this character. But it seems likely that the main root from which all types of drama sprang was the worship of the god at whose festivals they were performed. Dionysus—Bacchus—is pictured today as the god of wine, but to the Greeks he was much more than that. He was a son of the Earth, a god of vegetation, of trees and plants. His gifts were fruitfulness and growth. His incarnations, the most vigorously male of animals—the bull and the goat. The symbols of his power, the luxuriantly-growing ivy and the phallus. Because such a god, like the year, comes forth in full vigour in spring and summer but lies buried during the winter months, he also belonged to the realm beneath the earth's surface and was a lord of the dead. His earliest rites were fertility-magic, wild dances bringing ecstasy to the dancers and new life and growth (as they believed) to orchard and meadow. They were performed mainly by women. Wine was the vehicle of communion with the god and inspiration by his spirit—hence its special place in his worship. But there were stories of more savage things—of midnight revels on the mountains in which the Maenads, frenzied devotees of the god, sought to drink in vital power by tearing living animals and even human beings limb from limb and consuming the warm blood.

This deity of rustic orgies is a being far removed from Zeus or Apollo. The Homeric poems know him as a 'raging' god, but give him no place among the lords of Olympus. Tradition said that his worship came into Greece from the North, from the 'barbarians' of Thrace. A cult with such origins and such a character would hardly appeal to the noble families, the great landowners: it was among the peasantry that Dionysus found a welcome and a home. Simple fertility ritual and local gods of the countryside had existed among them from time immemorial. To the poor and oppressed countryfolk the Bacchic cult brought hope of transcending the hardships and miseries of reality by magic, of escaping from them by ecstasy. The new religion must have spread, absorbing the older rites in its path—a wave of religious emotion like the dancing-madness that swept across medieval Europe during the great plague. Legends indicate that in some places the rulers resisted the invasion and tried to prohibit the new cult, but its appeal was too strong for such methods. The defenders of the older faiths were obliged to adopt the wiser strategy of accepting the newcomer and reducing his worship to more sober and harmless levels. In the course of time he was admitted to the select company of the Olympians. The priests of Delphi eventually welcomed him as second only to Apollo, and at the same time subjected him to their golden rule: 'Nothing too much'. In many cities besides Athens his worship became an official cult with state festivals. At Thebes Maenads were appointed as public functionaries. Under such treatment the wild orgies of the mountain-tops became little more than dim memories of the past, but the old Dionysus, shorn of much of his barbarism, still had a warm place in the peasant's heart. Every village of Attica had its mid-winter celebration in his honour. Secret groups of worshippers devoted themselves to his service. Every farmer dedicated a tree-stump to Dionysus in his orchard.

From many forms of ritual, as an earlier chapter showed, came choral song and dance. The worship of Dionysus gave birth to the type of song and dance known as the 'dithyramb', performed, like other types, by a group and its leader. 'I know how to lead off the pretty tune of Lord Dionysus', says Archilochus, 'my wits thunderstricken with wine'.[1] What was the original nature of the dithyramb? Obviously the answer lies in the ritual itself, and our knowledge of the ritual is not enough to give us a clear picture. Here more than anywhere else in Greek literature comparison with primitive communities has been used to fill the gap, attributing to the Dionysus-cult the rites of other vegetation-spirits or features of initiation ceremonies. Such conjectures can give no certainty, but they are nearer the truth than those who would make the dithyramb a specialised art-form from the first. Artists ascribed to Dionysus, says Plutarch, 'a certain variability combined with playfulness, wantonness, seriousness, and frenzy'.[2] Was the manner of the dithyramb gay or serious? Probably both—and in any case the early Greeks did not make our distinction between the two. Were its themes joyous or sorrowful? Again, both. The year's round brings winter as well as spring, mourning as well as gladness. Dionysus was a god of the dead as well as of new life. Out of dance and song in his honour both tragedy and satyr-drama and comedy could arise.

It was 'from the leaders of the dithyramb', says Aristotle, that tragedy arose.[3] Strongest among several criticisms which have been levelled against his statement is the objection that the dithyramb as we know it is not 'mimetic': the members of the dithyrambic chorus are the mouthpiece of the poet, but unlike the chorus of tragedy they represent nobody but their normal selves. At what stage 'mimetic' choral songs—common elsewhere in primitive ritual—were first performed in honour of Dionysus, we do not know. Whether they were ever included under the

---

[1] *Fr.* 77. Tr. Edmonds (Heinemann, Ltd.).
[2] *The 'E' at Delphi*, 9. Tr. Babbitt (Heinemann, Ltd.).
[3] *Poetics* 1449 a.

term 'dithyramb' (thereby justifying Aristotle) is equally uncertain. But there can be little doubt that it was from such performances that drama evolved, when an 'interpreter' or 'answerer' (*hypokritēs* was the Greek word) was added to the choral rite to make it more readily intelligible to the populace. It was this essentially democratic step that led to the evolution of the form of literature which was to reach its climax in the heyday of Athenian democracy.

What brought about this transformation of simple Bacchic song and dance into something which could be called literature? A change in society itself: not the change to democracy, but the development which opened the way towards it. We must return to the history of the seventh and sixth centuries B.C. When the growing commercial class of that period came into conflict with the landed aristocracy, and 'tyrants' seized power in many states, they sought allies among the discontented peasantry, winning their support by dividing up confiscated estates. But the power and privilege of the noble houses was based on more than material wealth. A mainstay of their ascendancy was their place in the all-important sphere of religion—their domination of the worship of Zeus and Apollo and, above all, their control of the local hero-cults. To loosen their opponents' spiritual grip on the minds of the people the tyrants did not of course attack religion itself. They put new emphasis on other forms of religion, including the worship of the peasants' own beloved deity, Dionysus. To the delight of the countryfolk they raised his cult to a status it had never had before, but in doing so they carried still further the process of changing the orgies that had come from barbarian Thrace into a respectable institution of the civilised state.

Let us look at three instances. The first city on the Greek mainland to set up a 'tyranny' was the natural trade centre, Corinth, where Periander came to power near the end of the seventh century B.C. To his court came Arion from Lesbos. (The fact that later legend made Arion ride on a dolphin's back does not disprove his existence, but connects him with Dionysus, whom dolphins were said to escort across the sea.) It was Arion —encouraged no doubt, by his patron—who turned the crude Bacchic song and dance into the 'dithyramb' as later generations knew it: an 'ode' with definite form and subject, performed by an organised chorus. After this step forward the dithyramb took its place as one of the recognised types of choral song, and became the only type which was popular under democracy. The greatest choral poets included it in their repertoire—Simonides, Pindar, Bacchylides. Six of the latter's dithyrambs still survive. There is little excitement or ecstasy in them. Only one refers to Dionysus: like other kinds of 'ode', the mature dithyramb drew on the whole realm of legend for its material, and often dealt with themes far removed from the ritual out of which it sprang.

At Sicyon, a dozen miles from Corinth, Cleisthenes was 'tyrant' early in the sixth century B.C. The historian Herodotus tells us[1] that when Sicyon was at war with its neighbour, Argos, Cleisthenes did away with the worship of the Argive hero, Adrastus, and transferred to Dionysus 'tragic choruses' with which Adrastus had been honoured. The story shows that here at any rate some kind of dramatic performance had sprung up as part of a hero-cult. One may suspect that Cleisthenes' motive for the change was more complex than Herodotus suggests: that he hoped both to rally the peasantry to his support and to weaken the nobles who opposed his rule and would readily have tried to overthrow him by acting as a fifth column for the enemy from without.

Corinth and Sicyon were both Dorian states, and these events lend some colour to the Dorian claim to have originated drama. But its true birthplace was Athens, and Pisistratus was the infant's

[1] v, 67.

beneficent uncle, though not its father. To dim the importance of the local hero-cults which the aristocracy controlled, the Athenian ruler in the middle of the sixth century not only used the splendour of the Panathenaea with its Homeric recitals: he also built a new temple of Dionysus, and enriched the religious calendar by founding or reorganising a spring festival of the god, the most magnificent of them all—the 'Great Dionysia of the City' which I have already described. The dithyrambic contest which Pisistratus included in the festival gave new importance to the advance made by Arion. The tragic competition was based on the achievement of Thespis, himself the victor about 534 B.C. It was Thespis who in a performance at Icaria, a village north-east of Athens, had taken the crucial step for the change from choral song to drama, introducing an actor (*hypokritēs*) who could deliver speeches and converse with the chorus-leader. Here was the first step towards dramatic dialogue, the beginning of tragedy. The meaning of the name, 'goat-song', clearly connects it in some way with Dionysus—perhaps through the tradition that in Thespis' day a goat was the prize.

Thespian drama, if one can call it such, must have been a simple and unpretentious affair. But once it had become a state institution, a spectacle for all the citizenry of Athens to watch, no village mummery would suffice. The choral song and dance—still the main part of the performance—must have taken on new dignity and elaboration from the example of other choral poetry, including the dithyramb. And in their need for themes to put before the public, poets here too deserted Dionysus, and naturally turned to the same rich storehouse in which the choral poets found material for their songs and the vehicle of their thoughts—all the wealth of heroic legend which was then becoming common property. Stories told at length in the *Iliad* and *Odyssey* were generally avoided: their place was the Panathenaea. But else-where in the saga there were dramatic themes in plenty. By resorting to the treasurehouse of epic poetry these first play-wrights found figures of more than human stature for the actor to represent, characters already moulded by epic into beings suitable for drama. Agamemnon could walk straight out of the *Iliad* into the theatre. So to the Bacchic ritual was added all the glamour and adventure of the heroic age; to the crudity of the early mimetic dithyramb (or whatever it should be called), all the splendour of Homer. Here was stuff of which great drama could and would be made. But it is not surprising that many among the audience complained, as we are told, that all this had 'nothing to do with Dionysus'.[1] When Pratinas about the end of the sixth century came to Athens from the Northern Peloponnese and brought with him the Bacchic satyr-drama which had developed there, the novelty was welcomed by the populace as a means of reinstating their beloved Dionysus at his own festival. A few years later the dramatic contest was reorganised, and a play with satyr-chorus and characters usually suited to such stuff was included with the three tragedies which each competing poet must present.

With the introduction of one actor tragedy had begun to emerge from its choral shell. To give it freedom of movement and growth two actors were needed, between whom there could be dialogue and action in which the chorus took no part. This second vital move towards drama as we know it was made by Aeschylus about the beginning of the fifth century B.C. Yet the striking feature of the history of the outward form of tragedy—not of its inner meaning or dramatic quality—in the hundred years that followed is not the speed of its development, but the slowness. Here more than anywhere else in Greek literature the sequel to the rise of a new form was its transformation into a fixed convention, and once again environment and circumstances were the cause. Although only the dithyrambic contest at the

[1] E.g. Plutarch, *Convivial Questions* I, I, 5.

148

Great Dionysia was organised on a tribal basis, the citizens of Athens at their common festival had much of the conservatism of the tribe—far more than had been felt among the aristocrats of Ionia or in the atmosphere of the tyrant's court. In the performance of a religious ceremony—and drama continued to be that—they would not easily accept change. The nature of the theatre in which the contest was held, with the great dancing-ground as its central feature, helped to keep the plays within the same ritual mould. Strongest of all restraining influences was the contest itself: a playwright who went too far in flouting public conservatism had little chance of being accepted as a competitor, still less of winning the coveted first prize.

Convention left its mark on every aspect of tragedy: themes, language, chorus, actors. Let us look at each in turn.

The themes. After the great extension of the subject-matter by the inclusion of heroic legend some poets went even further, and turned to contemporary history for their plots. Soon after Ionian Miletus, greatest city of Asiatic Greece, had fallen to the Persians in 494 B.C., Phrynichus dramatised the catastrophe in a play called *The Capture of Miletus*. Its reception is reported by Herodotus:

> The whole theatre burst into tears, and the people sentenced him to pay a fine of a thousand drachmas, for recalling to them their own misfortunes. They likewise made a law, that no one should ever again exhibit that piece.[1]

Playwrights thereafter took care to dramatise the Athenians' successes, not disasters which touched their consciences. Phrynichus' *Phoenician Women* in 476 and Aeschylus' *Persians* in 472 both celebrated the victory of Salamis. Even in these the scene is set in Persia, and, as a recent commentator has put it, 'remoteness of place compensates for nearness in time'.[2] Although

[1] VI, 21. This and all other quotations from Herodotus are from the translation by George Rawlinson (John Murray).

[2] Kitto, *Greek Tragedy*, p. 35.

both won the prize, the experiment of historical drama was not repeated. Throughout the rest of the fifth century legend was the playwright's sole material, and even within the sphere of legend a few favourites were repeated again and again. Tragedy might be a product of democracy, but the main characters were always the kings and queens and nobles of the past. Only the heroic figures of saga, figures who could move on the same plane as the gods, fitted the great religious occasion and the heightened language for which it called. Thought, it is true, could give the legend new shape, new emphasis. But it is equally true that legend shaped the dramatists' thought: with the partial exception of Euripides, they did not use the ancient stories as means of presenting ideas which they could equally well have expressed in more rational terms. They brought gods and heroes into the theatre because such were the terms in which they saw the problems of human life.

The use of traditional legendary themes not only moulded the thought of tragedy: it also affected the quality of the plays as plays. There was little room for original plots or novel characters. When the performance began, the audience already knew the outline of its contents. New turns of plot, new subtleties of intrigue could only be achieved by reshaping the old material. But the audience's knowledge brought the poet advantages as well as limitations. He could be confident that the vast throng would follow the familiar theme. He could put into the mouths of his characters remarks with an added significance for those who knew what was to come. No drama excels Attic tragedy in the use of tragic irony.

The language. The diction of Aeschylus, as we shall see, was all his own, but in employing such magnificent 'heightened language' in the theatre he was not unique. The few lines and phrases which have reached us from other early dramatists suggest that the tragic chorus took its manner of speech not from its first crude origins, but from the developed choral ode. As long as the actor remained closely bound to the chorus, his language would echo theirs. To many of the Athenian audience such stuff must have seemed as Euripides describes it in Aristophanes' *Frogs*:

> Long words, with crests and beetling brows, and gorgons round the
> That no man ever heard on earth.   border,

'Intelligible—not one line!' cries Euripides.[1] One change in tragedy during the century was the development of the dialogue, at any rate, towards something which the humblest member of the public could understand, something nearer to the simplicity and directness of prose—a change that went hand in hand with the growth of rationalism of thought.

The chorus. It was at the expense of the chorus that the dramatic aspect of tragedy, the dialogue, came into its own. The number of dancers was reduced: according to Aristotle, it fell from fifty to twelve and then rose to fifteen. Their share in the lines of the play dropped to a quarter or less. But their continued importance is shown by the number of plays named after them. Each dramatist, as we shall see, has his own way of handling this legacy from the past, yet to a large extent its character and function remain the same. The songs of the chorus, like the odes of Pindar or Simonides, are generally a mixture of myth and moralisation. Often they have little to do with the action. Their leader's part in the dialogue rarely goes beyond a repetition of conventional maxims evidently expected by the Athenian audience, but boring to the modern reader. The chorus of tragedy, like Pindar's chorus, links the particular with the universal, places the incidents and characters of the play against the general background of Greek legend and tradition. But its very existence also had a profound effect on the entire performance. Although

---

[1] Ll. 925-7. Tr. Murray (George Allen and Unwin, Ltd.).

Attic tragedy by no means always follows the 'unities' of time and place which have been mistakenly read into Aristotle's account, although lapses of time are frequently taken for granted—as in the *Agamemnon*—and in two of our extant plays there are changes of scene, yet the presence of the chorus from its entry to the end made change of place difficult and encouraged 'unity of action'—the treatment of the action, without break or by-plot, as one organic and continuous whole. Because of the chorus a fifth-century tragedy could not easily be a serial drama, leaping from incident to incident and place to place. It usually embodied the climax of the story, the culminating episode in the familiar legend on which it was based. If the three plays of a trilogy dealt with the same theme, they presented three culminating points. Hence another consequence: such plays leave no great scope for development of character. The hero's nature may be revealed to the audience step by step, but in most of the extant tragedies it does not change. In emotional tension, in the mood of the characters, in the tone of the whole spectacle there tends to be little variation, little rise and fall, only a continuous and ever-growing intensity which some find monotonous, others overwhelming.

The actors, of course, remained masked, and female roles continued to be played by men. When a state prize for acting was instituted in 449 B.C., voice and gesture must have been the keys to victory. Facial expression could not be seen: quick movement was impossible. A third actor was introduced by Sophocles, and the innovation was adopted by others, including Aeschylus: the *Agamemnon* needs three. But there the increase in the number stopped. One actor per character was never the custom in the Greek theatre. Silent roles, even crowd scenes, could be performed by 'extras', one of whom occasionally might speak a line or two, but all considerable speaking parts were shared between the three actors: with negligible exceptions, never could more than three speaking characters be before the audience at once. Even these were not fully used: the habits of earlier times remained. Dialogue in the extant tragedies is mostly duologue, three-cornered conversation is rare. A character who enters normally speaks first to the chorus, as in the old one-actor days. Murder and violent death (except, sometimes, suicide) take place 'off' and are reported by a messenger—an inevitable arrangement when only one actor took all parts, but probably also a reflection of some feature of the ritual background, at which we can only guess. From the same background, and perhaps from imitation of the choral ode, comes the strange formality of the dialogue—the symmetrical balance of line against line in rapid give and take, of speech against speech in debate.

Tragedy as I have described it was not only a creation of democracy. It was a product of the particular phase of Athenian democracy which reached and passed its climax during the fifth century B.C.—a democracy whose temporary unity was cemented by a common outlook, by the common heritage of legend and mythology from which drama drew its material. When that unity disintegrated, when the common outlook was undermined, tragedy also declined. So far I have stressed the sameness of this fifth-century product, the common features which strike one at first acquaintance, especially in translations which cannot fully reproduce differences of language and style. But within the limits of the convention each of the three great tragic poets whom we can still read has his own individual stamp, reflects a different aspect of the democracy for which they all wrote, reveals a different stage in the growth or decay of its unity and its traditions. It is time to turn to Aeschylus, Sophocles, and Euripides and contrast the different content and significance which they put into the conventional form, the different effects which their treatment

had on the form itself. First it may be useful to list the names
and (where possible) the dates of their extant plays.

AESCHYLUS (525-456)

	B.C.		B.C.
Suppliant Women		*Agamemnon*	458
Persians	472	*Libation-Bearers*	458
Seven Against Thebes	467	*Furies*	458
Prometheus Bound			

SOPHOCLES (496-406)

Ajax		*Electra*	
Antigone	441	*Philoctetes*	409
Women of Trachis		*Oedipus at Colonus*	
Oedipus the King			

EURIPIDES (484 or 480-406)

Alcestis	438	*Ion*	
Medea	431	*Iphigenia among the*	
Hippolytus	428	*Taurians*	
Children of Heracles		*Electra*	413
Andromache		*Helen*	412
Hecuba		*Phoenician Women*	
Suppliant Women		*Orestes*	408
Mad Heracles		*Bacchae*	406
Trojan Women	415	*Iphigenia at Aulis*	

Satyr-play: *Cyclops*
Attributed to Euripides: *Rhesus*

AESCHYLUS: THE MAKING OF A DRAMATIST

Little is known about the life of Aeschylus. He was born
during the last years of 'tyranny' at Athens, and lived to see the
final stages in the growth of Athenian democracy. All his life
seems to have been spent in Attica except for two visits to the

court of Hieron of Syracuse. He fought at Marathon and probably at Salamis, and his epitaph at Gela, in Sicily—composed, according to one authority, by himself—points to the Persian Wars as the central event in his experience:

> This tomb the dust of Aeschylus doth hide,
> Euphorion's son, and fruitful Gela's pride.
> How tried his valour Marathon may tell,
> And long-haired Medes who knew it all too well.[1]

The lines make no reference to his plays. Aeschylus lived in the day when poetry came second to citizenship.

Aeschylus is a difficult author: difficult in language, difficult in thought. Even his contemporaries found him puzzling, although they shared the same background of experience and tradition. The few facts of his biography make little or no contribution towards an understanding of his work. But there is one point on which not enough stress has been laid: his position in the growth of tragedy, in the process of the transformation of ritual into drama. Aeschylus is not a playwright using an already developed instrument. He is a great choral poet gradually mastering the new offshoot from choral poetry, gradually learning to be a dramatist. Contemporary with Pindar, he belongs to the maturity of the choral ode, and handles it with expert assurance. But his work represents the youth of tragedy, its vigorous early life, its growing pains. The outward signs of his achievement are simple. It was he who made real drama possible by introducing a second actor. His earliest extant tragedy, the *Suppliant Women*, has two, though the second is scarcely used; the *Oresteia*[2] has three. The *Suppliant Women* has a chorus of fifty, who fill most of the play; in the *Oresteia* they number only twelve or fifteen, and their share of the lines

[1] Athenaeus xiv, 627 c. Tr. Plumptre.

[2] A collective title often used for the 'trilogy', *Agamemnon, Libation-Bearers, Furies*.

has dropped to about a third. But the organic growth of choral song into drama was responsible for more than technical changes: it left its mark on every aspect of Aeschylus' works—their themes, their characters, their plots, their language.

Because maturity had not been reached, because tragedy had not yet become a fixed convention, Aeschylus was more adventurous and more experimental, more varied in choice of subject-matter and scene, than any of those who came after him. Titles and fragments from the eighty or ninety plays which he may have written are enough to show the diversity of his themes. At least eleven tragedies were concerned with Dionysus. One trilogy was based on the *Iliad*. Others drew on the whole range of heroic saga and local myth. Even the seven extant plays are very different from each other. I have already described the *Oresteia* and mentioned the *Persians*—a national thanksgiving for the victory of Salamis adapted to tragedy by placing the scene at the Persian court. The *Suppliant Women*, earliest play in European literature, was the strange legend of the fifty daughters of Danaus who fled from Egypt to Argos to escape marriage with their fifty cousins—a tale in which some see a memory of the struggle between matriarchy and patriarchy, others a reflection of the conflict between endogamy and exogamy, but which in the Athenians a few years before Marathon must have roused thoughts of the threat from 'barbarian' Persia against Greece. The *Seven Against Thebes* tells part of the story of the family of Oedipus, a favourite subject with later dramatists—the fatal struggle between Oedipus' sons, Eteocles and Polynices, for possession of Thebes. The *Prometheus Bound* draws its material from Hesiod and a local Athenian cult, transformed by Aeschylus into a vast drama of the battle between the champion of mankind and the tyranny of Zeus. The scenes of the plays are as varied as their subject-matter—not only Athens or Thebes or Argos, but the Persian capital or the wild Caucasus. Aeschylus knows nothing of the limitations of scale commonly accepted by later dramatists, ancient and modern alike. He crosses the seas as nimbly as the beacon message of the fall of Troy. In the *Prometheus* the tale of Io's wanderings carries us across continents: the play as a whole is set against the background of the entire universe.

The makers of epic had told such stories as these for the sake of story-telling. The choral poets had a different approach to legend. For them the familiar saga was the accepted material for poetry on great occasions, the traditional mould which gave shape to the traditional beliefs which were their stock-in-trade. They turned without question to the stories of the heroic or mythical past as the traditional examples of the working of those forces which, as they saw it, dominated human life—not only the will of Zeus and Apollo and the other Olympians, but older and more shadowy deities, often seen as servants of Zeus: Temptation which could lead a man to sin; Infatuation which could drive him to folly and ruin; the Curse upon a family which brought disaster to generation after generation; Avengers swift in punishment and ruthless in pursuit. For the choral poet these forces were no abstractions. Though they might enter into human beings and use human character as their instrument, they were living creatures with an existence of their own.

Aeschylus is such a choral poet. He too is concerned with religious and moral problems, which he sees not in terms of abstract or rational ideas, but of the legends handed down from the past. Many of his choral odes retell the familiar stories, full of all the figures that move in his mythical world—men, spirits, gods. But he not only describes: he also tries to *represent* these figures, to make them step out of the picture given in choral song and come alive. Apollo, Athena, Prometheus; Force, Might, the Furies; avenging ghosts of the dead; men and women in whom unseen Powers are at work—all these constitute the people of his plays. Like a stereoscope, the art of Aeschylus makes these figures stand out in a new perspective, though the picture to which they belong remains the same as before. The increasing vividness with which they come alive is the measure of his growth as an artist. Significantly enough, he progresses farthest towards realism in portraying minor, nameless characters who had no place in the traditional background—the watchman, herald and nurse of the *Oresteia*. His main figures are increasingly vivid, but never realistic. Each of them embodies one striking characteristic—Hate, Pride, Anger—implanted in them by forces beyond their control. That simple fact, dramatised with appalling intensity, is all that we see. Eteocles goes to his death because Anger, the Curse of his family, comes upon him and he cannot resist. After murdering her husband Clytemnestra cries:

> You say this is *my* work—mine?
> Do not cozen yourself that I am Agamemnon's wife.
> Masquerading as the wife
> Of the corpse there the old sharp-witted Genius
> Of Atreus who gave the cruel banquet
> Has paid with a grown man's life
> The due for children dead.[1]

Because his characters are not realistic Aeschylus does not hesitate to use them as his own mouthpieces, to give them speeches which fit neither them nor the situation. When the ghost of Darius in the *Persians* rises from his tomb he surveys Persian history—interesting to the Athenian audience, but scarcely necessary at this crisis in the Persian court. Although he has to be told of his country's present plight, he knows and forecasts the future: Aeschylus wanted to introduce the victory of Plataea as well as Salamis.

The growing life of Aeschylus' characters has a corollary: growing differentiation of the actors from the chorus. In his earliest plays both chorus and actors moved on the same

[1] *Agamemnon*, ll. 1498-505. Tr. MacNeice (Faber and Faber, Ltd.).

unrealistic plane, and at first the chorus, which had been 'mimetic' before individual 'interpreters' were thought of, was less stiff than the actors in playing its part: Danaus' fifty daughters are more alive than their father. But the chorus could not follow the dialogue on the path to greater realism. Their traditional function was to dance and sing; the form of their utterances was already stereotyped. They lost life and vigour as the actors gained it. In the *Agamemnon* and *Libation-Bearers* there is a gulf between the chorus and the individual characters: the dancers no longer share effectively in the action. To suit their impotence Aeschylus has made them old men, helpless women—colourless creatures compared with the vigorous Danaids. It is typical of Aeschylus' versatility that in the *Furies* he returns to a chorus with a key part in the plot. But he has shifted the gulf, not removed it. Like all the characters of the *Prometheus*, Apollo, Athena, Clytemnestra's ghost, even the Prophetess move on the same supernatural level as the Chorus. It is the human figure's turn to be colourless: Orestes is no more than a puppet amid the divine debate.

Life brings movement. As Aeschylus' individual characters become more vividly alive, they create new possibilities of dramatic action, intrigue, the collision of conflicting wills. Amid the stiff splendour of the *Suppliant Women* there is only one dramatic moment: the clash between Pelasgus and the Herald. Compared with this the *Libation-Bearers*, thirty or forty years later, is full of melodrama. Yet Aeschylus is no deviser of skilful plots: he does not try to be. The movement of his characters, like their nature, is still shaped by the origins of his art, still takes place within the framework of the picture as the choral poets saw it, still reflects the ritual atmosphere in which the whole performance took place. The ritual structure of the plays is more obvious in scenes where the chorus takes part, but it is there even when the dialogue is most free from the chorus. The situations which Aeschylus puts before his audience often have a ceremonial content—the rite of seeking sanctuary which forms the whole framework of the *Suppliant Women*; the prayers which summon Darius from his tomb in the *Persians*, and the solemn mourning at the end; in the *Libation-Bearers*, the long rite at Agamemnon's grave which gives the play its name. Where the content is not ritual there is still a ceremonial quality—the formal parade of champions which leads up to the moral climax of the *Seven Against Thebes;* Agamemnon's walk across the royal carpets to his death; the great trial scene and procession which close the *Oresteia*. The dramatic effect of these spectacles does not depend on surprise. It is the dramatic power of ritual itself: the raising of emotion to an ever higher pitch, the gradual fulfilment of foreboding felt from the beginning. The Persian court is uneasily aware from the first of the disaster of Salamis. In the *Agamemnon* the watchman's opening speech strikes the notes of fear and horror which swell into a deafening crescendo as the play proceeds.

In all these ways Aeschylus' nearness to the choral origins of tragedy helps to explain the puzzling nature of his plays. It throws still more light on the feature which modern readers find most difficult of all—his language. Aeschylus' use of the Greek tongue was all his own. No other poet goes so far as he in the use of strange compound words, in piling adjective on adjective, in the creation of metaphors which cram the force of a whole Homeric simile into a single phrase. Metaphor, it has been said, is 'Aeschylus' natural speech'.[1] But if the species is unique, we can at any rate see the genus to which it belongs—the language of the choral ode. Like Pindar, Aeschylus had his own highly individual version of the complex and splendid diction to which choral song had risen. And because choral poetry set the keynote for his plays, he put into the mouths of his characters language

[1] Norwood, *Greek Tragedy*, p. 123.

little less strange and metaphorical than he employed in his odes. His boldness did not decrease with time. If his use of words changed, it was in the same direction as the rest of his development: increasing adaptation to the needs of drama. In the later plays strange words and phrases and metaphors are used less for ornament, more to express essential meaning and represent character, until there is much justification for the claim which Aristophanes puts into the poet's mouth in the *Frogs:*

> When the subject is great and the sentiment, then
> of necessity, great grows the word;
> When heroes give range to their hearts, is it strange
> if the speech of them over us towers?[1]

Powerful and majestic figures must speak in a fashion suited to their strength and stature. Never have they been given more powerful and majestic language than Aeschylus built up for them out of the magnificence of choral song.

The ideas which Aeschylus conceived in terms of myth and legend cannot be translated into the language of rational argument. He is no problem playwright whose secret can be tracked down like the solution to a detective story, no dogmatist writing treatises on theology. Among the few surviving plays and the little we know of the rest it is difficult to find a common denominator, certainly impossible to discover a precise system of ideas. His thought is not systematic, any more than it is abstract. But by concentrating on our knowledge of certain trilogies as wholes, by remembering that any one tragedy of Aeschylus (except the *Persians*) is only one act of a three-act drama, it is possible to trace a more or less consistent trend—a trend coloured by the temper of the age in which he lived.

Aeschylus was a tragic playwright, but he did not see human life as a tragedy. Though death and horror were his constant theme,

[1] Ll. 1058-60. Tr. Murray (George Allen and Unwin, Ltd.).

he was one of the few exceptions to the fatalistic pessimism which pervades Greek poetry. Like the Victorians, he lived in times when material advance, though at the expense of others, could appear to open up an unending vista of progress, when the building of Empire could still seem a noble mission, when the optimism born of victory in a great struggle for survival still held sway. The key point in his political thought was the glory which Athens attained in unity against the Persians, and he believed that the unity of those Marathon days must be maintained through compromise between the conflicting classes and ideas. The ending of the *Oresteia* makes his outlook clear. He welcomes the new treaty with Argos, accepts the trial of homicide as the original function of the Areopagus, but magnifies to the utmost the Council's importance and dignity. The same attitude reappears in his handling of the wider conflicts which he dramatises — the clash between man's struggling intelligence and the apparent arbitrariness of the world in which he lives, or between the opposing forces which govern human life. Aeschylus was both more serious and more hopeful than Homer in his view of the gods and the world. He died before the unity of Greece disintegrated into the Peloponnesian War, the unity of Athens into violent class strife; before doubt and scepticism undermined tradition and faith; before the hidden cancer of slavery afflicted the whole body politic with incurable disease.

How then did Aeschylus explain the evils and horrors of existence, so strongly reflected in the legends on which he based his plays? 'Sing sorrow, sorrow, but let the good prevail!' cry the chorus in the *Agamemnon*.[1] Just as the dangers and miseries of the Persian War were the prelude to the great days of Athens, so through both sin and suffering the ways of Zeus work out for the best in the end. This was the theme of the drama of which the *Suppliant Women* was the first act: out of violence and murder

[1] L. 121.

emerged the wise decision of the one daughter of Danaus who accepted marriage and became the ancestress of the kings of prosperous Argos. But Aeschylus did not remain content with this justification of the ways of god to man. In his later plays he developed a concept foreign to modern belief in natural law or a fixed divine order, but easy for the flexible anthropomorphism of the Greeks: the gods, even Zeus himself, learn by experience, change with the passage of time. Homer's Zeus was a king like Agamemnon. Aeschylus interpreted the myth in terms nearer to his own times. For him Zeus was originally a tyrant who seized power by force and exercised arbitrary rule. But the tyrant could become a philosopher-king. Shelley, the revolutionary dreamer, ended Prometheus' struggle by the overthrow of Jupiter: Aeschylus closed his Prometheus trilogy with reconciliation between a wiser and more just King of Heaven and the Champion of Man. The final scene of the *Oresteia* brings divine and human peace on to the same plane, makes the new unity of the gods and the glory of united Athens part of the same picture. Apollo, son of Zeus, and the Furies are reconciled by the human court set up by Athena, daughter of Zeus. Their new harmony exemplified the growing wisdom of Zeus, for all of them are his servants. The Furies become the Kindly Ones, future guardians of Athenian prosperity, and as gods and citizens form a triumphant procession to escort them to their new home the assurance rings out that there shall be no more strife among the deities, no more strife in Athens. In the words of one of the greatest of the Victorians:

> God's in his heaven—
> All's right with the world!

SOPHOCLES: THE ARTIST

Sophocles' long life covered the whole brilliant period of Athens' rise to leadership of Greece, and ended two years before

her defeat in 404 B.C. Tradition represents him as a typical
Athenian of the upper class. His father was a rich manufacturer,
but of noble birth. As a handsome boy Sophocles led with his
lyre the chorus in honour of the battle of Salamis—the victory
which Aeschylus celebrated in the *Persians*. Later he held high
political and military office. He was associated with Cimon,
opponent of extreme democracy and friend of Sparta. In his old
age he probably took part in the limitation of democracy towards
the end of the Peloponnesian War.

If he prospered as a citizen, he fared still better as a playwright.
His early plays may have had Aeschylus' simplicity: none has
survived from his first twenty years of writing. But in the seven
we now possess he is the conscious master of technique, the
conscious artist—the man who, we are told, gathered round him
a 'company of the educated', and wrote a book on tragedy. Of all
the fifth-century dramatists, Sophocles was the most skilled in
exploiting the limited possibilities which the convention allowed.
His purpose was to write successful plays, and he achieved it. He
learned from Aeschylus, and in craftsmanship far surpassed him.
Victorious over the older poet with his first production in 468 B.C.,
he composed perhaps 123 plays, and won the first prize with 96
of them. He never sank below second place.

> How blest was Sophocles. His many plays
> Were beautiful, and after many days
> Of a good life, he suffered no great ill,
> But died as he had lived, an artist still.

So wrote a comic poet[1] soon after Sophocles' death, and the
picture of him as a happy artist is the common verdict of antiquity.

With Sophocles, tragedy becomes a mature form of art. But
much more than his technique and craftsmanship must be

[1] Phrynichus, *fr.* 31 (Kock). Tr. Sheppard, *The Wisdom of Sophocles*
(George Allen and Unwin, Ltd.).

examined if one is to understand the advance he made. The starting point for study of his work, as of the other dramatists, is his attitude towards the myths and legends he used in his plays.

This prosperous aristocrat was not likely to become a follower of the new ideas or the new scepticism which spread at Athens during the latter part of his life. In religion he is the most orthodox of the three great tragic poets. For him Zeus is supreme—an unchanging Zeus—but the god who matters almost more than Zeus is Apollo. In five of the seven extant tragedies the fulfilment of oracles (which contemporary doubters were already attacking) plays a large part. Occasionally scepticism is put into the mouth of his characters, but only to be refuted. Unlike either Aeschylus or Euripides, Sophocles takes the traditional stories as they stand, and without questioning their value or their truth accepts them as the subject-matter of his plays. Yet there is one way at least in which he is deeply affected by the tendency of his time. The individualism which had arisen earlier in Ionia and now reared its head once again in Athens, finding its strongest spokesmen in the Sophists and Socrates, had a profound influence on Sophocles' conception of human character, human motives, human relationships. Every one of the extant plays focuses our attention on individual character. Two of them dramatise a clash between the individual and the state or the collective welfare—the *Antigone* and the *Philoctetes*, where Neoptolemus' conscience conflicts with the needs of all the Greeks at Troy. One tragedy—the *Oedipus at Colonus*—raises the question of man's individual responsibility for his fate. Sophocles has not Aeschylus' wide sweep across vast areas of space or time. Though the gods are always present—and all-important—in the background of his work, in the foreground they have little place. Except for Athena in the *Ajax* and Heracles at the end of the *Philoctetes* the figures he brings into the theatre are all human. They are not beings possessed, mere embodiments of Pride or Hate, mere victims of a Curse passing from generation to generation. Their driving force is within them. Their actions spring from their own complex personality, as heredity and environment have moulded it. Aeschylus stamps Agamemnon or Clytemnestra or Eteocles with a single striking quality, continually intensified as the play goes on. Sophocles uses all his technique to show us the whole personality of Oedipus or Electra. One aspect after another is revealed by clashes with other characters, by the impact of events. Minor figures are introduced as foils to the great. Antigone's passionate determination is thrown into sharper relief by the 'common sense' attitude of her sister, Ismene. Electra gains stature by comparison with Chrysothemis, who in the corresponding play of Aeschylus—the *Libation-Bearers*—does not appear at all.

As the characters of the dialogue acquired flesh and blood, the chorus also was affected by the change. Sophocles had no counterpart to Aeschylus' Daughters of Danaus or Furies. His chorus was always on a different level of reality from the actors. Not only had they fewer verses to sing than before. Their vitality dwindled as that of the individual characters increased. If they had personality, it was personality in a minor key. The same process of differentiation can be seen in the development of Sophocles' use of language: the dialogue in his later plays becomes simpler, more natural, more suited to the speakers, less and less like the elaborate and partly conventional style which he at first adopted (as far as we can judge from the fragments of his early work) from choral song, and which he retained to some extent in his odes. Yet although in this way the gap between chorus and dialogue has widened, it does not destroy the unity of the play. The two have not broken away from each other, but the tables have been turned, and the chorus, which for Aeschylus still set the tone and provided the framework for the tragedy, is now secondary to the actors. Nowhere does Sophocles show greater artistry than in handling the choral sections of his dramas, in subordinating them to his dramatic purpose. Often the chorus is used to place still more emphasis on the hero or heroine: Electra's women help us to see the story through their mistress' eyes. In every play (the *Philoctetes* is the outstanding example) the chorus is worked into the plot. It plays its part in the intrigue. Like the actors, it is unaware of the catastrophe to come. Songs shared between the chorus and an actor often replace choral odes. The odes themselves—some of the finest of all Greek poetry— are always relevant to the dialogue.

Because the words and actions of individual characters con- stituted the essential core of a Sophoclean tragedy, because their movements were no longer so restricted by the framework of choral ritual, because he was less concerned with the religious problems which his themes involved, Sophocles was able to develop complexities of plot far surpassing anything we find in Aeschylus. Aristotle rightly regards him as the greatest master of plot among the Greek dramatists, although only three plays— the *Electra*, *Oedipus the King*, and *Philoctetes*—now reveal his mastery to the full. The ritual atmosphere of so many scenes in Aeschylus finds little place in Sophocles, except perhaps in his last play. Where Aeschylus reaches the goal of his story by the direct and obvious route, Sophocles makes brilliant twists and turns on the way. Where Aeschylus prepares for his climax by foreboding in which both characters and audience take part, Sophocles brings it about with a shock of surprise. And because the audience knows the outcome of his play but the characters— or some of them—do not, he can fill line after line, scene after scene, with dramatic irony: Electra mourning over the urn which (as she thinks) holds her brother's ashes, while the living Orestes stands beside her; Oedipus uttering a terrible curse which, we know, must fall on his own head.

A single example will illustrate the kind of change which

Sophocles made. Aeschylus ends his *Libation-Bearers* with Orestes' murder of Aegisthus and Clytemnestra. The story is simply told. Aegisthus, fetched by the nurse, enters a wing of the palace and is killed there. A servant hurries out shouting for Clytemnestra, but even as she comes through the main door Orestes rushes upon her and after a moment of hesitation at her plea for mercy drives her in to her death. The two bodies are displayed with Orestes standing over them, but while he stands there his mind fills with terror. The Furies are already at work.

In Sophocles' *Electra*, Orestes and his friend Pylades gain entrance to the palace by pretending that they are strangers bringing news of Orestes' death and carrying his ashes. There they kill Clytemnestra. Aegisthus, away from home when they arrived, returns in haste and asks Electra where the strangers are. 'In the house', she replies. 'To the heart of their hostess they have found their way.'[1] Soon Orestes and Pylades are revealed standing over Clytemnestra's body, which is covered with a sheet. Aegisthus does not recognise them, but pretends sorrow at sight of the remains (as he imagines) of Orestes, and then turns to an attendant:

Aegisthus Go call me Clytemnestra through the house.
Orestes (*as Aegisthus removes the sheet*). She is beside thee: look not far off for her.
Aegisthus What sight is this?
Orestes   So scared? Is the face strange?
Aegisthus Who are the men, into whose net I have
               Thus helpless fallen?
Orestes   Hast thou not yet discerned
               Thou dost accost the living as the dead?[2]

Aegisthus, realising the truth at last, is driven within and struck down, and the play is over. To the Furies no reference is made. The two versions are similar—and yet how different!

---

[1] L. 1451. Tr. Whitelaw (Rivingtons).
[2] Ll. 1473-9. Tr. Whitelaw.

Aeschylus moulded the story to fit his conception of its significance. His climax is the mother-murder and its sequel. Sophocles' object is to produce a dramatic—almost melodramatic —thrill. His magnificent *coup de théâtre* is clearly an advance in craftsmanship, in dramatic technique. Whether it raises the play to a higher level than the close of the *Libation-Bearers* is a matter for dispute.

Sophocles' characters, I have emphasised, are individual human beings. They have complex interrelations with each other, move through complex plots. But they are not ordinary people, nor have they ordinary fates. All of them, of course, are taken from heroic legend—kings, princes, nobles and their underlings. But the poet's picture of them is not fixed by saga or tradition: even in the surviving plays he gives us two sharply contrasted portraits of Odysseus, three very different Creons. He himself said that he depicted men as they ought to be depicted, while Euripides depicted them as they are.[1] Sophocles was no realist. His field of vision of humanity was limited by the aristocratic conception of what characters should be—a conception which owed much to Homer, but is often foreign to the modern mind. Low-born folk like the semi-comic sentinel of the *Antigone* have their own low attitude, far removed from the aristocratic ideal, but the great figures move on a higher plane. The virtues prized among them are those which aristocrats valued most highly: courage, frankness, a sense of honour. Their faults, like those of Achilles, are noble faults: pride, anger, ambition, vengefulness, not cowardice or meanness.

For Sophocles, the proper subject of tragedy is the downfall of such beings when success brings catastrophe upon them. There are figures in his plays who, with or without understanding, obey the gods' precept of wisdom and restraint and, echoed by the chorus, advise others to do the same: Odysseus in the *Ajax*,

[1] Aristotle, *Poetics* 1460 b.

Theseus in the *Oedipus at Colonus*; on a lower plane, Ismene in the *Antigone*, Chrysothemis in the *Electra*. But fortunately it is not such sober creatures who play the main part in the tragedies. Sophocles writes dramas, not sermons. Not the upholders but the breakers of divine law, beings with the qualities which aristocracy admired, but whom passion or self-will brings to the brink of disaster or plunges down to the depths—these dominate Sophocles' plays just as Satan dominates *Paradise Lost*, or Dido the fourth book of the *Aeneid*. The *Ajax* may be a lesson in wisdom and moderation which is incomplete till the end, but it is Ajax himself, proud and vengeful but neither wise nor moderate, who steals the play. In the story of Orestes it is Electra who absorbs Sophocles' attention—the embittered daughter who cries:

> No shame? You may be sure I am ashamed
> Although you think not so. I understand.
> I know that what I do passes all bounds
> And is unworthy of me, but your hate
> Forces me, and your evil deeds compel me
> To forget shame because my life is shameful.[1]

The longest role in the *Antigone* is given not to the heroine but to Creon, who in the name of the state and political expediency denies the higher law of the gods—and is punished with horror and misery. Sometimes the heart of the tragedy lies in the victim's realisation of his mistake: it is not only Oedipus' quickness to anger, but his obstinate determination to find the truth that entangles him in a web of calamity from which he cannot escape. Elsewhere after coming near to disaster the play ends on a note of relief or even triumph, once the main figure has seen the error of his ways. The *Philoctetes* closes with Neoptolemus saved from dishonour, Philoctetes himself enlightened by new understanding, and both agreed that the wish of Heaven must be fulfilled.

If Sophocles has a lesson to preach, it is the theme that stands

[1] *Electra*, ll. 616-21. Tr. Sheppard (Bowes and Bowes, Ltd.).

out most strongly in his last play, in which Oedipus, having learned wisdom through suffering, departs from life amid supernatural glory. 'How wonderful a thing is man', sing the chorus of the *Antigone*,[1] giving utterance to what many Athenians must have thought in the middle of the fifth century B.C. To Sophocles man is indeed wonderful, but the greatest of his qualities is his ability to retain his human dignity, his moral stature, amidst all the hardships which the gods in their wisdom and justice impose upon him. It is the power of endurance that gives Sophocles' greatest characters a certain noble serenity—a serenity which pervades all his plays and softens the effect of the horrors they portray.

Euripides: 'The Most Tragic of the Poets'

Although Euripides was probably only twelve years junior to Sophocles and died a few months earlier, such information as we possess about him reveals a very different figure: an intellectual standing aloof and detached, a critic of men and things rather than one who takes his part. The highest public office attributed to him is membership of an embassy to Syracuse. He collected a library—as much a sign of eccentricity in fifth-century Athens as of respectability today. He is said to have studied and written in seclusion in a cave overlooking the sea. Such a mind was fertile soil for the burgeoning of novel ideas. His contemporaries saw him as an apostle of the new thought, the new radicalism and individualism, the new scepticism questioning convention and tradition and religion itself—a trend which emerged from Athens' own development, but which they regarded as an importation by the foreign visitors who first stimulated it. Even behind the comic playwrights' gibe at the poet's pedigree—the false allegation that his mother was a greengrocer—may lie the

[1] L. 332.

suggestion that he was of alien descent, an upholder of foreign ideologies, of un-Athenian ideas, of an attitude far different from the spirit in which Marathon had been fought and won. Euripides was placed beside Anaxagoras, the scientist from Ionia, accused of blasphemy and exiled for describing the sun as a red-hot stone and the moon as earth; beside the Sophists, purveyors of doubt and heresy; beside Socrates, with his subversive catechisms in the market-place. To many the playwright was the worst of all: he applied the new ideas to myth and legend, the stuff of which tradition was made; he brought them into the theatre, the stronghold of Athenian culture. No wonder the comic poets constantly attacked him! For all his dramatic skill, for all the enthusiasm he roused among the young, Euripides gained only five first prizes. His days of popularity came only when history caught up with his ideas. Later generations repeatedly performed his plays and used them in the education of the young, so that no fewer than eighteen (or nineteen, if we include the *Rhesus*) have survived. The works that shock one century become the schoolbooks of the next.

How far Euripides differed from his predecessors in mentality and outlook is manifest from even a superficial glance at the extant plays. It is easy to run through them and pick out passages in which item after item in the prevailing tradition is challenged. The subordination of women, for example:

> Of all creatures that live and have a soul
> We women are the most unfortunate.[1]

Or the importance of noble birth:

> For heaven's sake speak not of 'noble birth':
> 'Tis wealth's the thing. One has, another not.
> And in whose house wealth makes the longest stay,
> He is 'noble'.[2]

[1] *Medea*, ll. 231-2.   [2] *Fr.* 22 (Nauck).

172

Or the inferiority of the 'barbarian':

Iphigenia: It is their mother that the men have killed.
'Barbarian' King Thoas: God! No barbarian would have dared that deed![1]

Even slavery is called in question, though Euripides shows no realisation of its importance as the foundation of contemporary society:

> One thing alone causes the slave his shame—
> The name. In all things else he is no worse
> Than free men, if he be good.[2]

More than once Euripides makes fun of Aeschylus, ridiculing the tokens by which his Electra realised the presence of Orestes, or the long account of the heroes arrayed against Thebes. But commonest of all targets for his shafts is religion:

> Doth someone say that there be gods above?
> There are not; no, there are not. Let no fool,
> Led by the old false fable, thus deceive you.[3]

And again:

> Flushed with joy,
> Let Jove's illustrious consort, in the dance,
> Strike with her sandals the resplendent floor
> Of high Olympus: for she now hath gained
> Her utmost wish, and from his basis torn
> The first of Grecian warriors. Who can pray
> To such a goddess, who, with envy stung,
> Because Jove loved a woman, hath destroyed
> The benefactors of the Grecian realm,
> Those blameless objects of her hate?[4]

These passages are not consistent. Their inconsistency is typical of their author. Verrall and other modern writers are wrong in

[1] *Iphigenia among the Taurians*, ll. 1173-4.   [2] *Ion*, ll. 854-6.
[3] *Fr.* 286 (Nauck), ll. 1-3. Tr. Symonds (*O.B.G.V.* 391).
[4] *Mad Heracles*, ll. 1303-10.

transforming him into an atheist who disproved the existence of the gods by subtle problem plays which only a minority could understand. Sometimes Euripides denies the gods: more often he accepts them as an evil reality. He is not a consistent or systematic thinker in any sphere. He is a critic, not a missionary. He rejects the old: he is not sure of the new.

Euripides' critical approach did more than put unconventional views into the mouths of his characters. It affected his whole attitude to the theatre, made him see drama itself with different eyes. Though even he did not break loose from the conventional form of tragedy, he had no hesitation in adapting it to novel purposes. He was the first dramatist who deliberately used plays as an instrument to secure a desired effect. Among his works was a type new to the great theatre of Dionysus—propaganda plays in the widest sense of the term, performances aimed first and foremost at putting across an idea. Through some of these—the *Children of Heracles*, the *Andromache*, the *Suppliant Women*, the *Trojan Women*—we can trace one chapter in the making of a sceptic: the evolution of Euripides' attitude to the Peloponnesian War, which overshadowed his latter years even more than the struggle against Persia dominated the life of Aeschylus. War was less totalitarian then than in modern times. Freedom of speech, one of the first casualties today, survived till late in the long struggle between Athens and Sparta. War literature— including anti-war literature—was produced during the war itself.

The *Children of Heracles*, first performed in the early years of the conflict, breathes the spirit of idealistic faith in the Athenian cause. Athens is the protector of the helpless, the champion of freedom. She does not want war, but, says the chorus to the foreign tyrant,

> If 'gainst this city thou comest,
> 'Twill not be thy hope that is fulfilled.[1]

[1] Ll. 373-4.

'We don't want to fight, but, by jingo, if we do . . . !' Then, 'Athens expects every man . . .'

> Then Athens' king
> Cried to his host, as noble spirit should:
> 'Countrymen, now 'tis each man's task to aid
> The land that bore and fed him'.[1]

There is plenty of idealism here, but little hatred. Behind the *Andromache* lies the bitterness of over-populated and plague-ridden Athens, hemmed in by the Spartan invasions of Attica. The sufferings of Hector's wife after the fall of Troy give Euripides good material for a dramatic 'hymn of hate' against Spartan pride, Spartan treachery, Spartan brutality. Even the shocking ways of Spartan girls come into the picture, racing and wrestling with young men half-naked. No wonder Helen was a wanton!

In the *Suppliant Women*, probably composed about the time of the inconclusive peace which ended the first ten years of war, Athens is again the champion of the oppressed and of the common law, the upholder of democracy against dictatorship. But an element of doubt creeps in. Adrastus, soliloquising on the folly of the human race, includes among his list of fools states that prefer war to a peaceful settlement of their quarrels:

> O foolish states, which might by parley end
> Feuds, yet decide them in the field of blood![2]

And the Theban envoy begs Theseus not to let his championing of freedom cause disaster:

> Dear is Peace
> To every Muse; she walks her ways and sees
> No haunting Spirit of Judgment. Glad is she
> With noise of happy children, running free
> With corn and oil. And we, so vile we are,

[1] Ll. 824-7.   [2] Li. 748-9. Tr. Way (Heinemann, Ltd.).

Forget, and cast her off, and call for War,
City on city, man on man, to break
Weak things to obey us for our greatness' sake![1]

These plays make poor reading today, like all propaganda of the moment once the moment is passed. Not so the *Trojan Women*, performed in 415 B.C. The temporary peace had been smashed. In 416 Athens sent an expedition against the island of Melos, whose only sin was neutrality, and after a short siege put to death all the men of military age, enslaved the women and children, and sent five hundred settlers to establish a colony. This was no championing of the helpless. It was unprovoked aggression, imperialism naked and unashamed. Euripides put his protest into a form which he had already used in the *Hecuba*— a grim picture of the sequel to the Trojan War. In some ways the *Trojan Women* takes us back to Aeschylus. It is the third part of a trilogy on a connected theme. It is a tragic pageant with a ritual atmosphere. But it is a play of disillusionment such as Aeschylus never wrote. Euripides boldly strips off all the glamour which the recitals of the *Iliad* at the Panathenaea cast over the struggle with Troy. Though even here the captured women pray to go to Athens, not Sparta, they face nothing but misery. Why was the war fought? It is obvious that Menelaus will make it up with Helen on the way home. What have the conquerors won? Even in the hour of triumph fear drives them to sordid murder, and the gods who open the play forecast disaster for the Greeks as well as Troy. By 413 B.C. the Sicilian Expedition had ended in catastrophe.

About half the surviving plays were written after the *Trojan Women*, but Euripides never returns to the same violently anti-war tone. War-weary audiences prefer entertainment to propaganda, would rather be thrilled and amused than think. In composing his later plays Euripides often put theatrical effect

[1] Ll. 489-93. Tr. Murray (George Allen and Unwin, Ltd).

first, thought second. Our one complete satyr-play, the *Cyclops*, probably produced early in his career as a dramatist, shows that he could write for the theatre without the intrusion of ideas. In 438 B.C. he tried an innovation, replacing the satyr-play at the end of a trilogy by the strange tragi-comedy *Alcestis*, in which there is little evidence of an underlying idea, despite modern critics' efforts to find one. Towards the end of his life he tended to apply the same approach to tragedies, if such they can be called. Scepticism, radicalism, even propaganda are still there, but they form the background, not the foreground of the play. The poet's primary concern is with thrills, even with amusement. Plots well known to the audience offered narrow scope for shocks and surprises. Resort to pure fiction, the easiest way out, was contrary to convention and probably did not occur to Euripides, but he came near the same end by other means. Sometimes he boldly reshaped familiar tales. In the *Phoenician Women*, a portentous affair—portentous for the Greek theatre—with eleven characters and four messenger-speeches, he put a whole saga into a single play—not a narrative drama, but a new version of the Theban legend bringing together at a single focal point all the figures of the stories and their destinies. More often he turned into little-trodden byways of legend. Out of the well-worn material of the history of the House of Atreus he constructed not only an *Electra* like (though how unlike!) Sophocles, but a sequel, the *Orestes*—a nightmare melodrama of the escape of the murderers from execution by the people. The fate of their sister, Iphigenia, provided the subject-matter of two other 'tragedies'. *Iphigenia at Aulis*, a play full of surprises, tells of the preparations to sacrifice her to Artemis to obtain a fair wind for the Greek fleet, until (if the final messenger scene is Euripides' own work) the goddess herself saves the girl and puts a hind as victim in her place. *Iphigenia among the Taurians* dramatises what followed: Orestes, still pursued by some Furies whom the trial at Athens did not appease, voyages on Apollo's advice to the remote and savage Crimea and finds his sister serving as priestess there. Excitement follows excitement in the ancient equivalent—tame, perhaps, to a modern reader—of a tale of rescue from a cannibal isle. The *Helen* repeats the same theme in lighter and more fantastic style. As Stesichorus had said, it was only a phantom Helen that went to Troy. Menelaus finds his real wife in Egypt when shipwrecked there on the way home, and together they devise their escape.

Implicitly or explicitly all these plays condemn the wickedness of the gods—Apollo whose oracle led Orestes to matricide, Artemis who demands human flesh, Hera the deceiver and Aphrodite (as Helen describes her) 'insatiate in mischief'. The same thought is even stronger in the *Ion*, where Apollo is a liar and a raper of innocent girls. Yet in this brilliant melodrama of shocks and emotional crises it is again the thrills that matter most.

The plays mentioned so far do not include several of Euripides' greatest works. Of them, more later. But we have already considered some of the most distinctive. Is there a characteristically Euripidean technique? What is the effect of the poet's outlook and his varying purposes on his art? The keynote of his handling of the traditional form is not the subtlety with which some scholars have credited him, but an almost crude directness, typical of the new rationalism, in manipulating and exploiting the material which tradition put before him. One result is a simplicity which makes Aeschylus seem cryptic and Sophocles complicated, and which must have strengthened Euripides' popularity in later times. But we shall see that his handling of the conventional form often subjected it to a strain which it could not well bear. The new way of looking at the world did not fit easily into the traditional mould.

Glance first at the language of Euripides' plays. Variability is the keynote of his style. Most of his dialogue, though Gilbert Murray's brilliant but romanticised versions hardly suggest it, is near to prose—the medium in which the new rationalism was commonly expressed. It has a simple clarity which the modern reader often finds all too plain. Yet on occasion, especially in his choral songs, Euripides uses elaborate poetical diction as a means of ornament. Metaphor is not his natural speech, but an instrument deliberately employed with telling effect.

Turn to the aspect of his technique which has troubled critics from Aristotle onwards: the structure of his plots. Aeschylus builds his plays out of dramatic and spectacular situations. Sophocles writes dramas of excitement and intrigue, but each is a single connected whole and the action always has its roots in the personality of the characters. For Euripides a plot is a series of events, a section of legend to be deliberately manipulated according to the purpose of the moment. Dramatic unity and consistency are not essential. Sometimes, as in Sophocles, character-drawing moulds the tragedy into a single whole, but by no means always. In the 'propaganda plays' the only connecting link is the idea. The two halves of the *Andromache* would fall apart but for their common anti-Spartan theme. The *Trojan Women* is a succession of episodes only held together by the fact that they all illustrate the sufferings of the conquered and the horrors of war. When thrills and excitement are the poet's main aim dramatic unity is more likely, but here again Euripides takes any liberty he pleases with the ordinary sequence of cause and effect. Many of his plots abound in startling twists and turns, in amazing coincidences. The corpse of Hecuba's murdered son is washed ashore at the very moment when she is burying her daughter. When Andromache is being led off to execution the aged Peleus turns up in the nick of time. Such surprises may seem near the technique of the Wild West in fiction. So they are.

The Athenian audience, unlike intellectual commentators through the ages, probably enjoyed them.

Directness and clarity, I have said, are the keynote. It is consistent with this that Euripides not only takes a slice of legend and puts it before his audience, but also shows them where it was cut from the cake. Aeschylus and Sophocles expected the public to know the traditional context from which their plots were drawn. Euripides, often treading less familiar ground, takes nothing for granted. Where a subtler writer might have indicated the background in the course of an opening dialogue scene, Euripides is straightforward and direct. He puts a formal speech into the mouth of a single character—divine or human—and so the modern 'prologue' is born. Sometimes the speaker of the prologue sets the tone for the rest of the play or gives some hint of its meaning. Sometimes he foretells the future, not always correctly. But his chief function is simply to give a narrative of the past and describe the present. 'Let me remind you', says the poet in effect, 'of the old stories of so-and-so. This-and-this has happened before my play begins. Now the situation is such-and-such. Watch what will happen next.'

So most of Euripides' plays begin. At the end he again forges a link with the legendary context, often through the intervention of a god or goddess who in some performances appeared in the air suspended from a 'machine.' Some have seen in this strange convention a survival of an apotheosis scene in the original ritual from which drama sprang. In any case, the notion of divine interference at a climax in human affairs was familiar from Homer. But why did Euripides use it? To underline the absurdity of belief in such a story and such deities? No. If Euripides had had any such ingenious intention, he would not have carried it out so cryptically that it could remain unrealised for more than two thousand years. To extricate himself from the tangle in which he had involved his plot? Again no. The 'gods from the machine' are not to be placed in the same category as the miraculous Chariot of the Sun which rescues Medea. Sometimes the god makes no change in the situation. Where he does, it is to reverse some turn made only a moment before or some move that could well have been avoided. One more surprise, apparently, won't do us any harm, but the play could easily have ended without him. The solution of the mystery is, I believe, that there is no mystery. Here again it is Euripides' simplicity that has defeated the critics, not his subtlety. Just as the prologue linked the plot with the past, so the epilogue connected it with the future—not only with the remainder of the legend, but with local ritual and local institutions which brought the theme close to the Athenians' own doorstep. Although Euripides usually takes some pains to dovetail the epilogue into the rest of the play, its main function is to prophesy what is to come. Sometimes a human character acts as prophet, but who can do it better than a god?

Prologue and epilogue were Euripides' own additions to the conventional form of tragedy. What did this rebel against tradition make of the chorus, the chief convention which tradition had bequeathed to him? That the presence of fifteen musically-minded commentators should be inconvenient in the midst of swift-moving melodrama or intimate domestic tragedy is shown by their apologies for their existence, by the promises of secrecy that are extracted from them lest they upset the plot. A modern playwright, faced with the same dilemma, might use the chorus as mouthpiece of his own views. It was possible for Aeschylus, but not for Euripides. His views on the lips of his characters were bad enough. To express them through the sacred chorus would have started a riot in the theatre.

Euripides' solution of the problem varied, and continued to vary up to the time of his last two works. The chorus of the *Bacchae* is not only relevant: it almost dominates the play. In the *Iphigenia at Aulis* we could well do without the fifteen female strangers from Chalcis: we feel they are there only because they have to be. But in most of the dramas the chorus has a twofold function. It not only moves on a separate spiritual level from the actors, but has two distinct levels of its own. Where it takes part (usually through its leader) in the dialogue episodes, it is relevant and has its share in the action, however ineffective (fourteen of Euripides' choruses are women; the rest, old men). Like Sophocles in the *Philoctetes*, Euripides often turned the entry of the chorus into a dramatic scene. The songs, usually limited to three, are in a different category. Their relevance is often indirect, sometimes non-existent. The point of odes on the Trojan War in the *Hecuba* and *Trojan Women* is obvious enough, but why interrupt the *Helen* for a song about Demeter's search for Persephone? The original edifice to which dramatic dialogue was added has become a superfluous and somewhat antiquated wing—a beautiful decoration, a lovely but pointless *entr'acte*. Music and song were in danger of disappearing from the drama, but Euripides found other means of keeping them alive. As the words became less important, he made the music more complex. If the odes were fewer and shorter, he gave more singing to the actors. His emotional solos were famous, if not notorious. In the *Orestes* a terrified barbarian from Phrygia (well known for its music) delivers even a 'messenger's speech' in a series of excited arias. Tragedy has come near to opera.

Dialogue scenes and choral odes were the framework of drama. What of Euripides' characters? Sophocles' remark gives an answer: 'I portray men as they ought to be portrayed, but Euripides portrays them as they are.'[1] King Telephus in a beggar's rags, a figure in a play now lost, became a symbol of Euripidean realism for the Athenian audience and the comic poets. There are examples in plenty in the extant plays: Jason,

[1] See p. 169 above.

the self-centred husband; Agamemnon, ambitious yet weak and vacillating; Clytemnestra, fussy mother-of-the-bride, nursing hatred of the king in her heart; Electra, childless, embittered, sinister; Orestes, irresolute murderer in one tragedy, half-crazy desperado in another. Euripides' conception of character is not restricted by tradition: like Sophocles, he pictures the same person differently in different plays. Nor by any aristocratic limitation of outlook: in the *Electra* the only praiseworthy character is the peasant. Euripides still keeps to legend and legendary figures, but strips them naked, reduces them from heroes and heroines to ordinary—or not so ordinary—human beings. He is the first great realist of the theatre. Yet he is far from fully realistic. In handling his characters he does not imitate life. It is not merely that they do not stop for meals or suffer from the common cold. His treatment of them is artificial because here again he is aloof and detached, because he does not identify himself with them (nor, consequently, do we) but tends to use them as puppets, pulling the string of this or that emotion just as deliberately as he manipulates his plot. He often makes them too simple. He effectively but all too readily switches them from one mood to another, transforming Hecuba, for instance, from a helpless victim into a resourceful fiend, Iphigenia from a frightened child into a resolute patriot. He exploits the feebleness of old age for comic effect. Most disturbing of all to the modern reader, he does not hesitate to turn the theatre into a debating-hall. 'See!' cries the chorus-leader in the *Hecuba*, 'how a good cause always gives an opening for a good speech!'[1] His comment, the reader feels, is all too true. The teachers of rhetoric who flourished towards the end of the fifth century are said to have practised their new craft by inventing mythical debates, and the habit is reflected in Euripides. Few of his characters are deficient in the art of public speaking. Where plot is his main concern he

[1] Ll. 1238-9.

does not allow mere discussion to interrupt it: there are no debates in the *Ion* or the *Iphigenia among the Taurians* or the *Helen*. But in most of the plays no chance is lost. In the *Trojan Women* Helen and Hecuba match each other in eloquence and in the length of their orations. So do Clytemnestra and her daughter in the *Electra*. In the *Medea* even husband and wife wrangle· in set speeches. The procedure is formal, the style standardised. Opposer answers proposer point by point, while the chorus-leader takes the chair. We enjoy this sort of thing when it is done by the modern Euripides, Bernard Shaw. So also, no doubt, did the Athenians. But these debates are one more sign of the invasion of Athenian life by rationalism, one more indication that the expression of ideas through dramatised legend was becoming out-of-date.

Episodic plots; incredible coincidences; the 'god from the machine'; characters handled like puppets; set debates. All this suggests that Euripides can sometimes be a second-rate dramatist. So he can—even third- or fourth-rate. Yet Aristotle writes: 'Euripides, even though he manages badly in all other points, is seen to be the most tragic of the poets'.[1] Everyone who has read Euripides must feel that there is truth in Aristotle's statement. Few playwrights in history have rivalled him in plucking at the heartstrings of the audience. Few have equalled the pathos of Andromache parting from her little son in the *Trojan Women*, Medea hesitating over her children's fate, Electra and Orestes in horrified despair after they have killed their mother, the Queen in the *Bacchae* returning from the hills with her son's head held triumphantly aloft. There is a humanitarian pity here nearer to modern than ancient sentiment. But the tragic quality of such scenes goes far deeper than humanitarianism.

To attempt analysis of that quality is as dangerous as to

[1] *Poetics* 1453 a.

explain humour: in the course of the diagnosis the quality itself
may disappear. But this much may be said: Euripides' greatness
as a tragic writer is intimately linked with his rationalist point of
view. Just because he was a rationalist he was keenly aware of the
irrational forces in human life—forces whose power made an ever
deeper impression on his mind as the Peloponnesian War moved
towards its catastrophic close. He saw them at work in the sudden
and violent reversals of fortune. 'Change succeeds to change, and
man's life veers and shifts in endless restlessness', sings the chorus
of the *Hippolytus*.[1] Chance, the goddess of later centuries, already
overshadows Euripidean drama. He saw the effect of unreason still
more in human character, especially (as he believed) in the
character of women. Tradition, particularly aristocratic tradition,
stressed the value of moderation, self-control. But even in the
strongest personality self-control can break. Euripides boldly
put into his plays example after example of its collapse—women
in love, for instance, whom his predecessors had never portrayed.
He shocked the audience, but that was not his main aim. His
contemporary, Socrates, maintained that he who knows what is
right will do it. For Euripides the tragedy of humanity was that
Socrates was wrong: Medea, resolved on killing her children, is
aware of the wickedness of the plan—but passion is too much for
her. As Phaedra says in the *Hippolytus*:

> That which is good we learn and recognise,
> Yet practise not the lesson.[2]

Sometimes the poet hints that irrational emotions have a root in
heredity. Sometimes he represents them as the devilish handiwork of the gods—whether because he really thought so or as a
piece of allegory, matters little. Whatever their origin, these
forces bring disaster not only on the individual, but on the
whole community around him.

[1] Ll. 1109-10. Tr. Coleridge (Random House).
[2] Ll. 380-1. Tr. Way (Heinemann, Ltd.).

This emphasis on the instability of character and circumstance, on the power of the irrational, is present in nearly all of Euripides' works. This is the mental background which makes possible many features of his theatrical technique—the somersaults of fortune, the coincidences, the sudden changes of mood or personality, even the 'god from the machine', divine symbol of the irrationality of fate. The same fundamental conception underlies propaganda plays and melodramas alike: in the last analysis the theme of the *Trojan Women* is the suffering brought on humanity by the unreasoning folly of war; the theme of the *Electra*, the horrors to which an overriding passion can drive us. But the thought finds its strongest expression in Euripides' greatest tragedies, where idea, character-drawing and action are most completely fused: the *Medea, Hippolytus, Heracles, Bacchae.*

The *Medea* has its propaganda aspect. Through his heroine Euripides denounces the contemporary treatment of women and contempt for 'barbarians'. But it is not these ideas that dominate the play: it is Medea herself, a being impelled by suffering and jealousy to murder not only her rival but her own children. Medea is no ordinary woman. She is an enchantress with a spectacular past. She makes her final exit in the chariot of the Sun. But Euripides puts her before us as an extreme example of something that is in every woman's heart. The *Hippolytus* is a very different variation on the same fundamental theme. The young prince's scorn of sexual love, his neglect of Aphrodite and devotion to the virgin goddess Artemis, sets forces in motion that bring disaster to all the royal house. Aphrodite is capricious and arbitrary. Her ways have no relation to reason or morality. But she exists, and no man or woman can withstand her attack.

Other poets had voiced traditional ideas about the destruction brought on humanity by the gods. Man himself, they said, was guilty. It was his own fatal insolence and ambition that made the wrath of heaven strike him down. Unreason, mad folly, was inflicted on him as the divine punishment for sin, and so brought him to disaster. Euripides makes it clear that he will have none of all this. Like Oedipus in Sophocles' last play, he claims that the individual cannot be held responsible for excesses to which overwhelming passion has driven him. This is Helen's defence in the *Trojan Women*. It is the theme that holds together the two halves of the *Heracles*, in which Euripides delivers a rationalist broadside against the conventional conception of sin and guilt. Once again he takes from legend an extreme case. Heracles is the benefactor of mankind. When he returns home from his labours he shows no arrogance. He greets the gods with all due piety. After slaying the tyrant who threatened his family he is performing the due purificatory rites, when the demon of Madness, sent by Hera, swoops down upon him and drives him to murder his own wife and sons. The demon herself protests at the injustice she is compelled to commit. When the mad fit has passed and Heracles becomes conscious of what he has done, Theseus— from enlightened Athens—persuades him that he is not morally polluted. Convinced of his own freedom from sin he finds he has strength to endure—not as a hero, but as a man, a victim of the tragic brutality of the powers that rule the world.

Shortly before his death Euripides left war-torn Athens for Macedon, whence the final overthrow of the city-state and its traditions was later to emerge. Perhaps because he found the Bacchic worship still flourishing there in something like its original form, he turned back to the old theme of tragedy which Aeschylus had several times dramatised—the legend of Dionysus himself. Out of it he fashioned the supreme embodiment of his conception of the tragedy of human life. The *Bacchae* brings together many features of Euripides' theatrical technique: brilliant turns of plot, powerful character-drawing, fine messenger-speeches, magnificent poetry. It has both pathos and comedy. But it is far more than a theatrical triumph. The god of wine stands for all the forces in nature—including human nature—which reason can neither explain nor control. They are put before us in all their beauty—and all their horror. They summon us away to the hills, to superhuman joy and sublime ecstasy—but we return with blood on our hands. Euripides has not turned mystic in his old age, as some commentators on the *Bacchae* have imagined. It is true that he anticipates many features of the religions of later centuries—the liberation of the soul through direct communion with the divine, the triumph of the miraculous over science, of conversion over reason, of individual faith over official cults. But he looks into the distant future only to turn his back on it. He remains rationalist to the last, as fully conscious of the evils of unreason as Agave becomes when she sees that it is her son's head that she is carrying. Euripides finds no answer in mysticism to the problem of life. He offers us no answer at all. He has none. Andromache weeps and he has no comfort to give her. Aeschylus believes the beings who rule the universe can learn wisdom and mercy. Sophocles accepts the inevitability of fate, but achieves a certain serenity through belief in the noble virtues and the endurance of the human spirit—a thought which Euripides approaches at the end of the *Heracles*, but nowhere else. For Euripides the optimism of the early years of Athenian democracy has gone. Aristocratic confidence in human nobility has been discarded. A society based on slavery, a society sick yet unaware of the nature of its own disease, can show him no way forward. Breaking free from the past without finding hope in the future, alive as none of his predecessors had been to the problems of existence yet seeing no solution, he is indeed the most tragic of them all.

The Comedies of Aristophanes

Once more we are in the huge theatre of Dionysus, and the benches are crowded for the god's spring festival. It is 421 B.C.:

the first performance of Aeschylus' *Agamemnon* is a dim memory in the minds of the older generation. Except for a number of visitors from oversea, the audience here today are men and women who have spent ten years in a city at war. Some families among them have lost men in battle: few escaped bereavement in the epidemic that ravaged Athens soon after the struggle began. Many are countryfolk, who every summer from the walls of the overcrowded town have watched the Spartan army pillaging farms, hacking down vines and olive trees. Yet this is not a gloomy crowd. As they wait for the next play they talk optimistically of peace. Moves towards an armistice have had no lasting result in the past, but now there is real hope. Brasidas, the enemy's most outstanding general, is gone. So is Athens' own war-leader, Cleon, the leather-merchant. Both were killed in the same battle last summer. Negotiations have been opened. 'Yes, neighbour, any day it may be home-sweet-home for us. Any day now.'

It is early afternoon. The tragedies and satyr-play are over, and there is a comedy to come—one of the three accepted for the competition at this festival. Today's author is that brilliant young man, Aristophanes. The title of the play: *Peace*.

The herald calls for the play to begin, and the hubbub of talk among the vast throng dies away. The scene at the back of the dancing-circle now represents the front of a house, and beside it a stable, with closed doors. To the other side, a pile of stones. Two figures appear, their bodies stuffed out with padding in front and behind, and clad in tunics short enough to expose a large leather phallus. By their grotesque masks the spectators recognise them as slaves. One of them is kneading cakes of dung and throwing them into the stable: the other gives him orders. The cakes, it seems, are for a beetle—'a most stinking, foul,

voracious brute'. As the audience grow more and more curious
Slave *A* anticipates their questions:

> Now I suspect some pert young witling there
> Is asking, 'Well, but what's it all about?
> What can the beetle mean?' And then I think
> That some Ionian, sitting by, will answer,
> 'Now, I've nae doubt but this is aimed at Cleon,
> It eats the muck sae unco shamelessly.'

While the citizens are laughing at his mimicry of the Ionic
dialect Slave *A* disappears into the stable, and Slave *B* makes an
explanatory speech. His master is mad, he says. In a frenzy to
get to Zeus and persuade him to stop draining the life-blood from
Greece, he has tried climbing by ladders to heaven, but 'came
tumbling down, and cracked his skull'. Now he has brought a
huge beetle home, and keeps on saying:

> 'Wee Pegasus, my flying thoroughbred,
> Your wings must waft me straight away to Zeus!'

The mention of Pegasus gives the audience a clue: this must be a
burlesque of Euripides' hero, Bellerophon, who flew to heaven
on his winged horse to remonstrate with the king of the gods.

While the slave was speaking his master could be heard com-
plaining to Zeus behind the scenes. Now the stable doors are
flung open and the giant beetle appears, just being hauled by the
theatre-crane into the air. On his back rides the master, dressed
much like the slave except for his mask. He chants encouragement to his steed amid protests from the slave, who desperately
summons the daughters of the house. One of them pleads with
her father, but as she utters a last warning that he should not

> tumble off,
> And (lame for life) afford Euripides
> A subject, and become a tragic hero

the rider soars into the air, mixing quotations from the *Bellero-phon* with cries of alarm lest the all too earthly activities of a man down by the harbour should distract the beetle from its skyward course. At the climax of his flight he nervously appeals to the scene-shifter to take care, and is lowered again to the ground. The house, he says, must be the dwelling of Zeus, and he is right: when he shouts for a porter the door is opened by the god Hermes, who greets him with the abuse to be expected from the butlers of the great. At last the strange visitor to heaven reveals his name: he is Trygaeus, 'Mr Grape-Gatherer', from the Attic village of Athmone.

Hermes' bluster is soon checked by a bribe—a piece of meat. Even in heaven, it seems, there is a food shortage. But when Trygaeus adds 'Just step in and summon Zeus', the divine butler explains that the gods have left these premises: in disgust at the Greeks' continual failure to make peace, they have retired to heights beyond contact with humanity. War has taken over, and has thrown Peace into a deep pit under the pile of stones. Hermes departs and Trygaeus runs to hide as the grim figure of War himself enters, carrying a huge mortar into which he throws ingredients for his salad, each symbolising the cities he intends to pound—leeks for Prasiae, garlic for Megara, cheese for Sicily, honey for Attica (*Trygaeus:* 'Hey, use some other honey. That costs sixpence.'). The preparations complete, War shouts for his slave, Tumult, to fetch a pestle. There's none in the house? Then borrow one from Athens! But Tumult returns empty-handed:

> Just look here, sir:
> The pestle the Athenians had is lost,
> The tanner fellow that disturbed all Hellas.

An errand to Sparta is equally fruitless, and War retires to make a pestle for himself. Trygaeus leaps up. The moment has come

'to pull out Peace, the joy of all mankind', and he shouts for
helpers:

> O all ye farmers, merchants, artisans,
> O all ye craftsmen, aliens, sojourners,
> O all ye islanders, O all ye peoples.

Enter the chorus—twenty-four men representing Attic farmers.
They are dressed less grotesquely than the actors, and wear no
phallus. With them come others—the war-monger Lamachus,
different types of Athenians, people from various Greek states.
Their entrance is noisy and gay, a wild dance of joy in anticipation of the end of parade-ground days. Even Trygaeus' warning
that they may waken Cleon from the dead does not stop them.
When he at last turns to the task of removing the stones, Hermes
reappears and threatens to tell Zeus, but is won over with a golden
cup and a promise of a future monopoly of sacrifices. Libations
are poured, prayers said for the discomfiture of warmongers and
arms-sellers, and with Hermes shouting 'Heave!' all tug at ropes
that go down into the pit. At first their efforts are a failure:
Lamachus sits on the rope; some states will not pull, others are
too weak; the Athenians themselves haggle too much to tug
together. Only when the job is left to the farmers is the giant
image of Peace dragged out, and with her—what is this?—two
living young girls whom Trygaeus greets as Harvest home and
Holiday. While the representatives of the cities fraternise and
among the spectators—as Trygaeus points out—the sellers of
pitchforks and sickles cock a snook at the arms-makers, farmer-
hero and chorus gaily sing the joys of the return of Peace:

> Figs and olives, wine and myrtles,
> Luscious fruits preserved and dried,
> Banks of fragrant violets, blowing
> By the crystal fountain's side.

Presently Hermes gives Trygaeus Harvest home for himself and

Holiday for the Council of Athens, but when the farmer looks for his beetle, he finds it has vanished. 'Yoked to the car of Zeus, it bears the thunder', explains Hermes, and leads Trygaeus and the girls off to show them another way down to earth.

The actors have gone and the chorus is left alone on the dancing-circle. At their leaders' bidding they throw their cloaks to attendants, and turn to face the great audience. The leader speaks. He is no longer a farmer, no longer concerned with Peace and Trygaeus and Holiday and Harvest home. He is the mouthpiece of the poet. Bald-headed Aristophanes, he claims, has cut out the old low jokes and uplifted Comedy. He has dared to attack the mighty, not mere nobodies. All bald-headed men must help him to victory, since if he wins — the leader gabbles these last ten lines, for he must say them in one breath — it is the baldheads that will thrive. When he has finished, the chorus sing an ode in which they praise the Muse and satirise three contemporary tragedians.

Re-enter Trygaeus, with Holiday and Harvest home. Limping with weariness after his long journey, he speaks to the spectators:

> How small ye seemed down here! Why, from above
> Methought ye looked as bad as bad could be,
> But here ye look considerably worse.

From now on the play continues on an earthly level. A sacrifice and prayer to Peace are interrupted by the oracle-monger Hierocles, whose fussiness over the ritual and cryptic announcements end in a beating. Chorus and chorus-leader celebrate the joys of country life. Trygaeus prepares his marriage-feast, but again there are intruders: a sickle-maker and cask-maker, bringing presents in gratitude for the rise in the price of their wares; a series of arms-makers, in despair because the bottom has dropped out of their market. Trygaeus converts a breastplate into a chamber-pan, a trumpet into scales 'to weigh out figs for labourers on the farm'. As to the spears:

> Saw them in two,
> I'll buy them all for vine-poles, ten a penny.

Boys enter to rehearse their songs for the ceremony. When one who quotes warlike lines from epic proves to be Lamachus' son, Trygaeus drives him away and calls for the son of the notorious coward Cleonymus, who sings Archilochus' poem on throwing away his shield. The comedy ends with a marriage procession, and the chorus, with a final joke on the coming wedding night, carry Trygaeus off in triumph shoulder-high.

A few days later the signing of a treaty between Athens and Sparta is announced. Peace has come to Hellas, and the country folk of Attica go back to their farms.

The *Peace* is one of eleven surviving plays of Aristophanes, the only complete examples of Greek comedy. Their chronological order is as follows:

	B.C.
Acharnians	425
Knights	424
Clouds	423
Wasps	422
Peace	421
Birds	414
Lysistrata	411
Women Celebrating the Thesmophoria	411
Frogs	405
Women in Parliament	391?
Plutus	388

Although each of these comedies has its individual characteristics of form and tone, all of them bear the stamp of the same convention. There is a great gulf between these dramatic extravaganzas, these uproarious farces, and Greek tragedy. They are gross, often obscene; topical, often libellous; fanciful, often fantastic. They treat legend as material for burlesque, the gods as figures of fun. Not only their spirit is far removed from the *Agamemnon* or the *Medea*. They have peculiarities of structure which may seem unimportant in a single play, but become full of significance when they recur again and again. Most striking, of course, is the interruption of the show for an address to the audience, known to the ancients as the *parabasis*, or 'coming forward' of the chorus. In its complete form (it is divided in the *Peace*) the *parabasis* itself has an elaborate internal construction of its own. Before the *parabasis* there is an explanatory speech or dialogue, the entry of the chorus, and often a conflict in which fisticuffs give way to verbal debate—a feature lacking in the *Peace*, where all the emphasis is on harmony. After the *parabasis* come episodes in which various unwelcome intruders force themselves on the hero and are driven away. The play ends with feasting and women, one or more of whom may be introduced solely for the purpose of the final scene.

What are the background and origins of this type of drama, strange to the modern reader and unique in theatrical history? Aristophanes, like the Homeric poems, represents the last phase in the development of a convention. Old Comedy, as it was called by scholars of a later day who looked back on it from very different times, had existed in some form for generations before the performance of Aristophanes' first play in 427 B.C. At the spring festival of Dionysus official competitions in comedy began in 486 B.C. At the god's winter festival, the Lenaea, the institution may have been older, though state recognition was delayed until the middle of the century. Look back still further and the story fades into obscurity which neither the scanty ancient evidence nor the plethora of modern conjectures can dispel. But there is fairly general agreement on a path which leads some distance into the darkness.

The Greek word *komodia* means the song of the *komos*, a 'revel' or 'band of revellers'. Aristotle, who admits that even in his day the early phases of comedy were unknown, states that it originated 'from those who led the phallic songs'.[1] What revel? What phallic songs? Are the two points consistent? Such information as we have suggests that they are, and guides us towards that part of Greek life where we should most expect to find the roots of comic drama—the worship of the god of fertility and wine at whose festivals it was performed. In Aristophanes' *Acharnians* Dikaiopolis, another comic hero of the Trygaeus breed, makes a separate one-man peace with Sparta, retires to his farm, and celebrates all on his own the rural winter festival of Dionysus from which the Lenaea in Athens must have been derived. Dikaiopolis himself leads a miniature procession, his daughter follows with a basket holding the instruments of sacrifice, two slaves carry a phallus on a pole, while Dikaiopolis' wife—the crowd—looks down from the roof. After a miniature sacrifice and prayer Dikaiopolis—both chorus-leader and chorus—sings to Bacchus' companion Phales a song which mixes bawdiness and personalities. One man does not make a *komos*, but multiply Dikaiopolis, and the band of revellers is before us. Later sources provide other pictures of phallic revels, which evidently survived in various parts of Greece long after Old Comedy had come into being and passed away. They include an element barely present in Dikaiopolis' celebration, but common elsewhere in Greek ritual: impromptu lampooning of the bystanders. Although neither Aristophanes' version nor any other is close enough to Old Comedy to give a complete explanation, together they provide a background against which some of its main features

[1] *Poetics* 1449 a.

196

gain new significance. They indicate a seeming paradox: that the aspects of these plays which the modern mind regards as most irreligious are those which are most likely to have had a religious origin. They show that the obscenity which translators omit or minimise was no mere incidental boisterousness, no mere product of high spirits or a low mind, but the very core of the performance—the descendant of fertility magic in which *komos*, phallic songs, and *komodia* itself had their distant source. They suggest that the invective, which no twentieth-century law of libel would allow, also had its roots in magic. The earliest origin of the lampooning which passed from the reverent procession into comedy was the primitive employment of ritual abuse to drive away evil spirits and malign influences. Behind Trygaeus' dung-beetle and the jests about his wedding-night, behind the (to us) outrageous attacks on individuals sitting among the audience, lie the practical needs of the peasant whose life depended on his meagre crops.

The phallic fertility ritual known to us from the *Acharnians* and elsewhere clarifies much that is otherwise puzzling in Old Comedy, but it leaves one key factor still a mystery—the same problem to which we have no answer in the history of tragedy. There is nothing dramatic in these pictures of the *komos*, no element of impersonation. Yet except in the *parabasis* (and sometimes even there) the chorus of fifth-century comedy was always dramatic. Its metamorphoses were many and various. In different plays its members appeared as farmers, miners, Lydians, Thracian women, savages, even as twenty-four Hesiods; as wasps, flies, ant-men, fishes, beasts, birds, even as clouds. A background to this aspect of the problem is provided by paintings on vases, which prove that the animal masquerade, found by anthropologists as a part of fertility ceremonies and totemic rites among many peoples, was no stranger to the early days of Greece. Perhaps a century before Aristophanes delighted the Athenian audience with his chorus of birds, an Attic wine-jar bears figures of dancers in bird disguise. What was the relation between such masquerading and the Bacchic *komos*? We do not know. But that a combination of the two formed the basis of comedy is the most likely conjecture we can make.

How much of a play like the *Peace* can be explained from such beginnings? When the search for origins turns to the details of the form of comedy, all is guesswork. Is the *parabasis* 'a nugget of unassimilated ritual embedded in the structure of the play'?[1] Is the conflict a relic of a mock struggle between revellers and bystanders, or different sections of the revellers themselves? An attempt has been made to derive the whole framework from an Attic folk-play with roots in a single ritual, but most modern commentators see the Attic *komos* as the foundation only of those parts which a certain symmetry distinguishes from the rest: the entry of the chorus, the conflict, the *parabasis*, possibly the final scene. To explain the remainder—the opening dialogue and later episodes—and to account for the extraordinary costume of the actors, they look beyond Attica. Vases and statuettes from both the Peloponnese and the West portray just such padded and phallic figures. At Megara, across the Attic frontier, there was improvised comedy in the sixth century B.C. In Sicily comedies were written by Epicharmus, contemporary of Aeschylus, who must have met him at the Syracusan tyrants' court. The fragments of his plays—the earliest remnants of Greek comedy that we possess—show no trace of a chorus, but several of the features that reappear at Athens: burlesque of legend, social satire, conflicts or debates. These are the beginnings of the 'mime'—not the acting without speech which the word 'mime' normally suggests today, but simple drama with no apparent connection with religion, which in one form or another continued its existence long after Old Comedy was a thing of the past, and

[1] Murray, *Aristophanes*, p. 12.

reached its highest popularity in Hellenistic and Roman times. Comedy as it was performed in fifth-century Athens was in a sense a temporary divergence from this more lasting trend, but Athenian poets too, it is supposed, took over elements from the mime. Aristotle's reference to 'the leaders of the phallic songs' seems to imply that in comedy, as in tragedy, the actors were an offshoot from the chorus. In spite of the evidence of costume he may be right, but at any rate some dialogue scenes and stock characters were imitated from Dorian models and loosely joined with the Attic *komos* to form such plays as we now possess. The result of the combination remained a ramshackle affair compared with the closely-knit unity of *Hippolytus* or *Oedipus the King*. Yet it must have been the influence of tragedy, the effect of performance in the same theatre as tragedy, that moulded Old Comedy into its final shape. From imitation of tragedy came the length of the plays, their poetical choral odes, the limitation to three actors. And—irony of literary history—can one in Aristophanes' explanatory speeches hear an echo of the prologues of Euripides?

Whatever the details of the story, one thing is certain: *komos* and *komodia* emerged from the lives of the common people. Trygaeus' antics and Dikaiopolis' mock ceremony are no products of a royal court or limited aristocratic circle. They come from roots deep in the needs and hopes and fears of simple folk— the man-in-the-street; still more, the man-on-the-farm. Comedy made the humble peasant its starting point, not the heroic and legendary past. Here was a seed which in the right soil could grow into one of the most truly popular art forms the world has ever known. Megara was a democracy when comedy came into being there, but not enough is known of either Megarian plays or Megarian politics to show the connection between the two. Epicharmus' work was produced under the autocratic regime of 'tyrants', and the fragments maintain a significant silence on political affairs. Only fifth-century Athens provided conditions in which the young plant could flourish and reach full bloom. Old Comedy was part and parcel of the life of Athenian democracy. During the comic performances in the huge theatre beside the Acropolis players and spectators were a single unity, a single body of citizens of Athens. The *parabasis*, of course, provided the most complete contact between poet and audience, but it did not break a barrier between them: there was no barrier to break. The repeated remarks to the spectators in the *Peace* are typical of the extant plays. Again and again they strike the same note as the *parabasis* of the *Birds:*

> Truly to be clad in feathers is the very best of things.
> Only fancy, dear spectators, had you each a brace of wings,
> Never need you, tired and hungry, at a Tragic Chorus stay,
> You would likely, when it bored you, spread your wings and fly away,
> Back returning, after luncheon, to enjoy our Comic Play.[1]

Because Old Comedy had its roots in the life of democratic Athens, it is an invaluable picture of that life. Trygaeus provides us with a specimen of all the 'little men', all the thousands of his kind, who sat and watched him from the benches of the amphitheatre. Aristophanes' plays have a unique historical function: they place the political leaders, the literature and art of the most brilliant period of Greek culture in their everyday contexts, their normal setting. But the picture is not photographic. The reflection is that of a distorting mirror, which shortens some features and elongates others; and the cause of the distortion is not only the poet's own point of view (of which more presently) but the spirit of Old Comedy itself. Anthropologists are familiar with the existence of occasions in primitive society when licence is permitted to break all the rules, when words and actions are allowed, even prescribed, which at other times are entirely taboo.

[1] Ll. 785-9. This and all other quotations from Aristophanes (except the *Frogs*) are from the translations by B. B. Rogers (G. Bell and Sons, Ltd.).

The same spirit reappears in the medieval Feast of Fools. This must have been the spirit of the Bacchic *komos*, and from the *komos*, gradually brought within limits by ritual and convention, it passed into comedy. Hence the violent contrast between the dignified tragedies presented in the morning and the fantastic farces that followed in the afternoon. Hence the uniqueness of fifth-century comedy in Greek literature, its violation—amazing to the modern reader, but taken for granted by the ancients—of most of the precepts of religion and morality. Greek tragedy repeats continually the theme of 'nothing too much', but the vigour of Old Comedy knows no moderation, no restraint. Its very essence is abnormality, the smashing of taboos. Even its most serious passage—the chorus-leader's address in the *parabasis*—ends in a ridiculous scurry to utter several lines in one breath. Trygaeus is John Citizen, but not John Citizen of Athens as he normally lived. 'My master is mad', says his slave: his madness—the madness of all Old Comedy—gives him seven-league boots, a freedom from restrictions which every John Citizen in the audience momentarily shares. 'Little man' that he is, space and gravity lose their grip on him, and a flight to heaven presents no difficulties. He can be obscene: women and boys sit and listen in the theatre, philosophers do not object. He can reduce ancient legend to absurdity, though Euripides was heavily criticised for treating it in realistic terms. He can ridicule oracles and ritual procedure, and make fun of the gods (though not Athena), can even overthrow them. He can assail with lies and laughter individuals sitting in the theatre, the heads of the state, the sovereign people itself. He not only *can* do all these things. He *must* do them: they are expected of him. For a couple of hours it is his function to violate the rules, to kick over the traces. His *raison d'être* is to be obscene and libellous, to be 'agin the Government'—and his Government includes the gods. These excesses were as expected in fifth-century comedy as they were forbidden in other forms of art. Just as distortion is taken for granted in a caricature, so it must be allowed for in looking at these plays as a mirror of Athenian life. It must not be imagined that because in comedy tradition was torn to pieces, either audience or playwright was against tradition, or anything but conservative; that because Aristophanes lampooned and misrepresented Socrates in the *Clouds*, he could not be on friendly terms with him in private life; that because a play trouncing Cleon was given the first prize, Cleon was unpopular, or the spectators who guffawed at this satire on him in the theatre were different from the crowd which applauded him in the Assembly. The comedies must be read with Heine's brilliant—indeed, Aristophanic—comment in mind: 'A deep idea of world-annihilation lies at the base of each Aristophanic comedy, which, like a fantastically ironic fairy-tree, shoots upward therein bearing gorgeous blossoms of thought, melodious nightingale-nests and climbing monkeys.'[1]

What happened to the fantastic spirit of fifth-century farce? Why did the 'fireworks of destruction' (to use another phrase of Heine) splutter and die away into the damp squib of later comedy? Not only is Old Comedy a mirror of contemporary life. Its final development and decline, mainly known to us through a chronological survey of Aristophanes' surviving plays, present a striking reflection of social change, a striking illustration of the effect of such change on the form as well as the content of literature.

Of Aristophanes' predecessors and contemporaries in the history of Attic comedy we know little. The few hundred fragments that remain from their works only enable us to guess the tone of their plays; in three or four instances, to attempt reconstruction of the plot. Not all were equally topical, or equally

[1] *Reisebilder* III, ii, 11.

maintained the spirit of uproarious and indecent farce. One group—Crates, Phrynichus, Pherecrates, Plato—anticipated the development of later times by turning to social and domestic life rather than politics, cultivating ingenious wit in place of topical satire, elegance in place of bawdiness. But the greatest figures—Cratinus, Eupolis, Aristophanes himself—were in the true *komos* tradition. Probably most to be regretted is the loss of Cratinus, satiriser of Pericles and master of burlesque, who in his old age made a telling reply to the young Aristophanes' description of him as a drunken old sot. In a play called the *Wine Flask* he portrayed himself with Comedy as his wife and Drink as his mistress, and won first prize in a competition in which Aristophanes came third.

Compared with such rivals, Aristophanes could declare in more than one *parabasis* that he had refined comedy and raised it to higher levels. The claim is surprising to the modern reader of his plays, but there can be no doubt that he had qualities—whether or no refinement was one of them—which elevated him above the rest. Within the limits imposed by the conventions of his art he is a sublime poet: there are few things in Greek literature better than his bird-songs or his descriptions of country life. As a weapon for his wit he possesses amazing skill in the use of language: Aristophanic dialogue scintillates with apt quotation, parody, different dialects, coined portmanteau words of the poet's own, one of which, a monstrosity beloved by schoolboy students of Greek, runs to 169 letters. A playwright with such individual talents must also have had his individual point of view. Unfortunately we are almost entirely ignorant about Aristophanes' life and personal background. Few passages in the comedies offer any direct proof of his outlook, and we can only guess at the distinction between the ideas and prejudices likely to have been his alone and those that were typical of his generation. But the general impression gained from reading the comedies is clear enough. Like Aeschylus, the comic poet looks back to the time and the men of Marathon as the glorious model which Athens should imitate. His sympathies, like those of Sophocles, lie with the old aristocracy whose conservatism objected to the excesses (as they regarded them) of democracy and its leaders after Pericles' death. In Aristophanes these trends of outlook become more openly political: admiration of the past goes hand in hand with condemnation of the present 'demagogues'; sympathy with the old noble families comes near to support for the new would-be oligarchs.

In considering Aristophanes' portrayal of his contemporaries allowance must be made for this political bias as well as for the distortion and exaggeration normal in Old Comedy. But the comedies' success with their audience ensures that on the whole they reflect the Athenian public's taste and prejudices. What version does Aristophanes give of life in war-time and post-war Athens?

The first five extant plays—*Acharnians*, *Knights*, *Clouds*, *Wasps*, *Peace*—were produced amid the atmosphere of the first long period of the war. What picture is there here of the common folk in the overcrowded city? They cannot be called proletarian or working-class. The majority still look to the soil as the citizen's natural home and livelihood. They own slaves to do their dirty work—even to feed a giant dung-beetle if the need should arise. They are far from revolutionary. Despite the slum conditions and acute discomfort (as the twentieth-century A.D. would see it) in which they live, they have no desire for fundamental change. They show all the conservatism of the primitive community which has reached what seems to be a stable way of life. Towards the old noble families they are respectful: no jokes are cracked against the aristocratic statesmen of the past. But they welcome a jibe against the younger generation of aristocrats, the gilded youth of the city and its foppish ways. Any suggestion of dictatorship rouses their opposition. They are prepared to laugh at attacks on the memory of 'Olympian' Pericles, as at Cratinus' ridicule of him during his lifetime. They regard Pericles' 'upstart' successors, Cleon and Hyperbolus, as fair game for comedy. Aristophanes three times made Cleon his chief target. His assault on him in 426 B.C. in the *Babylonians* (now lost) was so vigorous that the politician ignored the licence allowed to comedy and brought the poet to trial, but Aristophanes returned to the attack with a virulence which no modern nation at war— or even in time of peace—would permit. In 424 B.C., when Cleon was at the height of his power after a military success and probably occupied a seat of honour in the front row of the audience, the young playwright savagely caricatured the leather-merchant as a villainous barbarian slave who eventually lost to a still more villainous Sausage-seller his place as favourite of the People. The *Knights*, so called after the chorus of well-to-do conservative citizens whom the poet sees as the state's champions against such villainy, was awarded the first prize. Two years later, when Aristophanes satirised as *Wasps* with giant stings the old citizens who loved to spend their days as jurymen and order confiscation of the property of the rich, 'Cleon-lover' was the name he gave to the stupid old man whom his son, 'Cleon-hater', persuaded to change his ways.

In comedy the audiences of this first decade of the war were ready to accept any fantasy, any blasphemy. But not elsewhere. Unless Aristophanes' plays completely misrepresent popular taste, the common folk of Athens showed all their conservatism in their reaction towards the new ideas, the new modes of thought, that were winning a warm reception among the young aristocrats. The 'immoral' playwright, as many modern readers would consider him, was a champion of traditional morality. In his first work, the *Banqueters* (427 B.C.), he contrasted the old-style country education with the new-fangled teachings of the town. Four years later he gathered together all the current highbrow notions of philosophy and science and represented—or mis-represented—them by the familiar figure of Socrates, whom every Athenian knew. As a portrait of Socrates the *Clouds* is obviously not to be trusted; as part of the background to his execution twenty-four years later, it tells us much. Innovations in the drama were, of course, the special field of the comic poet's wit, and Euripides its special target. In the *Acharnians* (425 B.C.) Dikaiopolis, turning suppliant, goes to Euripides to borrow the rags of Telephus. From this first surviving play onwards, through quotation and parody, gossip and burlesque, Euripides is never left alone.

What was the people's attitude to the war itself during this early phase? Pacifism, antagonism to war as such, was unknown. Poet and audience still looked back to the glories of Marathon. But against the incidental sufferings and injustices of wartime there was grumbling in plenty: against overcrowding in the city, against profiteers, against lack of the goods that in peacetime reached Athens by land. The playwright made good use of these complaints to further his own policy of ending the war—a demand not found in the fragments from other comic writers of the time. Feeling against war hardships was intensified as the conflict went on: even between the *Acharnians* and the *Peace* there is a striking change of mood. Dikaiopolis in his crusade for peace has no easy task. The chorus of charcoal-burners from Acharnae (they fought at Marathon sixty-five years earlier!) are out for the blood of this traitor with all the old soldier's wrath against the suspected fifth-columnist: only when he prefaces his plea for a truce by saying that he too hates the Spartans, he too has had his vines cut down, does he divide these tough patriots and then win them over. Aristophanes is being cautious in his approach to what may be an unpopular theme. But in the *Peace* there are no two sides to the question. All are ready for an end to the struggle. All are willing that the goddess be pulled out of the pit—except fire-eater Lamachus, who sits on the rope.

These first five plays plunge us right into the hurly-burly of Athenian politics, but Aristophanes never does it again. During the seven-year gap between the *Peace* and the next extant comedy developments took place the effect of which we have already seen in Euripides. The hopes raised by the treaty of 421 B.C. were short-lived. Hostilities were soon resumed, and in 418 the Spartan army won a great victory in the Peloponnese. Defeated on land, Athens turned to fresh aggression by sea: the brutal subjection of Melos which called forth the *Trojan Women*; the expedition to Sicily which raised wild hopes and ended in crushing disaster. It was not the renewal of the war itself and its privations that mainly influenced comedy, but their effect on the political situation in the city. Even in the theatre the outspoken argument of the *Acharnians* and the violent satire of the *Knights* were only possible while there was equilibrium between the classes, while the compromise to which Aeschylus had looked as the future of Athens remained a reality. In the first decade of the struggle there had been signs of what was to come. Cleon put tolerance aside and indicted Aristophanes. A significant passage of the *Wasps* makes fun of the rising popular fear of an oligarchic *coup d'état*. When the chorus accuses him of conspiracy and aiming at tyranny, Cleon-hater replies:

> Ay 'Conspiracy' and 'Tyrant', these with you are all in all,
> Whatsoe'er is brought before you, be the matter great or small.
> Everywhere the name of Tyrant, now for fifty years unknown,
> Is than cheap salt-fish at Athens commoner and cheaper grown.[1]

After the war was resumed, feeling between rich and poor, oligarch and democrat, rapidly became more bitter, till 411 B.C. brought the beginning of an open conflict which culminated in 'tyranny'—the rule of the 'Thirty Tyrants' after Athens' surrender. During the last fifteen years of the century the conditions

[1] Ll. 488-91.

under which Old Comedy had flourished were disappearing. The most typical literary product of Periclean democracy was nearing its end—thanks to Aristophanes, a brilliant end.

The answer of Aristophanes' contemporary, Eupolis, to the critical situation of this later phase of the war was a play called the *Demes*, in which he brought statesmen of the past up from Hades to give Athens their advice. Aristophanes also had counsel to offer: in the year before the final defeat he used the *parabasis* of the *Frogs* to call for unity in the face of the common peril—unity to be obtained by the dubious means of recalling the oligarchs who had been exiled. But as topical comment and satire became more dangerous he avoided openly taking a side in the political struggle, and showed his genius by exploiting more fully the other possibilities of his art.

First and foremost, Utopianism. The Greeks usually placed their Utopia in the past, looking back to a Golden Age of peace and plenty from which mankind had followed a downhill path to the degenerate present. But amid the hardships of peasant life men naturally dreamed of a day when the Golden Age would return. The practical and conservative Hesiod gives a moral twist to such dreams by picturing them as the happy state of those who 'go not aside from what is just':

> As a garden bloometh their city; her people are prosperous. Peace,
> Nursing-mother of children, abides in their land. Zeus never decrees
> Against them cruel war, for the Far-seeing King loveth these.
> Upon givers of righteous judgments famine and ruin ne'er
> Descend, but with gladness they till the fields which are all their care.
> The Earth bears food in abundance for them: on the mountain's crest
> The oak wears crowns of acorns, within him the wild bees' nest.
> Their wool-clad sheep with fleeces heavily laden go.
> Of their wives are children born that their parents' features show.
> So with all good things they abound: they need not on ships set foot
> For the Earth corn-bounteous yieldeth all that they need of fruit.[1]

[1] *Works and Days*, ll. 227-37.

The fantastic spirit of fifth-century comedy constantly turns towards such themes. The fertility-magic of the early phallic rites had tried to extract from nature more than the meagre subsistence which primitive agricultural technique could produce: the imagination of comic playwrights dwelt on the happy results of thus miraculously transcending natural laws. They described rivers of wine or soup, fish that offered themselves for eating or turned themselves over in the pan to be fried on the other side. They talked of automatic cooking gadgets which science has still not equalled. They fancied the day when the gold of Persia would put an end to poverty in Greece, or when workers in the silver-mines would fall through into a subterranean eldorado of food and drink. Pherecrates portrayed (perhaps only to satirise it) a land of 'noble savages' in whose life—preposterous thought! —there were no slaves. In Aristophanes' earlier plays such ideas make a partial appearance in Dikaiopolis' private achievement of peace and return to his farm, in Trygaeus' flight to heaven, in the repeated rejuvenation motif—probably a relic of early ritual. But after the period of silence which follows the *Peace* Utopian-ism blossoms forth into a riot of phantasy. At the spring festival of Dionysus in 414 B.C., while the fate of the great Sicilian Expedition was still undecided, two of the three plays in the competition for comedy were concerned with escape from the troubles of mankind—Phrynichus' *Hermit* and Aristophanes' *Birds*, in which two Athenian citizens, weary of the worries and discomforts of war-stricken Athens, joined all the fowls of the air in building a Cloudcuckootown between heaven and earth, stealing sovereignty from the gods and making the birds—with one of the Athenians as their king—masters of the universe.

The whole of this magnificent play perhaps ridicules the extravagant ambition of Athenian democracy in sending the fleet to Sicily, but otherwise contemporary allusions are few. There is little obscenity. This can hardly be said of the *Lysistrata*, presented three years later, but here again escape from present miseries is Aristophanes' theme. Amid the desperate struggles to rebuild Athenian strength which followed the catastrophe in Italy, a few months before the first move against democracy, the playwright returned to the subject of peace, but on a Utopian plane. Argument in *Acharnians* style for an immediate end to the war was now impossible: surrender was the only settlement acceptable to Sparta. Aristophanes carried his audience once more into the realm of extravaganza, and invited them to dream with him of a peace secured by a reversion of the subjection and seclusion of women, a wild caricature of the feminist ideas which were part of the New Thought—refusal of all Greek wives to let their husbands touch them till the fighting was brought to an end. This earliest proposal of a strike as a weapon against war is in the true *komos* spirit, but there is a grim note in the laughter, a serious undertone which bodes ill for the future of Old Comedy. In phantasy the women may reject their husbands, but the tragic reality peers through the comic mask: far too many women have no husbands at home to spurn, the girls of Greece are growing old unwed.

The other aspect of his art which Aristophanes now developed was literary criticism, though hardly the modern conception of literary criticism. His main target was still Euripides.

At the Great Dionysia in the spring of 411 B.C., a few months after the *Lysistrata*, another play dominated by women and full of obscenity—the *Women Celebrating the Thesmophoria*—gave Athens an afternoon of brilliant wit, parody and burlesque at Euripides' expense. But the highlight of Aristophanic 'criticism' comes six years later, in the *Frogs*. Both Sophocles and Euripides have now joined Aeschylus among the dead, and Athens has no great tragic poet. Why not fetch one of them back to life? And who could be better fitted for the task than Dionysus, the god of drama himself? Once more Aristophanes takes his audience out of their hard-pressed city into another world—the realm of Hades. Accompanied—of course—by a slave, and disguised as that experienced underground traveller, Heracles, the god in whose honour the whole festival is being held becomes himself a figure of Bacchic fun. But in the second half of the play, when the Conflict (contrary to the usual structural order) takes place between Aeschylus and Euripides, Dionysus is transformed: he turns into Trygaeus, Dikaiopolis, the Athenian man-in-the-street, enabled for once not only to choose his favourite tragic poet, but to cock a snook at tragedy itself. This judgment scene of the *Frogs* must not be taken too seriously. The 'madness' of Old Comedy is not dead, though its distortions are less grotesque and less libellous than in the *Clouds*.

Within a year of the production of the *Frogs*, the war was over. Peace had come to Athens, but it was the peace of surrender and defeat. Life in Attica could now 'return to normal', but the Athenians, like other peoples after great wars, discovered that the 'back to normal' they had dreamed of was an illusion. The farmers returned to their fields to find them ruined. Tribute from the 'Allies' no longer filled Athena's treasury. War had ceased to pound Greece in his mortar, but Poverty (as Aristophanes was to show) had taken its place. Class conflict dominated politics, and though the Panhellenism of the *Peace* and *Lysistrata* was a pointer to the future, the 'little man', pushed down from middle-class complacency to proletarian want and discontent, saw no practical way out. In imagination, but not in action, there was a swing towards revolutionary ideas, economic panaceas which Plato was to adapt to his own purposes in the *Republic*. A number of years before the philosopher's version of them was published, Aristophanes ridiculed such notions in the theatre, but he did not assail their authors directly as he had attacked Socrates in 423 B.C. Such hilarious libel was a thing of the past. The *Women in Parliament* (probably 391 B.C.) is a burlesque of political

Utopianism: the women again seize power—this time, to bring prosperity, not peace. Their communist Utopia is thoroughgoing, but for citizens only: food, drink, land, money, women, children are common property, but there are still free men and slaves.

For all its fantasy, the *Women in Parliament* is a sober affair compared with the earlier plays. The form of comedy has changed to suit a changed world, and the *parabasis*, most distinctive feature of Old Comedy in its heyday, has dwindled till here it entirely disappears. The obscenity of the final scenes, for the first time in Aristophanes, leaves a bad taste in the mouth: it was natural amid the gaiety of the phallic revel, but here it is mechanical and nauseating. In the *Plutus* (388 B.C.) the sobriety has sunk into dullness, the bawdiness has nearly vanished. The chorus, descendant of the original *komos*, has become so unimportant that its songs, if they ever existed, are not included in our version of the play. The theme—the restoration of sight to the blind god of Wealth, and its happy sequel—is a Utopian conception typical of the time: money and the lack of it are the things that matter now. But the handling of the plot is nearer to allegory than fantasy. The debate between Poverty and the follower of Wealth is more like a dialogue on elementary economics than the Conflicts of earlier plays—with Poverty proving herself the better economist of the two. Fifth-century Athenian democracy could afford to welcome farces that broke taboos and smashed conventions, but the unstable society of the post-war years had too little confidence in its traditions to laugh when they were turned upside down in the theatre. The realism of some scenes of the *Plutus* makes it credible that in future comedy should learn more from Aristophanes' butt, Euripides, than from the spirit which inspired the *Peace* or the *Birds*. The fantastic fairy-tree has withered, the nightingale-nests are silent, the climbing monkeys have become tame chimpanzees. For many generations after this plays were still produced in the theatre of Dionysus, but the great days of

Greek drama—indeed, of Greek poetry—were over. These last two surviving works of Aristophanes were by-products of a century that found its natural medium in prose.

CHAPTER VII

THE RISE OF PROSE

ONLY in middle age did Molière's Monsieur Jourdain make the delightful discovery that all his life he had spoken prose. Ancient Greece was equally late in passing through the same exciting experience. Greek culture was near its prime before prose was consciously recognised as a vehicle of narrative or thought. The Muse was already a little grey around the temples when she produced prose literature that could rival the poetry of her more youthful days. But of course the peoples of the Aegean during the adolescence of their civilisation did not lisp in numbers: not only was unmetrical speech always the medium of ordinary talk, but if early Greece was true to the general rule, if we are to make sense of the growth of Greek prose literature when it did come into being, this same ordinary talk must long have been used for story-telling. The teller of stories in prose could not claim the lofty inspiration of Demodocus, with his lyre and his language specially adapted to his art. Prose tales were the pàstime of the market-place, not the nobles' hall. Yet some of the qualities of epic narrative—clarity, simplicity, speed, vividness—must also have been the aims of the humblest entertainer of the crowd.

Whereas verse was conventionalised and easily committed to memory because of its metre, and could be handed down in more or less fixed form by oral tradition, a piece of prose could hardly survive from generation to generation without being written down. It seems probable—as probable as anything amid the mists that surround the earliest prose almost as thickly as they envelop the origins of poetry—that the use of the alphabet, at first applied to accounts or records, lists of names or codes of law, where there was no place for metre or rhythm, was soon extended to narrative. Certainly the sixth century B.C. found writing regularly employed, especially in Ionia, for something more than utilitarian ends. While epic declined, while choral song became linked with aristocracy and 'tyranny' and personal poetry was the pastime of the few, social change and the spread of knowledge on the eastern side of the Aegean created a new public with new needs and new tastes. Among the popular stories now put into writing were the first version of Aesop's fables, known to us only in much later form, and of those *Milesian Tales* in which Hellenistic and Roman times found their equivalent of the *Decameron* and the *Arabian Nights*. Here were the simple beginnings of the mass of 'fiction' which fills our modern libraries. Other prose authors—if they deserve the name—were more ambitious. Using the straightforward story-telling style but strongly influenced by the epic tradition, they reproduced the contents of records for public consumption. They wrote annals, chronicles of cities and peoples, genealogies—often intended, no doubt, to provide divine or heroic roots for a patron's family tree. Sometimes they retold epic myth or legend in prose.

These early prose-writers, who all used the Ionian dialect, were little known to fifth- and fourth-century Athens. Their works were collected and studied by the scholars of Alexandria— hence our own knowledge of them—but time has preserved only the most meagre fragments: Herodotus is the earliest prose author whose book we now possess complete. If we still had his predecessors' writings, they would probably seem little different from epic except through inferiority and lack of metre—no more than a feeble reflection of hexameter verse. Yet a great destiny lay ahead of these humble beginnings. The situation which produced them contained a trend very unlike the story-teller's point of view, a trend which was to give prose new subject-matter;

even where its subject-matter was old, a new and distinctive spirit. Let us glance once more at the Ionian scene.

The seventh and sixth centuries in Ionia, when her cities were ruled by 'tyrants' who looked to the monarchs of the East for support, were a time when growing intercourse with Lydia and Persia and Egypt meant fresh prospects of trade and travel, a new world of opportunity. The older civilisations were a mine of information, hitherto untapped. Technical developments were required to keep pace with the expansion of commerce and industry. The leaven of new knowledge and new needs created an intellectual ferment which did not restrict itself to practical affairs. The spirit of enquiry—*historiē* was the Greek word— marched boldly beyond the confines of local tradition to seek understanding of the whole world. Here were the crude origins of geography as well as of history in the limited modern sense, the first steps towards natural science. Typical of his time—the first decades of the sixth century—was Thales of Miletus, traveller, engineer, inventor, astronomer—and, incidentally, the first to look for one substance underlying the universe.

The conventional assumptions of the small aristocratic city-state could not satisfy this spirit. Nor could the conventional medium of literary expression. An intellectual revolt had begun, and a literary revolt accompanied it. It was this wider transformation of outlook, turning to prose as its natural means of expression, that gave the new medium a status and importance of its own. The transition from poetry to prose as the main component of Greek literature began as part of a shift from mythological ways of thought to rationalism, as one aspect of a growing revolt against the authority of tradition and the poets, as one way of asserting the right of the individual to challenge the assumptions of the community. The process was not sudden. It affected some early prose writers more than others—some, doubtless, hardly at all. Even the boldest of them were far from entirely turning their backs on the material or the spirit of the poets. They did not distinguish myth from history, and attempted a more rational account of the old legends instead of discarding them altogether. Amid the little evidence that we possess it is sometimes difficult to see any clear trace of the new rationalism at work. Yet it is there. Three early Ionian authors of whom we have some definite knowledge will serve to illustrate how the first development from the language of conversation and dry records towards something like literature was linked with the slow disentanglement of reasoning from earlier ways of thought. Two of them—Anaximander and Heraclitus—may perhaps be described as scientists, although their 'science' was little more than an attempt to bring the universe within their comprehension by projecting into it their own personality and activities. The other—Hecataeus—has been called 'the father of history', though modern historians would scarcely recognise their distant ancestor.

Anaximander was a citizen of Miletus, chief Ionian trade centre and one of the greatest cities of the ancient world till its destruction by the Persians. The dates of his birth and death are uncertain, but there can be no doubt that he reached his prime during the first half of the sixth century. He was reputed to be the inventor of the sundial. To his contemporaries he seems to have been best known as the maker of the earliest map, picturing in new form the world that was opening up before Ionian eyes. That his geography was linked with practical aims and needs is suggested by the fact that he himself led a body of colonists to start a new settlement on the Black Sea coast. Like his fellow-townsman, Thales, Anaximander extended his *historiē* to the universe as a whole. Unlike Thales, he published a book, in which he set forth his conclusions in prose. His theories, known to us through the late fourth-century scientist Theophrastus, belong to the realm of philosophy; what matters for the history of literature is that one statement by Theophrastus is almost certainly a quotation from the original work: 'Into that from which things take their rise they pass away once more, as is meet; for they make reparation and satisfaction to one another for their injustice according to the ordering of time'.[1] 'Somewhat poetical terms' is Theophrastus' description of this language. Not only the style recalls the poets. Like Homer's Achaeans who modelled the Olympian gods on their own society, Anaximander sees the changing universe in terms of the administration of justice in his time. But his analogy is new: it is applied not to gods, but to material things. Science, rationalism, the prosaic outlook are being born.

Hecataeus, also of Miletus, lived late enough to warn his fellow-citizens not to revolt against Persia and to see the city sacked when they failed to follow his advice. Previously he had travelled through the Persian Empire, including Egypt, and he not only improved Anaximander's map but published a prose work, of which we have more than 300 fragments, embodying all his knowledge of foreign lands—their cities and peoples, their religion, their laws, their animal life. Hecataeus, like Anaximander, did not break completely with the past or with the old ways of thought, unless his claim to be descended from a god in the sixteenth generation is to be regarded as ironical. He wrote a book entitled *Genealogies* mainly concerned with mythology. But its opening sentences, which with over thirty other fragments survive, breathe the spirit of critical and rather arrogant rationalism: 'Thus speaks Hecataeus of Miletus. What follows I write as it appears to me to be true; for the writings of the Hellenes are many and in my opinion ridiculous'.[2] These simple and abrupt statements contain all the essentials of the literary revolt that brought prose an independent status: the assertion of individual opinion; the emphasis on truth; the contemptuous rejection of

[1] Diels, *Fragmente der Vorsokratiker*, A 9 and B 1.
[2] *Fr.* 332 (Müller).

'the writings of the Hellenes' by one who has seen all the wonders of Egypt and the East.

Heraclitus, probably contemporary with Hecataeus, was born at Ephesus, thirty miles north of Miletus. Even ancient readers found him obscure and nicknamed him 'the dark one', and the 130 fragments confirm their verdict; yet there are few early writers whose personality and experience are so clearly reflected in their work. A bitter aristocratic opponent of the 'tyrants' and their supporters, he thoroughly despised 'the many'. Partly because of the difficulty of expressing new ideas in old terms— the problem today of the exponent of 'popular' science, who usually turns to metaphor and analogy as the solution—and partly through a desire to veil his meaning from vulgar minds, he imported into prose the cryptic manner of the oracles, and rivalled Pindar and Aeschylus in the picturesqueness of his style. Heraclitus is a sweeping critic: he condemns all other writers, from Homer to Hecataeus; even traditional ritual is a target for his attack. His own views transfer to the universe all the instability and strife of the society in which he lived. Everything is in a state of flux: 'You cannot step twice into the same rivers; for fresh waters are ever flowing in upon you.'[1] Conflict is perpetual: 'We must know that war is common to all and strife is justice, and that all things come into being and pass away through strife.'[2] Yet the key to it all is a rational principle which the understanding mind must grasp—the principle that the only permanence *is* change, the only unity *is* conflict, embodied and symbolised in the equation 'all is fire'. For all Heraclitus' obscure and picturesque language, even here prose and rationalism go hand in hand.

Some of these fragments of early prose are more poetical than

[1] *Fr.* 41. Tr. Burnet, *Early Greek Philosophy* (A. & C. Black, Ltd.).
[2] *Fr.* 62. Tr. Burnet.

many of the poets. Neither in Ionia nor in the rest of Greece did prose immediately oust verse, even for topics which to the modern mind are thoroughly prosaic. The precedent set by the *Works and Days* was kept up. Just as the *Theogony* described the beginnings of the universe in hexameters, just as Solon chose the elegiac couplet for expounding his political policy, so even some of those who deserted the old ways of thought still wrote in verse, which with its Homeric language could reach a more Panhellenic audience than a local dialect of Ionia. Xenophanes, a striking example from Ionia itself, composed poems on the founding of his native Colophon and the colonisation of Elea, where he later settled, as well as satirical elegiacs. In the West, where the early growth of philosophy was an offshoot of the Orphic religion rather than secular *historiē*, Parmenides produced a strange literary paradox by telling in hexameters how a goddess revealed to him a logical approach to the problem of the universe —the initial step towards the thoroughly prosaic science of logical argument. Empedocles used the same medium to expound his theory of four elements, combined with the Orphic doctrine of the transmigration of souls. Even contemporary history could still in the fifth century be written in hexameters—by Choerilus, for example, who published a verse account of the Persian Wars. The verse convention died hard. Nevertheless, in the generations that followed Hecataeus and Heraclitus prose became established as the normal medium for philosophy, science, history. It was in prose that Anaxagoras published at Athens the heretical views which caused his exile, Democritus set forth his atomic theory, the followers of Parmenides maintained and applied his logic. Among the most extensive remains of fifth-century writing, vitally important for the history of science, is the large collection of prose medical treatises found by third-century scholars in the archives of the medical school on the island of Cos and attributed to Hippocrates, a collection now

best known through one document—the Hippocratic oath.
Besides various authors who wrote prose histories of Persia or
parts of the Persian Empire there were others, including Herodotus and Thucydides, who turned the searchlight of enquiry or
rationalism on the history of Greece. But before considering
them we must retrace our steps for a moment to glance at another
factor which completed the development of prose.

Up to the middle of the fifth century B.C. rational argument
was still not the dominating feature of Greek prose. Nor had
prose style crystallised into any fixed or conventional form. The
simple, almost rambling manner of the story-teller was usually
maintained: otherwise each author gave his writing what shape
and character he pleased—simple or obscure, plain or poetical.
Yet later prose bears the marks of convention no less clearly than
the epic or the drama, and argument rather than narrative is the
keynote of its style. What brought about the change?

At this point a new figure enters the pageant of Greek literature: the rhetorician, the deviser of effective and convincing
speech. His cue: the rise of democracy. Later he was to steal
the show, for in a literature composed mainly for hearers rather
than readers the art of oratory was bound to gain a leading role.

Eloquence, of course, was no newcomer. Some of the
Homeric heroes gave powerful displays of it in the councils of
the chiefs. Little is heard of it among the 'tyrants'—a contrast
with modern dictators—but in all phases of Greek development
there must have been some individuals, like Themistocles, who
possessed it as a natural gift. Because speeches were not reported,
we know of such early orators only by repute. The effect of the
coming of democracy to the city-state was to put oratory at a
premium to make natural talent worth developing and the art
worth acquiring even by those whom nature had overlooked.
Unlike the representative systems of modern times, democracy

in the small communities of fifth-century Greece brought to all and sundry the opportunity of joining in political debate. The replacement of the arbitrary 'justice' of autocratic rulers by law courts and legal codes, without a professional class of advocates, greatly increased the value of being able to plead one's case. Leisure, based on the growth of slavery, made it possible for more of the citizens to turn their attention to such things. And though Solon had put politics into verse, though the aged Sophocles is said to have convinced a jury of his sanity by reciting lines from *Oedipus at Colonus*, it was of course in prose that the would-be orator wished to learn to speak. The demand arose especially in two places: in Athens, and in Sicily, where the transition from 'tyranny' to democracy in 466 B.C. created both a political ferment and a flood of litigation on property disputes.

To meet this demand was the function of the Sophists, who exercised a profound influence on literature, although they were not primarily writers and little that they wrote has survived. Plato and most of our other sources about them paint a biased picture which gave the word 'Sophist' itself a bad sense, but modern comment has reinstated them. Brilliant sons of small states where they could find little scope for their ambition as citizens, they travelled elsewhere and sought their fortune in trade. The commodities they purveyed were knowledge and intellectual skill. In payment they exacted fees, and naturally their best market was among the sons of the rich. It was Alcibiades and his like, not Trygaeus, who had the money and the leisure for such a luxury as higher education. The Sophists were not specialists. One of them, Hippias, claimed to know and teach everything, and appeared at Olympia in an elaborate costume which was all his own work. But if among their various interests they had one common denominator, one common line in mental merchandise, it was the craft of rhetoric. When Strepsiades entered the 'thinking-shop' in the *Clouds*, there was one thing that he expected there—to learn to speak. The art of oratory was first developed by writers of law-court speeches in Sicily, and extended by the Sophist Gorgias, of the small Sicilian town of Leontini, to political and general themes. Gorgias is said to have shocked Athens by his novel eloquence when he came there on an embassy in 427 B.C., but other Sophists, including Protagoras, earliest of them all, had already introduced the new art to the Athenians. Aristophanes' Acharnian veterans—as old as the mythical Tithonus—complain bitterly against the tricks which the young have picked up:

> There we stand, decayed and muttering, hard beside the court-house
> stone,
> Nought discerning all around us save the darkness of our case.
> Comes the youngster, who has compassed for himself the Accuser's
> place,
> Slings his tight and nipping phrases, tackling us with legal scraps,
> Pulls us up and cross-examines, setting little verbal traps,
> Rends and rattles old Tithonus till the man is dazed and blind;
> Till with toothless gums he mumbles, then departs condemned and
> fined.[1]

With the growth of rhetoric the tradition of the story-teller and his influence on prose style were eclipsed. The rhetorical writer's object was not clarity of narrative, but persuasion, effective argument. It was from this that prose-writing acquired a technique, consciously formulated and applied, a conventional mould which has left its stamp on most extant Attic prose. The new craft was swiftly developed. Antiphon, in his old age a leader of the revolution of 411 B.C., published theoretical exercises in oratory as well as actual court speeches. Gorgias deliberately imported poetical words and phrases into prose, and worked out rhetorical devices—antithesis, balanced rhythm, assonance, even rhyme—which he was the first to call 'figures of

[1] *Acharnians*, ll. 683-9.

speech'. Some Sophists went beyond the teaching of persuasive speech to the study and analysis of language itself: Protagoras classified types of sentences and discussed grammatical genders; Prodicus pointed the way towards dictionary-making by differentiating synonyms. The first exuberance over the new discovery carried the cult of style for its own sake to extraordinary lengths, some slight idea of which can be gained from a translation (so far as it admits of translation) of part of a fragment by Gorgias himself, taken from a type of speech of which we have several examples—a funeral address for men killed in war:

What qualities did these men lack of those that men should possess? And what did they possess that men should not possess? May I be able to say what I wish and may I wish what I should, escaping the vengeance of the gods, avoiding the envy of men. For divine was the courage these men possessed, but human their mortality. Often they put temperate fairness before blunt insistence on their rights, often rightness of principle before the letter of the law, deeming this the most divine and the most universal law—rightly on the right occasion to speak or keep silence, to do or leave undone. Two things especially they practised of what is needful, thought and strength, the one in counsel, the other in action, as helpers of those who wrongly suffered ill fortune, and punishers of those who wrongly won good fortune. They were bold for the sake of the common good, easily moved for the sake of duty. They checked rashness of act by prudence of thought. They were violent towards the violent, orderly towards the orderly; fearless towards the fearless, terrible when all around was terrible . . .[1]

Even in translation, what a contrast with Anaximander or Hecataeus! One is reminded of the parody of Euphuism which Shakespeare puts into the mouth of Falstaff: 'Now I do not speak to thee in drink but in tears; not in pleasure but in passion; not in words only but in woes also.' In the original Greek this passage of Gorgias carries artificiality to extremes. But the same essence, in more diluted form, colours most later Greek prose.

[1] *Fr.* 6 (Diels).

The forces which produced the Sophists and their rhetoric not only affected the form of prose: by carrying rationalism into fresh territory they also extended the subject-matter of prose literature. As the questioning spirit which the Ionians had applied to the world around them invaded the life of the city-state itself, not only politics and legal cases, but all aspects of the citizen's existence became topics for debate and opportunities for eloquence. Prose became the medium for expressing all kinds of ideas very different from the traditional assumptions inherited from the past. Here is Protagoras on religion:

> With regard to the gods, I cannot feel sure either that they are or that they are not, nor what they are like in figure; for there are many things that hinder sure knowledge, the obscurity of the subject and the shortness of human life.[1]

And the Sophist Antiphon—not to be confused with the orator —on distinction of race and birth:

> We all in every way have the same nature, both Greeks and barbarians . . . In all these things no barbarian or Greek is different from us; for we all breathe into the air through mouth and nose, and all eat with our hands.[2]

Although the infection of tragedy by the new outlook is evident in Euripides, whose theatrical debates show how argument for its own sake flourished as well as style for its own sake, the main vehicle of such discussions continued to be prose. By the end of the Peloponnesian War prosaic rationalism, less than two hundred years old, had come into more than its own. The fourth century was an age of prose: though drama and other kinds of verse were still produced, little but prose survives from this period, and in most of this—as we shall see, there were important exceptions—rhetoric is the dominant note. Rhetoric itself, of course, made great advances on the form which the Sophists had

---

[1] *Fr.* 4 (Diels). Tr. Burnet, *Greek Philosophy: Thales to Plato* (Macmillan and Co., Ltd.).   [2] *Fr.* 44 (Diels).

given it. Its style became less artificial, nearer to normal speech. Antithesis became only one of the means employed in building up more flexible and more organic sentences, in which individual phrases and clauses were subordinated to a larger unity. The use of poetical words was abandoned. Yet the rhetorical flavour remained. The aim was still persuasion, effective argument. This was the age of the Attic orators, to whose outpourings, thanks to the value set on rhetoric in later centuries, time has been kinder than to some more deserving parts of ancient literature. The surviving remains include many law-court speeches, far more slanderous and emotional than those of today; many political harangues; a few orations—they might almost be called political sermons—designed for great public occasions such as the Panhellenic gathering at the Olympian Games. Among their authors are Andocides, high-born gentleman and amateur in the practice of rhetoric; Lysias, skilful advocate and professional writer of speeches for others; Isaeus, specialist on the law of inheritance; Lycurgus, die-hard patriotic opponent of Macedon; Aeschines, a tragic actor before he turned his wits to political opportunism; his antagonist Demosthenes, who carried Greek eloquence to its greatest heights both in the law-court and in his demands for a return to the spirit of Marathon and a stand against the Macedonian threat.

Rhetoric was by no means limited to the assembly and the law-courts. The orator and teacher of oratory trespassed everywhere on the poet's former preserves. Discourses on philosophical or political subjects were substituted for drinking songs at banquets. Exhibition speeches in the grand style ousted the rhapsode and his recitations from festivals. In the curriculum of the schools training in the art of speaking found a place alongside memorisation of the *Iliad* and the *Odyssey*. Still more important for the future of literature, though few of its immediate results are extant today, was the intrusion of rhetoric into areas once covered by the story-teller with his simple style. History, first brought under the influence of oratory by Thucydides, later became predominantly rhetorical. Biography, now becoming a recognised type of literature as individualism advanced, tended to model itself on the oratorical 'encomium'. The central figure in this development was Isocrates, probably a pupil of Gorgias, and chief fourth-century heir of the Sophists. Nervousness and poor delivery prevented Isocrates from being a great orator himself. His numerous writings, though in speech form, were published as pamphlets rather than delivered to an audience. But it was mainly he who developed rhetoric into a distinct and elaborate science. He was the principal architect of the 'grand style' which became the model for later Greek and Latin prose. Among his pupils were many of the writers of the time, including some of the historians. From now on not only the orator was expected to display the technique of eloquence, but any author of prose, and all too often it was by his possession or lack of this quality that his works were judged.

Most of these later rhetorical writings have now disappeared. With the orators themselves I shall not deal in detail. Their speeches stirred the emotions and absorbed the attention of the Athenians of their day, but like all oratory concerned with a particular and transient situation, they have lost their savour with the passing of time. However much excitement was once roused by such attempts to persuade contemporary audiences by contemporary arguments and appeals to contemporary feeling, however fruitful a field they still provide for the historian and the antiquarian, as literature they are dead. The Greek prose authors whose work has most literary appeal today are those who —with one partial exception—are most free from the influence of rhetoric: the historians Herodotus, Thucydides, and Xenophon, and the philosopher Plato.

CHAPTER VIII

THREE HISTORIANS

'THESE are the researches of Herodotus of Halicarnassus, which he publishes, in the hope of thereby preserving from decay the remembrance of what men have done, and of preventing the great and wonderful actions of the Greeks and the Barbarians from losing their due meed of glory; and withal to put on record what were their grounds of feud.' So begin the five hundred or more pages of the one and only work ascribed to Herodotus. The dialect is Ionian. The word translated by 'researches' is *historiē*. Although probably written in the second half of the fifth century B.C., this opening sentence still calls to mind the features of early prose—the art of the story-teller, the pursuit of 'inquiry'. Ionian Hecataeus and his travel-book are not far away.

Read on, and the impression is confirmed. As we turn the pages Herodotus takes us to one country after another of the ancient world: to Lydia (East of Ionia), Persia, Egypt, the rest of North Africa, India, Scythia (between the Carpathians and the Don), as well as the areas inhabited by Greeks. He describes each, stressing especially (like a modern newspaper) what is exceptional and strange. He explains their geography—a revelation to his contemporaries, even though he goes so far wrong as to think that Europe extends the entire length of Libya (Africa) and Asia, or to name 'the Carpis and the Alpis' as tributaries of the Danube. He gives an account of their animal life. The hippopotamus, for example, 'is a quadruped, cloven-footed, with hoofs like an ox, and a flat nose. It has the mane and tail of a horse, huge tusks which are very conspicuous, and a voice like a horse's neigh. In size it equals the biggest oxen, and its skin is

so tough that when dried it is made into javelins.'[1] He deals
with different aspects of their many peoples: physique ('the
Budini are a large and powerful nation: they have all deep blue
eyes, and bright red hair'); dress ('these Indians wear a dress of
sedge, which they cut in the river and bruise; afterwards they
weave it into mats, and wear it as we wear a breast-plate');
customs ('with this substance, which is of a thick consistency,
they plaster their faces all over, and indeed their whole bodies.
A sweet odour is thereby imparted to them, and when they take
off the plaster on the day following, their skin is clean and
glossy'); methods of warfare (the Scythians 'make it impossible
for the enemy who invades them to escape destruction, while they
themselves are entirely out of his reach, unless it please them to
engage with him'); agriculture, commerce, transport ('the boats
which come down the river to Babylon are circular, and made of
skins'); religious practices (the Egyptian priests 'bathe twice
every day in cold water, and twice each night'). Everywhere he
notes details of monuments, statues, offerings in temples, all kinds
of works of art. He narrates the past of some peoples, often mixed
with myth, but above all he tells the story—true or legendary—
of their famous men and women, frequently with genealogies
attached. His book is a portrait-gallery of kings, queens, nobles,
tyrants, political leaders, soldiers, from emperor Xerxes to the
Athenian infantryman at the battle of Plataea who anchored
himself to the ground rather than retreat.

The style of all this goes back to the story-teller in the market-
place. Directness and speed are the keynotes. Herodotus'
simple sentences are strung loosely together with the help of
stock phrases and idioms. Speeches and conversations are given
in the same style as the narrative. To the same tradition belongs
the arrangement of his material. There are many whole stories
or descriptions which could stand separately by themselves.

[1] II, 71.

Often they are introduced as digressions: 'Additions', says their author, 'are what my work always from the very first affected.'[1] Sometimes the inclusion of digression within digression is reminiscent of an old man's tales of family history ('Now let me see, where was I?'). With such methods it is hardly surprising if Herodotus' chronology is far from clear: he shows little concern over dates. Yet the pattern of the work as a whole is historical. The connecting chain that links all the various elements together is not geographical (as with Hecataeus) but the theme mentioned at the beginning—the story of the relations of East and West. Primarily it is an account of Persia and her imperial adventures. Even the long section on Egypt is introduced because of Cambyses' Egyptian expedition. Greek history is brought in incidentally: it is only through the tale of Lydian Croesus that Athenian Solon enters the picture.

Such are the contents and manner of more than half of Herodotus' book. But as we read further there is a change. He is still the story-teller, still keeps the same simple style, but now he concentrates his attention on a single tale—the Persian onslaught against Greece and its defeat. It is difficult to say where the transformation begins. Certainly in the last three of the nine books (named after the nine Muses) into which the Alexandrian scholars divided the work the narrative sweeps majestically forward almost without a break. Digressions here are few and brief. The stage is set for the drama by speeches that reveal Xerxes' megalomaniac ambition, by dreams and prodigies that show the Persians being driven by fate to their doom, by the King's vast preparations and the march of his enormous host into Europe across the bridge built over the Hellespont—with flaxen cables weighing no less that fifty pounds a foot! While the invaders advance on Greece drinking rivers dry and reducing cities to poverty as they pass, among the Greeks themselves there

[1] IV, 30.

is tragic division and delay, but even so scene follows scene in which the Hellenic David triumphs and the barbarian Goliath is laid low: Thermopylae, Artemisium, Salamis, Plataea, Mycale, Sestos—till the account ends abruptly with a paragraph that would be a footnote in a modern book.

Who was Herodotus? How does this 'history' fit into what we know of his life and background? It is clear from the book itself that he travelled very widely for his day, that his own 'researches' were the main basis of his work. He visited Babylon, Phoenicia, Egypt, the Black Sea coast, and probably other places far from Greece. Commerce may have been his principal object —he is remarkably interested in manufactures and methods of transport—but hand in hand with trade, as in sixth-century Ionia, went *historië*. 'In the wish to get the best information that I could on these matters', he writes in one passage, 'I made a voyage to Tyre in Phoenicia, hearing there was a temple of Heracles at that place . . . In Tyre I remarked another temple where the same god was worshipped as the Thasian Heracles. So I went on to Thasos.'[1] Of other aspects of his biography the book gives no direct information. Though full of anecdotes, it tells no personal reminiscences in the modern style. But partly by inference from his work, partly from other sources, we can piece together an outline of his life.

'The researches of Herodotus of Halicarnassus', says the opening sentence. Halicarnassus was a town on the fringe of the Greek world—a settlement established by Dorians who mingled with the local Carian 'natives'. Most of their culture must have come from Ionia further north, however much they (like Herodotus himself) professed to despise the Ionians. Here Herodotus was born a few years before the battle of Salamis—a member of 'the better class', and nephew of the epic poet Pany-assis. A struggle with Lygdamis, the 'tyrant' who ruled

[1] II, 44.

231

Halicarnassus with Persian backing, resulted in the uncle's death and Herodotus' departure, and though he may have returned later to join in Lygdamis' expulsion, he did not stay. Athens, then rising to be the foremost state of Greece, became his home and the centre of his thoughts. It was from Athens that he went to join in founding Thurii, in Italy, in 443 B.C. To Athens he later returned, and at Athens he probably died early in the Peloponnesian War—perhaps a victim of the plague which struck the city in 430 B.C. Where his travels come into the picture we cannot tell, but they must have taken up a number of years.

Put what we know of the historian's life alongside his book, and it is obvious that there can be no certainty about how and when he wrote. Later anecdotes may well be correct in saying that some sections were delivered orally before they were published in writing. The work as a whole is often divided by modern commentators into the final narrative—from Book VII or earlier to the end—and the preliminaries. The final part is clearly the climax towards which the rest leads up. It must have been composed as a single unit, probably in a comparatively short time. Was it written first or last, early in Herodotus' life or at the end? The arguments from cross-references are too complex to be dealt with here, but the best conclusion is the one that also fits both the entire historical context and Herodotus' place in the development of prose literature. Some or all of the earlier 'books' were written (and possibly published) first as a 'Persian history'—a subject fully in keeping with the traditions of Ionian prose. It was in the last years before his death, under stress of the new war which was splitting the Greek states into hostile camps, that Herodotus drew his dramatic picture of Greece triumphant against the barbarian invader, adapted his previous work to it as a prelude, and published the whole. In making little reference to events nearer to his own time he was merely following the precedent set up by epic and tragedy.

One of his motives for choosing the Persian War as his theme is clear enough: defence of his beloved Athens at a time when half Greece had turned against her and a Spartan army was ravaging Attica. Although he occasionally has hard things to say of the Athenians, they are for him the champions of Hellenic freedom against aggression and tyranny. It was they who assisted the Ionian revolt and so called down on their heads the wrath of Darius. It was they who at Marathon first faced the Persians and defeated them, when (as they later claimed) they 'stood alone, and conquered forty-six nations'. When Xerxes launches his great expedition, Herodotus comments: 'And here I feel constrained to deliver an opinion, which most men, I know, will dislike, but which, as it seems to me to be true, I am determined not to withhold . . . If a man should now say that the Athenians were the saviours of Greece, he would not exceed the truth'.[1] The long account of the battle of Plataea is contrived to make the Athenians the heroes of the day, though the role modern historians give them in the story is far from heroic. At Mycale 'the Greeks who behaved with the greatest bravery were the Athenians'. Surely, Herodotus implies, writing half a century later—surely the state with such a past record as this deserves better from her fellow-Greeks than the destruction of her vines and olives and the plundering of her farms?

According to a later writer[2] Athens showed her gratitude by awarding the historian the large sum of ten talents. Yet to describe him merely as 'pro-Athenian' is not enough. Class background and associations moulded his outlook, as well as loyalty to the city of his adoption. In Halicarnassus he belonged to 'the better class' and had an epic poet as his uncle. At Athens tradition links him with Sophocles. Passages in his book show a strong bias in favour of the Alcmaeonid family to which Pericles belonged. But Themistocles, strategist of Salamis and founder

[1] VII, 139.　　　　　　　　　　[2] Diyllus the Aristotelian.

of much of Athenian democracy's future greatness, receives little praise. He is 'a man who had lately made his way into the first rank of citizens', a trickster who 'never ceased his pursuit of gain'. Very different is his political enemy, the nobly-born Aristides: 'He was an Athenian, and had been ostracised by the commonalty; yet I believe, from what I have heard concerning his character, that there was not in all Athens a man so worthy or so just as he.'[1] Herodotus' sympathies, like those of Sophocles and Aristophanes, evidently lay with the Athenian aristocrats who accepted democracy as long as it did not go too far. He admired Pericles, but he would have been bitterly hostile to Cleon. These feelings, though never clearly stated, must have had some influence on his choice and treatment of his theme. The aristocrats above all looked back to the glories of Marathon and contrasted them with the more degenerate present. In place of the cleavage which reached its climax in the Peloponnesian War they stood for friendship with Sparta and other states—unity strongly advocated by Herodotus' idealised Athenians of the past: 'There is our common brotherhood with the Greeks: our common language, the altars and the sacrifices of which we all partake, the common character which we bear—did the Athenians betray all these, of a truth it would not be well.'[2] Herodotus is rarely a deliberate propagandist. His attitude, like that of the poets, is shaped by assumptions and trends of thought which he did not—and could not—clearly formulate. Yet through his selection and handling of his material his book carried a double message in those first years of the new war. To Hellas as a whole it preached the achievements and deserts of Athens, the dangers of strife among Greek states surrounded by a barbarian world. Before the Athenians it set their glorious past as a model, and counselled them to walk in the footsteps of Aristides, not Themistocles.

[1] VIII, 79.   [2] VIII, 144.

So much for Herodotus' political outlook. The same background conditioned other aspects of his work: his prose style, his method as a historian, his religious beliefs. He was roughly contemporary with Protagoras, and must have met him at Athens or Thurii. Here and there he echoes the ideas which the Sophists were encouraging—in the strange debate between Persian conspirators on the rival merits of democracy, oligarchy, and monarchy; or in the anecdote of the Greeks' horror at certain Indians who ate their dead fathers, and the equal revulsion of the Indians on hearing that the Greeks burned theirs. But rationalism and the Sophists have left no mark on his book as a whole. His prose, as we have seen, has no rhetorical flavour: his tricks are those of the story-teller, not the orator; his purpose, to narrate and describe, not to persuade.

Of his method (or lack of method) more must be said. What was Herodotus' attitude towards the mass of information which he drew from previous 'historians' like Hecataeus, from official documents and lists, from oracles and temple records, from tradition (especially Athenian tradition) handed down by word of mouth, from conversation—usually through interpreters, for his only language was Greek—with those whom he met on his travels? Did he accept every word without question, or did he discriminate?

Because much that he reports is to us incredible, because he tells of Indian ants 'bigger than foxes' and supposes that the sun can be driven off its course by storms, he must not be regarded as a Greek Munchausen. His aim is the truth, though he does not always achieve it. Nor is he a credulous fool. Herodotus is a sceptic. 'My duty', he writes, 'is to report all that is said, but I am not obliged to believe it all alike—a remark which may be understood to apply to my whole History.'[1] There are many tales which he refuses to believe:

[1] VII, 152.

The bald men say, but it does not seem to me credible, that the people who live in these mountains have feet like goats; and that after passing them you find another race of men, who sleep during one half of the year. This latter statement appears to me quite unworthy of credit.[1]

Sometimes he adds his own version:

Now the Persians had with them a man named Scyllias, a native of Scione, who was the most expert diver of his day. . . . In what way he contrived to reach the Greeks I am not able to say for certain: I marvel much if the tale that is commonly told be true. It is said he dived into the sea at Aphetae, and did not once come to the surface till he reached Artemisium, a distance of nearly ten miles. Now many things are related of this man which are plainly false, but some of the stories seem to be true. My own opinion is that on this occasion he made the passage to Artemisium in a boat.[2]

This is the scepticism of Ionia which leaves its mark on so much early prose, a tendency more prevalent in the environment of Herodotus' early years than in Periclean Athens. Its prominence in his account of Egypt shows that that section (Book II) was among the first to be written, not, as some critics have imagined, that it was the last. Like Ionian Hecataeus, Herodotus particularly ridicules the 'foolish fables' of the Greeks, including some which came from Homer. He turns the same weapon against Hecataeus' own claim that his sixteenth ancestor was a god.

Occasionally disbelief leads Herodotus into rationalisation of some myth or legend. But although he is a sceptic, he is not a rationalist. Reasoning plays little part in his treatment of his material. It is true that in the final books a tendency appears for which reasoning might well be responsible—the idea of relevance, of restriction to a single theme. But in Herodotus this limitation is a result of emotional concentration, not of rational plan. It is true that he talks of his 'exact investigations', that often he distinguishes between mere hearsay and things he himself has seen. But he neither states nor uses reasoned, systematic principles for

[1] IV, 25.   [2] VIII, 8.

sifting evidence. He has no scientific yardstick for measuring credibility. He accepts as 'the real facts' the Egyptians' ground for regarding the Phrygians as the oldest race—that when two children were isolated from birth from all human speech, the first word they uttered was the Phrygian name for bread. Yet absence of an eye-witness' assurance makes him doubt whether 'there is any sea on the further side of Europe', and in recounting the first Phoenician voyage round Africa he refuses to credit the very point which indicates the truth of the story—that 'they had the sun upon their right hand'. Nor does he only lack general scientific principles. He has no expert knowledge of any aspect of his subject. Although he writes of war, he is no practical soldier, nor even an armchair strategist. It is left to the modern historian to work out the real relation between the land and sea fights of Xerxes' campaign. Such an 'enquiring amateur', as he has been called, must for all his scepticism be easily misled by prejudice, easily persuaded to accept distorted and exaggerated reports. His version of the battle of Plataea has already been mentioned. A still more remarkable example is his estimate of the size of Xerxes' forces, which he adds up—in his eagerness to magnify Greek heroism—to the preposterous total of five-and-a-quarter million men. Yet the absence of a reasoned and scientific approach has its advantages. As a rule Herodotus transmits the information he has received, and leaves the reader to make his own selection from it and draw his own conclusions. 'This is the more likely of the two tales that are told', he will say. 'The other is an improbable story, but, as it is related, I think that I ought not to pass it by.'[1] His work is a mine of unspoilt ore from which the scientific historian can extract the true metal of fact and reject the dross. If Herodotus had omitted all that he disbelieved, we should not be aware that the Phoenicians sailed round Africa at all.

[1] III, 9.

Although Herodotus follows other prose authors in rejecting some of the legends and traditions of the past, in one important respect freedom from the influence of rationalism places him in line with the poets rather than with the further development of prose: he is a writer who thinks in concrete rather than abstract terms. His book is an ever-moving kaleidoscope of peoples and places, personalities and events, *bon mots* and anecdotes—nearly always the particular, rarely the general. In his eyes the mass of people have manners and customs, but no initiative. The motives of individuals are for him the driving force of history: Persian expansion was the result of the whims of despots; a series of legendary incidents caused the whole feud between East and West. If he seeks any general trend in the story of the human actors in his drama, his search takes him no further than the well-worn proverbs of Greek tradition, or the concept (familiar from his own experience at Halicarnassus) of a struggle for liberty against tyranny. If he looks for other forces behind the human scene, he sees the gods. Though he pushes direct contact between the deities and mankind as far back as possible, though in Book II he derives the names of the Greek divinities from Egypt, often questions divine legend, and states the belief that 'all men know equally little about the gods',[1] elsewhere his scepticism rarely touches religion. 'Many things prove to me', he declares, 'that the gods take part in the affairs of man.'[2] The inevitability of Fate, the envy and vengeance of Heaven against those who raise themselves above their proper mortal station— these are the notes sounded ever more loudly as his tale of 'barbarian' ambition and aggression moves towards its climax. His pages are thickly sprinkled with miracles and prodigies, from the heaven-sent rain that saves the life of Croesus to the priestess of Athena among the Pedasians, who whenever their neighbours are in danger grows a long beard. Sometimes it is reticence that

[1] II, 3.

[2] IX, 100.

shows his piety. Like his friend Sophocles, Herodotus gives a prominent role to oracles, and his narrative nearly always proves them right. He prefers Delphi's authority to Homer's, and faithfully repeats the Delphic priests' explanation of the fact that the invaders left the shrine and its treasures untouched—how by terrifying marvels and portents Apollo 'protected his own'.

'Homeric' is the adjective applied to Herodotus by one ancient critic. Despite the historian's own doubting attitude towards Homer, no epithet could be more apt. It was not for nothing that he was the nephew of an epic poet. Item after item among the characteristics of his book tallies with the Homeric list: scepticism, archaism, emphasis on leading individuals, acceptance of divine intervention in human affairs, digressions, speeches, conversations, even the cataloguing of forces. But the comparison goes deeper. What was Herodotus' purpose? Not only, like Achilles singing in his tent, to tell of 'the glories of men', to 'preserve from decay the remembrance of what men have done', but also to shed fresh splendour over the glorious past. Just as Homeric epic consolidated the Ionian saga of the Trojan War and its sequel, so Herodotus reproduced and raised to new heights the Athenian saga of the struggle against Persia. The same inspiration led to almost equally magnificent results. Other prose writers had also imitated epic, had retold its myths and legends in humbler form. Herodotus alone gave an account of historical events Homeric dimensions, raised prose narrative to a Homeric level. The architecture of his history towered above the work of Hecataeus and his other Ionian predecessors, just as the *Iliad* and the *Odyssey* surpassed the material out of which they grew.

Before Herodotus was thirty years old, perhaps about the time when he first went to Athens, a citizen was born there who was to carry the writing of history a further stage forward: Thucydides, described by Macaulay as 'the greatest historian that ever lived'. The two had much in common. For both Athens was the centre, the throbbing heart of the Greek world, yet both were connected with that world's outer fringes—Herodotus by birth with Halicarnassus, Thucydides by ancestry with Thrace, where he inherited a rich estate with gold mines. At Athens both were linked with the aristocracy—Herodotus by association, Thucydides by his kinship with conservative aristocrats like Cimon. Both suffered exile, and travelled as a result. In one of his rare autobiographical moments Thucydides tells how in 424 B.C., six years after surviving an attack of the plague from which Herodotus may have died, he was sent as commander to the Thracian area and failed to save its chief town, Amphipolis, from the Spartans. The sequel, he mentions later, was twenty years of banishment during which he journeyed to Sicily and elsewhere and associated with both sides in the struggle. Only when the war ended in 404 B.C. did he return to Athens, and probably there a few years later he died.

Put the lives of the two historians side by side, and there are many similarities. Compare their works, and it is the contrast that is striking. Herodotus' book was a glorification of the past, mingling historical events—despite all his Ionian scepticism—with myth and legend. Thucydides was the first writer of *contemporary* history. His 450 or more pages (divided into eight 'books' by later editors) narrate the events of the Peloponnesian War through which he lived, till the story breaks off, unfinished and unrevised, in 411 B.C. When in his opening paragraphs he deals with the past, his main purpose is to demonstrate not the greatness but the feebleness of antiquity—to claim that even the Persian invasion (remember Herodotus' five million!) was on a smaller scale than the conflict now dividing Greece. The main body of his work shows us the contemporary scene. In the foreground are the military operations of a war on which we in our turn can look back as a small-scale affair: the slow sieges with building of wall and counter-wall, the miniature naval raids and land invasions, the battles that end with the setting up of 'trophies' and collecting of the dead—details of a conflagration which spreads over the whole Hellenic world when minor flare-ups set light to the smouldering enmity between two great powers (each as large as Luxemburg!). In the background are the more general features of the age: class conflict, scarcely mentioned by Herodotus, but here constantly transcending the divisions between states; the presence of the 'barbarians' at the edge of the arena, gradually drawn into the struggle as it grows more desperate; the increasing number and importance of slaves —the attendants who serve free troops and desert them when defeat threatens, the 'more than twenty thousand' who flee from Attica when there is a chance of escape, the invitations to slaves to join oligarchs or democrats when they fight each other. Characteristically inconspicuous in the picture are women, whose highest merit is 'not to be talked about for good or for evil among men'. Thucydides does not paint in soft colours, or attempt to tone down the harsh realities of war. Although both sides are Greek, the brutalities they practise shock even the modern reader—the mass slaughter of defenceless men, the enslavement of women and children, the uprooting and shifting of populations. This is not the past, clothed in romantic splendour by the hand of time. It is the present in all its nakedness.

Difference of theme is one reason for the contrast between Herodotus and Thucydides. Another, no doubt, is difference in individual temperament. The personality behind Thucydides' book has an intensity and austerity which Herodotus lacks. But more important than either of these was the fact that the younger historian was strongly affected by influences which the older escaped. Whereas in Herodotus traces of the new intellectual trends associated with the Sophists are few and far between, in Thucydides they are everywhere. His conservative family background evidently did not prevent him from wholeheartedly embracing the New Thought when it came to Athens. It is the cold light of the new rationalism that shines through his work and dispels the mists of romance and sentiment. But the result is not pure 'realism' or 'objectivity'. Thucydides' rationalism imposes its own pattern on what he writes, fits his story into a mould of its own making, so that modern attempts to reconstruct the past may well find better material in the information transmitted, with little reshaping, by Herodotus.

Thucydides' reasoned approach to his task manifests itself in several ways, each of them a sharp contrast with Herodotus' outlook. First, the limits which he sets to his theme. In the last part of Herodotus' narrative the attention of writer and reader alike is focused almost entirely on Xerxes' invasion and its defeat. Thucydides throughout his book achieves a still greater concentration as part of a deliberate plan. His sole concern is with the events of the Peloponnesian War and the reasons (as he sees them) for those events. In selecting what to report he does not restrict himself to the remarkable: though there are some strange omissions, he records many incidents that are trivial and dull. But outside his self-imposed boundaries he rarely strays. There is no gossip in his book though comedy shows the streets were full of it, little or no reference to art or literature though he lived in a great period for both. If he digresses into geography or into the more distant past (or occasionally into the future) it is nearly always to give an explanation or proof relevant to the matter in hand—passages which nowadays would be either footnotes or appendices. His reticence has often been praised, but again his earlier rival can claim an advantage. Many readers find it easier to roam with Herodotus than to keep to Thucydides' straight and narrow path.

The framework into which he fits this limited material is his chronology, also rationally and carefully planned. Herodotus had shown little interest in such things, but Thucydides defines the date of the outbreak of war in four different ways. In describing its course he was confronted with a problem: the magisterial year differed in different states, and in Attica ran from July to July, from the middle of one campaigning season to the middle of the next. His solution was simple—a rational conclusion from the habits of warfare in his day. Because the ancients marched and sailed and fought chiefly in summer and little in winter, he divided his story into summers and winters, ending the year at the beginning of spring. To this scheme he rigidly adheres, even though it breaks up the narrative of episodes that last through more than one summer.

Equally deliberate is his handling of the material to be placed within this chronological framework. His opening paragraphs on earlier times give us an idea of what is to come, with their rationalisation (but not rejection) of legend and their treatment of Homer as a historical document of dubious value rather than as holy writ. He warns the reader that 'he must not be misled by the exaggerated fancies of the poets, or by the tales of chroniclers who seek to please the ear rather than to speak the truth'. Their accounts cannot be tested by him; and most of the facts in the lapse of ages have passed into the region of romance. At such a distance of time he must make up his mind to be satisfied with conclusions 'resting upon the clearest evidence which can be had'.[1] Religion is put on one side as firmly as 'romance'. Omens and prodigies are rarely mentioned, appeals to heaven shown to be ineffective, oracles slyly ridiculed. The gods and goddesses familiar in Homer and never far away in Herodotus do not haunt the pages of Thucydides. Chance, a great goddess in later centuries, plays a large part here, but is no divinity. The historian's positive principles are far from any

[1] I, 21. This and all other quotations from Thucydides are from the translation by Benjamin Jowett (Oxford University Press).

attitude that would give portents or prophecies an important role in the shaping of events:

> Of the events of the war I have not ventured to speak from any chance information, nor according to any notion of my own; I have described nothing but what I either saw myself, or learned from others of whom I made the most careful and particular enquiry. The task was a laborious one, because eye-witnesses of the same occurrences gave different accounts of them, as they remembered or were interested in the actions of one side or the other.[1]

How completely Thucydides fulfils this claim to precision we cannot judge, since on most points he is our sole authority. But no other ancient writer gives such an impression of painstaking care over details of geographical description, over names of commanders, over casualty figures or the size of armies or fleets. Nine times in the more unfinished sections of his work he quotes the actual texts of treaties: even if his ultimate intention was to incorporate them in his narrative in his own words, their presence is proof that he made documentary evidence his starting-point. Part of one of them we can check by an inscription on a marble slab discovered on the Acropolis, and despite the transmission of Thucydides' manuscript through many hands we find only minor differences between the two versions. In addition to general accuracy Thucydides (again unlike Herodotus) shows himself technically expert in some of the spheres most relevant to his theme. One is the mechanics and tactics of warfare (he had held military command, even if unsuccessfully). Another is medicine. His striking account of the plague follows the methods of contemporary medical writers—methods which affected his entire outlook. His book has been called a study in the pathology of imperialism and war.

Such deliberate and systematic treatment of evidence was only made possible by rationalism. But the rationalist trend and the

[1] I, 22.

influence of the Sophists have left their mark most clearly not in Thucydides' narrative but in the speeches—to the modern reader, the strangest and most puzzling feature of his work. Herodotus too, of course, had professed to report speeches and conversations. So had Homer. But here again Thucydides introduces system and deliberate planning. His handling of speeches is nearer to drama than to epic. He includes forty in all: statements by envoys (who usually conveyed verbal instructions, not a written document), political harangues before assemblies, commanders' exhortations to their troops, a funeral oration over the dead. Some are arranged in pairs to form debates presenting opposite trends of policy at Athens or Sparta: like the debates in Euripides, they recall the teaching methods of Protagoras and other Sophists. Once—before the Athenian attack on Melos—the historian follows another Sophistic practice and sets out a lengthy argument in dialogue form.

How far are these speeches historical? Thucydides makes it clear that they do not stand on the same level as his narrative:

As to the speeches which were made either before or during the war, it was hard for me, and for others who reported them to me, to recollect the exact words. I have therefore put into the mouth of each speaker the sentiments proper to the occasion, expressed as I thought he would be likely to express them, while at the same time I endeavoured, as nearly as I could, to give the general purport of what was actually said.[1]

There can be no doubt that the words of the speeches are Thucydides' own. Spartans, Corinthians, Sicilians, Athenians and others all speak the same Attic dialect; politicians, envoys, generals all use the same difficult style; most of them are incredibly brief. Often the thoughts attributed to them are historically impossible or inappropriate, and sometimes it seems dubious whether anything like Thucydides' version was delivered at all. He is nearer here to the dramatist whose aim is to reveal

[1] I, 22.

character than to the precise recorder of events. But the real function of the speeches and the dialogue at Melos can only be seen against a wider background—the general development of abstract and rational thinking at the expense of more primitive ways of thought. Thucydides, unlike Herodotus, was a pioneer in this development, but it did not equally permeate every aspect of his work. The new approach and the old stand side by side: they have not yet coalesced into a single attitude. Abstraction still clings to the branch of prose writing through which it first entered Greek literature—rhetoric, persuasive speech. While the narrative is concrete, factual, with few generalisations and little comment except a few paragraphs in distinctively rhetorical style, these passages and the speeches are overloaded with abstract argument. It is this above all that proves the speeches largely unhistorical. When Nicias writes home to the Athenian Assembly instead of only sending messengers to speak for him, his letter contains no such theorising. However much allowance is made for the influence of rationalism and the Sophists, it is incredible that among all types of speaker, at Sparta or Melos as well as Athens or Syracuse, abstract discussion of justice, honour, expediency and the like should play the leading part in debates that decided the issue between war and peace, life and death.

The dualism which characterises Thucydides' thinking leaves its stamp no less clearly on his style. Translations give his prose a false appearance of sameness and homogeneity, but would-be Greek scholars know all too well the difference in manner—and difficulty—between the narrative and the speeches or other rhetorical passages. A brief extract from the Funeral Oration put into the mouth of Pericles will show—even in translation—that for Thucydides prose-writing is a conscious art, nearer to the fragment of Gorgias' funeral speech than to the flowing ease of Herodotus:

They resigned to hope their unknown chance of happiness; but in the face of death they resolved to rely upon themselves alone. And when the moment came they were minded to resist and suffer, rather than to fly and save their lives; they ran away from the word of dishonour, but on the battlefield their feet stood fast, and in an instant, at the height of their fortune, they passed away from the scene, not of their fear, but of their glory.[1]

Fourth-century Greek rhetoric achieved clarity as well as effectiveness, but the style of Thucydides' speeches belongs to an earlier stage—the time before his exile from Athens, when rationalism was making its first impact on literature. Antithesis is the rather monotonous keynote of his sentences. His diction is often archaic or poetic. The obscurity of many passages has led some commentators to change the text, others to talk of the historian as a Thracian for whom Greek was a foreign tongue. But there is no need to rewrite Thucydides or to dub him a semi-'barbarian'. Individual temperament and historical circumstances moulded his prose along with the other aspects of his book: it must be read as the product of a tense and powerful mind struggling to master the new-fangled game of abstract thought.

The limited scope of Thucydides' history, its planned chronological structure, its treatment of evidence, its speeches and its style—all these are marks of the consciously rational attitude which divided him from earlier writers. The same spirit inspired his politics—for although the use of speeches in place of direct comment gives his work an 'objective' air, it is as definite in political outlook as anything in Greek literature. The historian's family background and early training must have imbued him with keen interest in the politics of the day, but he did not remain content with the conservatism inherited from his kinsfolk. Like many young members of the aristocracy in later decades, he turned against the traditions of his family—or brought them up

[1] II, 42.

to date. 'As in the arts', he makes the Corinthians say, 'so also in politics, the new must always prevail over the old.'[1] For him the new in politics was the leadership of Pericles, who opposed his family's point of view and defeated it. A devotee of Pericles he became. It was not as a democracy that he admired Periclean Athens (the city, he tells us, 'though still in name a democracy, was in fact ruled by her first citizen') but as a united community in which the populace accepted the wise guidance of their betters. Others of noble birth—Aeschylus, Sophocles, Herodotus—had also regarded this unity as the hope of Greece. The young Thucydides, seeking a rational ideal yet guided in his search by aristocratic upbringing and distaste for the 'mob', thought he saw in Pericles' regime the rational synthesis of opposites which he makes the statesman himself describe in his Funeral Speech[2]— the perfect compromise between labour and relaxation, thought and action, the democracy where 'the claim of excellence is also recognised', where freedom is tempered 'by respect for authority and for the laws', where 'we are lovers of the beautiful, yet with economy, and we cultivate the mind without loss of manliness'.

Thucydides' kinsmen had constantly accused Periclean Athens of imperialism. The historian does not deny the charge. He faces the realities of empire without cant or sentiment, often speaks of it in the same harsh terms—'tyranny', 'enslavement', and the rest—which his family must have used. Certainly Athens under Pericles is an imperialist state. Certainly she has used the situation after the Persian Wars—above all, her sea-power—to gain domination over much of Greece. Certainly she plays the game of power politics. Thucydides not only acknowledges all this: he finds rational grounds for welcoming it. Power, he claims, *is* the key to politics—and to the growth of human civilisation. When in his early chapters he looks back on former times, he sees them with Periclean eyes. Sea-power has always

[1] I, 71.   [2] II, 35-46.

been the way to greatness. In the distant past this truth was exemplified by Minos; in recent decades, by Themistocles (whom Thucydides admires as much as Herodotus belittles him). Now it is demonstrated by Pericles. Under his leadership Athens is no harsh mistress of her subjects—not because harshness is unjust or wrong, but because it is unwise. She shows the same rational spirit of moderation and compromise towards her Empire as in her internal affairs. She rules by right of her recognised superiority. She is 'the school of Hellas', and domination by such a city is good for the Greeks, just as domination by Pericles is good for Athens herself. Along this road lies the hope of Hellenic unity.

When war came, there was every reason to expect victory for go-ahead, imperial Athens over conservative, out-of-date Sparta. Pericles had a reasoned strategy which must make her victorious: she must not try to extend her Empire or risk unnecessary dangers; naval power—still the key to success—must be used to the full to harass the enemy. The city's great strength was shown by her resilience among the disasters towards the end of the struggle. Yet she was defeated. The reason for her failure is the central theme of Thucydides' book. His short answer to the problem is that the Athenians deserted the policy Pericles had laid down for them: 'they did all that he told them not to do', he writes. But he probes more deeply than this. Athens succumbed, he holds, to a disease which spread through most of Greece as a result of the war, seizing on men's minds just as the plague attacked their bodies: the disease (to give it a single modern name) of extremism, the very opposite of the wise spirit of moderation and compromise which Pericles had taught.

'In peace and prosperity', declares Thucydides, 'both states and individuals are actuated by higher motives, because they do not fall under the dominion of imperious necessities; but war which takes away the comfortable provision of daily life is a hard master, and tends to assimilate men's characters to their conditions.'[1] He is not writing of Athens, but of the bitter revolution at Corcyra, which he selects as the first outbreak of the sickness which later spread elsewhere. In highly abstract and rhetorical paragraphs of comment he describes how the violence of party-strife made men abandon reason. The correct use of words, a central point in the rationalism preached by the Sophists and Socrates, was thrown aside:

> The meaning of words had no longer the same relation to things, but was changed by them as they thought proper. Reckless daring was held to be loyal courage; prudent delay was the excuse of a coward; moderation was the disguise of unmanly weakness; to know everything was to do nothing.[1]

'Thus revolution gave birth to every form of wickedness in Hellas', says Thucydides. Though his immediate topic is Corcyra, he is thinking of Athens, where the removal of Pericles' controlling hand gave free rein to all the unreasoning passions, all the fickleness, of the 'mob'. Thucydides shows no 'objectivity' in his treatment of the low-born politicians who succeeded Pericles. Cleon is 'the most violent of the citizens', ignorant and cowardly yet over-confident, determined on war 'because he fancied that in quiet times his rogueries would be more transparent and his slanders less credible'. Hyperbolus is 'an Athenian of no character, who, not for any fear of his power and influence, but for his villainy, and because the city was ashamed of him, had been ostracised'. Goaded on by these men, Athens turned to extreme policies beside which Thucydides' own Periclean radicalism was conservative. Above all he stresses the two forms of degeneration most at variance with the tradition in which he was brought up—the replacement of unity by party strife, and of mild and wise treatment of the 'Allies' by stupid brutality. Most of his

[1] III, 82.

book tells the story of Athens' disastrous mistakes under evil leadership, until her desertion of Pericles' rational policy gives the victory to antiquated but comparatively stable Sparta: her failure (thanks to Cleon) to make peace after the lucky victory at Pylos; her decision (again thanks to Cleon) to punish the revolt of Mytilene by putting the men of the city to death and enslaving the women and children—a piece of political folly retracted only just in time; the performance of these brutalities eleven years later against the people of Melos although neutrality was their only crime—proof of the intensification of Athens' mental sickness as the war went on. Climax of the whole catalogue of errors is the Athenians' conduct of the Sicilian Expedition, on which Thucydides lavishes his powers of vivid description as generously as Herodotus in portraying the invasion of Xerxes. His final comment sounds the death-knell of Athenian hopes:

Of all the Hellenic actions which took place in this war, or indeed of all Hellenic actions which are on record, this was the greatest—the most glorious to the victors, the most ruinous to the vanquished; for they were utterly and at all points defeated, and their sufferings were prodigious. Fleet and army perished from the face of the earth; nothing was saved, and of the many who went forth few returned home.[1]

After the Sicilian disaster, political cleavage at Athens itself dominates the scene. As Thucydides puts it, the Athenians 'continued to resist, and were at last overthrown, not by their enemies, but by themselves and their own internal dissensions'. The historian dislikes both extremes in the struggle, although he goes out of his way to praise the oligarchic leader, Antiphon. He finds an echo of Periclean unity-through-compromise in the regime of the 'Five Thousand' which for eight months provided a middle course between democracy and oligarchy:

[1] VII, 87.

This government during its early days was the best which the Athenians ever enjoyed within my memory. Oligarchy and Democracy were duly attempered. And thus after the miserable state into which she had fallen, the city was again able to raise her head.[1]

The city's head was not high for long. If Thucydides had finished his task, he would doubtless have put still more emphasis on the class cleavage at Athens as the prelude to her final defeat. But his account breaks off soon after the conflict between 'the many' and 'the few' has come into the open. Why is the book unfinished? When was it written? Does it represent Thucydides' view as it developed during the war, or his final judgment?

The outlines of the manner in which the history took shape seem clear enough. From the beginning of the war Thucydides kept a kind of diary of events as they occurred, and some passages contain little more than these brief first notes. But most of his narrative consists of episodes which he selected for writing up in detail, partly because full reports from eye-witnesses became available, partly because the items chosen for such elaboration had some special interest, military or even medical, some special political importance, some special relevance to Thucydides' main theme. Theoretical discussion of these episodes he puts into the form of speeches or debates. That this was his general method is confirmed by the more unfinished sections of his book, where speeches are lacking and much of the narrative is close to note form. Turn to the question when the writing of episodes and speeches was done, and we face puzzling difficulties. The story falls into two parts, divided by the Peace of 421 B.C., and the second is introduced by a preface of its own: yet passages in the first part refer to the later phases and the end of the war. Was the history produced in two stages, or even three? There is one overriding reason for believing that the whole book reached its present form only in the last years of the conflict, or even after

[1] VIII, 97.

Thucydides' return to Athens in 404 B.C. Only when Athens' defeat was an imminent prospect or an accomplished fact could he have reached the view of the struggle that he maintains consistently throughout. The idealisation of the Periclean regime, the emphasis on Athens' decline from that ideal, the prominence of party strife in nearly every episode, all belong to the perspective of one who looks back on the story when Athens is torn by class warfare and her failure almost or quite complete.

'My history', says Thucydides, 'is an everlasting possession, not a prize composition which is heard and forgotten.'[1] His book is not like a play, composed for performance before an audience with victory in a competition as its main aim: it is a written record, of permanent value to readers. In claiming immortality for his work he was right. It still stands as an enduring monument to the rationalism of his age. Yet it demonstrates the shallowness of that rationalism as well as its brilliance and power —a shallowness characteristic of all ancient historians. Thucydides looks for the motives behind events, seeks an explanation of the course of history in the mental processes of politicians and communities. He shows little awareness of the need to probe more deeply. Inspired by a rationalist outlook which had little contact with the productive basis of Greek society, he did not sufficiently realise that human motives are themselves conditioned by the circumstances in which they arise. The limited knowledge available in his day did not enable him to regard the happenings of his little Hellenic world as a part of wider trends. The Periclean Athens of his youth, the Athens idealised in the Funeral Speech, was for him the highest achievement of human reason. When reason ceased to be the city's guide, he did not see the deeper social and economic causes at work behind her fall. Rationalism failed him, as it failed Euripides, and he turned for an explanation to other forces which, though brought down to a psychological

[1] I, 22.

level, had a mythological ancestry, and were nearer to the poets whose lines he had learned as a boy, nearer to Herodotus, than to science: forces like the Madness of Cleon, the intoxicating Hope that rouses the blind Insolence of the 'mob'. It has been disputed whether Thucydides' outlook was 'rationalist' or 'mythological'. It was both. After Pericles' death an attitude derived from mythology creeps into his narrative, not because of the influence of drama, but because the new rationalism has been found wanting and he falls back on older traditional ways of thought. A logical sequel to Thucydides' history is the ideal state of the most brilliant writer of the next generation, Plato—an imaginary Utopia where the rule of reason is imposed by force.

The last of our three historians is also the least—Xenophon, who was born at Athens about the beginning of the Peloponnesian War and lived till the middle of the fourth century B.C. Xenophon has none of Herodotus' breadth of vision or epic grandeur. Limitation to a particular subject has replaced the wide sweep of earlier *historië:* in each of his numerous works he keeps to the matter in hand, whether it be history proper (the *Hellenica*) or an account of his own adventures (the *Anabasis*), idealised biography (the *Education of Cyrus* and *Agesilaus*) or memoirs of Socrates (the *Memorabilia* and *Apology*), imaginary dialogues (the *Household Management, Symposium,* and *Hieron*) or treatises on military leadership or sport (the *Cavalry Commander, On Horsemanship,* and *Hunter*) or political essays (the *Spartan Constitution* and—if it is really by Xenophon—the *Ways and Means*). In his concentration on a particular topic and avoidance of digressions he recalls Thucydides, but there the resemblance stops. Although in the *Hellenica* he continues Thucydides' narrative down to 362 B.C., and in the first part (down to the end of the Peloponnesian War) he imitates his predecessor's method of chronology and use of speeches, yet he has neither Thucydides' insight nor his grasp of scientific principles. Thucydides stands alone, with no direct intellectual heir.

While Herodotus and Thucydides impress us by their greatness, their outstanding brilliance, much of Xenophon's attraction lies in the fact that he is ordinary. He was a man of talents, but no genius—a resourceful soldier, a sportsman, a farmer. His mind was filled with conventional piety. As a writer he is easy to criticise for his superficiality, his tediousness, his commonplace moralising, his obvious prejudices, his lack of historical sense. But his works reveal him to us as the ordinary middle-class Greek, all the more typical because of his mediocrity. It is significant that he uses prose as a medium taken for granted, the normal vehicle for what he wants to say. He rarely makes any conscious attempt at good style, but when he does his model is rhetoric. It was the simplicity of his prose, much admired during the Roman revival of 'Atticism', that led to the preservation of his works.

Like Herodotus and Thucydides, Xenophon spent much of his life in exile from his own state. In 401 B.C., at the age of about thirty, he was one of the thousand or more Greeks who were induced under false pretences to join the expedition which the Persian prince Cyrus organised to attack Babylon and drive his brother from the Persian throne. When the expedition failed and the Greek generals were murdered, it was Xenophon (according to his own account) who came to the fore and led the remains of the army northwards to the Black Sea. Other military adventures followed, and while still in the East he heard that a decree of banishment had been passed against him at Athens. He continued his soldiering under the Spartans, especially king Agesilaus, and was rewarded by the Spartan government with an estate in the Peloponnese. Here he must have written most of his works, although he later migrated to Corinth, and probably visited

Athens after his exile had been rescinded in 369 B.C. It is not surprising that he is generally biased in favour of Sparta, but more striking than his pro-Spartan feeling is his lack of any real patriotism, any real enthusiasm for any state. Xenophon turns, as many of his contemporaries were turning, from the city to the individual, from the search for good laws to the search for a leader. Hero-worship is his strongest emotion, and he must be seen as a biographer rather than a historian—the contemporary of Plato and his biographical dialogues, the predecessor of Plutarch rather than the successor of Herodotus and Thucydides. His memoirs of Socrates, his encomium of Agesilaus, his long account of Cyrus the Elder, founder of the Persian Empire, all portray Great Men for the reader to admire and imitate. The *Hellenica* comes to life only when it is most biographical: here again Agesilaus is the central figure. It is natural that such a writer should be most successful in *autobiography*—the narrative of his own adventures, his own problems of leadership, which he gives in the *Anabasis*, or *March of Cyrus up to Babylon*. In describing the journey and—at greater length—the retreat of the Ten Thousand he is handling his own experiences, not evidence that must be sifted and judged. He is dealing with individual people, not with institutions or abstractions. The intellectual powers of a Thucydides are not needed here. And as one reads the fascinating story it is not only the theme of a march into Persia that points forward to Alexander the Great. Individuals had been prominent in the work of Herodotus or Thucydides, but always subordinate to the history of communities. With Xenophon the individual completely dominates the scene. In his pages the Soldier-Leader, the Great Man, is already beginning to cast his shadow over the ancient world.

CHAPTER IX

THE PLATONIC DIALOGUE

WE have seen that after the fifth century oratory was the main-stream of Greek prose—a stream which not only flowed in abundance from its sources in the assembly and the law-courts, but spread into regions like history and biography, comparatively free from the influence of rhetoric in modern times. Yet today pride of place among the prose products of the fourth and later centuries does not fall to the orators: it goes to the dialogue. For every modern student of the speeches of Demosthenes there are a hundred who have read Plato's *Republic*. The motives for the preference, no doubt, are various. One reader studies Plato for his thought, still important in a world for which the topical arguments of the ancient politician or advocate have no signi-ficance. Another is attracted by the personality of Socrates, central figure in most of the dialogues. Another appreciates Plato as a great literary artist. But one reason why his works remain vivid and alive is that they recreate for us the living environment from which they arose. In modern literature the dialogue is a dead form, though radio discussions are doing something towards reviving it. Modern attempts to imitate it seem artificial, lifeless, stilted—characteristics which have infected some translations of Plato himself. But Plato's works were living products of the society of their day. Like the drama, like oratory, they had their roots in an aspect of the social life of the democratic city-state—a background which must be studied before either their form or their content can be fully understood.

Key feature of this background is the leisure which (thanks to the growing slave population) was enjoyed by at any rate a large number of the citizens of ancient Athens: leisure not whiled away by mechanical devices for entertainment such as the machine age has given us, nor devoted to sport organised on anything like the modern scale, nor passed in the bosom of the family, but spent in places where men of the well-to-do class came together: the gymnasium or the drinking-party, the market-place or one of the houses of the rich. The groups which met amid such surroundings were exclusively male, except perhaps for educated courtesans of the Aspasia type. The emotional relationships that sprang up in these circles were homosexual, and many an hour was passed in gossip about the feelings of X towards his young friend Y, as well as about the local happenings and political developments of the time. But amid the intellectual atmosphere of the close of the fifth century other less personal and more general themes were sure to be discussed, with a strong bias towards theory and away from practical life.

Out of this environment arose a habit of conversation which could be a fruitful source of both literature and philosophy, but it had little to contribute to either as long as it remained casual and unformed. Discussion was made deliberate and given shape by the Sophists, who found the majority of their pupils among those who had most leisure for these pastimes. About the middle of the century the philosopher Zeno had followed the method of taking a hypothesis held by other thinkers, and disproving it by drawing from it contradictory conclusions. The Sophists developed the art of disputation, of question and answer, along the same destructive lines, exploiting every possibility of verbal trickery to embellish their display of mental gymnastics. Yet this new and fascinating game (as many of their pupils must have seen it) was not the Sophists' main method. Their primary concern was rhetoric, not discussion: the technique of persuasion, not the technique of argument. In the midst of conversation they were likely to plunge into a lengthy speech. The greatest exponent of the art of question and answer was one who sharply contrasted it with rhetoric—Socrates, who more than any other Athenian embodied in his own habits and personality this aspect of the life of the democratic city-state.

Socrates, as we shall see, is a shadowy figure, and on many points about him there can be no certainty. But there is little doubt that among all the personalities of democratic Athens he went furthest in applying the searchlight of the new rational ways of thought to the assumptions and prejudices of his fellow-citizens. The son of a sculptor and probably himself at first a craftsman, he later joined the leisured minority, and his squat figure and satyr-like countenance became a familiar sight in the streets and market-place and gymnasia of the town. By some he was revered, especially the younger generation of the aristocracy; by many others he was regarded with a suspicion and hostility, partly political, which culminated in his trial and execution in 399 B.C. Talking—and making others talk—was his life-work. Many people classed him with the Sophists, and as a product of the same mental atmosphere he did to some extent bear the same stamp. It seems likely that his talk also was usually destructive. His practice was to take a hypothesis put forward by his companion—a suggested definition, for example, of courage or piety or friendship—and expose its inadequacy. Perhaps a better hypothesis would be proposed, but it would receive the same treatment, and the net result was more likely to be demonstration of the companion's ignorance than any positive conclusion. How close all this was to the Sophists' method of discussion, we cannot tell. But to the rhetoric that dominated their outlook Socrates' approach was entirely opposed, and the antithesis was all-important for the future of Greek literature and thought. His object was a search for truth, rather than either persuasion or display. Where rhetoric tried to gloss over ignorance, his aim was to expose it. Socrates was informal where the Sophists were elaborate. His colloquial simplicity was the opposite of their rhetorical striving after persuasive effect. History has shown which attitude could bring forth the better fruit.

The habit of discussion which the Sophists and Socrates thus developed has left its mark in many places on the literature of the time. Again and again in the plays of Euripides or Aristophanes one catches an echo of such theoretical disputations. We have seen that when Thucydides describes the bringing of an Athenian ultimatum to the island of Melos, he deserts his practice of speech-writing and turns to the dialogue form to expose this extreme example of imperialism. Sooner or later, amid the background I have described, the dialogue was likely to become established as an independent literary type, separate from the music and song and dance and religious atmosphere of the Theatre of Dionysus, and no longer subsidiary to history or any other form. Epicharmus had pointed the way in Sicily when he introduced philosophical argument into his verse mimes. Still nearer to the required realism, though unconnected with philosophy, were prose mimes like those of Sophron, also written at Syracuse. But it was the influence of Socrates, who himself wrote nothing, that brought the dialogue fully into being as a branch of literature. After Socrates' death, and especially after an attack on him published by the Sophist Polycrates sometime after 392 B.C., not only Plato and Xenophon but many others among his admirers rallied to his defence. Polycrates' onslaught took the form of a version of the speech for the prosecution at the trial. Plato and Xenophon produced versions of Socrates' own address to the judges, but the favourite way of paying a tribute to his memory was a prose portrait of the Master talking as was his custom when alive. We are informed—probably not always correctly—of numerous such 'Socratic conversations' composed by as many as twelve authors. There may have been many more. As Grote put it, they 'formed a recognised class of literature, noticed by the rhetorical critics as distinguished for plain, collo-quial, unstudied, dramatic execution, suiting the parts to the various speakers'.[1] All that has survived from this mass of Socratic literature is the complete output of Plato, which fills several volumes, a few works wrongly attributed to Plato but perhaps written in the fourth century, the *Memoirs of Socrates*, *Household Management*, and *Symposium* of Xenophon (also pro-bably all that he wrote of this type), considerable fragments from Aeschines, a few from Antisthenes. If all the dialogues produced at this time still existed, doubtless the extant specimens and the problems that arise from them would appear in a very different light.

One of those problems has caused enough controversy to become known as *the* 'Socratic problem'. How realistic are the pictures of Socrates in the surviving literature? How far can they be relied on as historically correct? Without a solution to this puzzle we know little or nothing of one of the most important figures in human history. Primarily of course it is a question for the student of philosophy, but literary considerations can throw more light on the answer than is often supposed.

Aristotle in his *Poetics* sees the 'Socratic conversation' as a form of prose drama, a branch of the same species as the 'mime'; and all drama, whether in prose or verse, he classes with 'poetry' as concerned with 'a kind of thing that might be', as opposed to 'history', which 'describes the thing that has been'.[2] The content of the 'Socratic conversation', in short, is not fact but fiction, though realistic fiction. Modern sentiment demands an attempt at historical accuracy in representing the talk of anyone recently

[1] *Plato and the other Companions of Socrates*, vol. III, p. 469.
[2] *Poetics* 1447b and 1451b.

alive—every Boswell must correctly report his Johnson—and some modern commentators insist that the same principle must have applied to the ancient dialogue. But the evidence indicates no such feeling among the Greeks. Not only Aristophanes gives free rein to his prejudices and his imagination in portraying the personalities of his time, alive or dead. Thucydides, most painstakingly accurate of ancient historians in relating facts, feels himself at liberty to make his characters utter speeches of his own composition, embodying his own ideas. Ancient writers did not consider such methods improper, but rather hoped to gain by them additional prestige for what they had to say. Of the extant Socratic dialogues themselves some are manifestly unhistorical: Plato's *Menexenus*, for example, which puts into Socrates' mouth an account of events after his own death; or Xenophon's *Household Management*, a dialogue including Socrates but obviously just as fictional as the same author's *Hiero*, an imaginary conversation early in the fifth century B.C. between the 'tyrant' of Syracuse and the poet Simonides. Plato's picture of Socrates' manner and interests varies in different works. The natural inference is that Aristotle was right: all dialogues belonged to the sphere of fiction, and were more likely to take their colour from the outlook and personality of the author than from the real Socrates himself. There was a growing tendency among fourth-century authors to express their own points of view by embodying them in figures from the past. Thucydides had come near to this in his portrait of Pericles. Xenophon put forward his ideas on education in a book on Cyrus, the first king of Persia. Aspasia became the ideal emancipated woman. The Socratic dialogue belonged to the same trend.

The conclusion is a strange paradox. We possess more contemporary evidence about Socrates than about any other of the ancient Greeks—the pictures by Aristophanes, Plato, and Xenophon, all of whom knew him; yet none of these can be relied on by the historian. The points on which the different portraits agree—Socrates' appearance, the main events of his life, his love of discussion, his insistence on the importance of the individual and the sovereignty of reason—are probably true to the original. To these must be added the statements of Aristotle, who, writing 'history' and not 'poetry', and obviously distinguishing the historical Socrates from the figure presented in Plato's dialogues, describes him as a thinker concerned only with the moral sphere, in which he used inductive reasoning and sought definitions of general terms. For the rest, the real Socrates must remain an ill-defined figure, taking various shapes from the ideas of those who write about him, just as he did in the decades after his death. The Socratic myth will change with the times. The Socratic problem will never be solved.

Slavery, leisure, the mental atmosphere of Athens, the habits of the Sophists and Socrates, the mime, the writing of 'Socratic conversations'—all this forms the literary background to Plato. Like the *Iliad* and the *Odyssey*, his dialogues did not spring out of nothingness; but—again like the Homeric masterpieces—they were outstanding in their kind and more than any others deserved to survive. Concentration on Plato as a thinker has often obscured his greatness as an artist. But an artist he was—and a conscious one. In his earlier years he was a poet, perhaps a writer of dithyrambs and tragedies. Certainly the epigrams of his which now survive are among the best we possess. He applied the same artistry to prose as he displayed so brilliantly in verse. 'You will allow', he makes Socrates say in the *Phaedrus*, 'that every discourse ought to be a living creature, having a body of its own and a head and feet; there should be a middle, beginning, and end, adapted to one another and to the whole.'[1] The

[1] 264c. Tr. Jowett (Oxford University Press).

reference here is primarily to speeches, but it could well be extended to Plato's own works. The apparently casual style of the dialogues must not lead to the conclusion that they were composed without attention to literary form.

Plato learnt much, a biographer tells us, from Epicharmus. Also he admired and imitated Sophron. He was the first to bring Sophron's mimes to Athens, and even slept with them under his pillow. The story is likely enough, but clearly Plato was no mere imitator. He experimented with the art which the writers of prose mime had begun. Sometimes he uses indirect narration instead of direct dialogue, and so gives a far more colourful picture of the scene, the occasion, the personalities involved. Or he introduces other elements besides question and answer—speeches, for example, often parodying the style of the speaker as it was known to those who had heard him in the flesh. Each dialogue is a dramatic sketch of a neatness and subtlety probably far superior to Sophron, vividly bringing before us—as Plato saw them—all the characters among whom Socrates moved: Sophists and politicians, rich merchants and young aristocrats, rhetoricians and poets. In the fifth century, drama had come from the Theatre of Dionysus, but the finest dramatic products of the fourth century are the dialogues of Plato. Yet the greatest quality of his works is not their dramatic skill, but something less obvious at first reading—a unity of form and content, expression and thought, which results from the common origin of both in the personality of Socrates.

This unity can be seen from either point of view. First, the dialogues take their shape not (as a first glance may suggest) from the casual ramblings of ordinary conversation, nor from a desire to gain dramatic effect, but from Socratic practice and Plato's development of it. Often the discussion is tiresome to the modern reader because, as Professor Richards says, 'Plato's style deployed endless exquisite devices for meeting attitudes and expectations in his readers which sprang from their milieu. These attitudes and expectations never arise in us; we have our own.'[1] The conversation deals at length with points which now seem obvious, or dwells on verbal difficulties peculiar to the Greek language, or treats argument as a game worth playing for its own sake. Nevertheless, at the heart of it all is the method of Socrates, giving shape and purpose to the whole.

In this way the content moulds the form. But the form also moulds the content. The dialogues are not merely popular versions of thought which could be equally well expressed in a systematic work like a modern text-book of philosophy. For Plato, deliberation *is* discussion. Even the individual mind thinks by asking itself questions and answering them. 'Plato's thought in its farthest reach', writes Professor Dorothy Tarrant, 'still carries the quality and the limitations of a Socratic discourse, as being the outcome of a human agreement.'[2] Modern attempts to give a systematic account of Plato's philosophy inevitably suffer from distortion and simplification. The aim of the Platonic dialogue at its best is not to expound a system of beliefs, but the aim of Socrates: to make others think for themselves.

Because of this unity of form and content in his writings the twin aspects of Plato's development—as a literary artist and as a thinker—are inseparably connected. It is only within the last century that study of his development has become possible, for until then little or nothing was known of the chronological order of his works. But the use of tests of style and language has at any rate separated them into groups, though within each group the sequence is still uncertain. The following are those generally recognised as Plato's own handiwork, in an order which cannot be very far from the sequence in which they were produced:

[1] *The Republic of Plato*, p. 9.
[2] *Classical Quarterly*, vol. XLII (1948), p. 28.

Hippias Minor	*Cratylus*
Laches	*Symposium*
Charmides	*Phaedo*
Ion	*Republic*
Lysis	*Phaedrus*
Euthyphro	*Parmenides*
Apology	*Theaetetus*
Crito	*Sophist*
Protagoras	*Statesman*
Gorgias	*Philebus*
Meno	*Timaeus*
Menexenus	*Critias*
Euthydemus	*Laws*

How was the composition of these works related to the events of Plato's life? We can now reconstruct his biography in some detail, largely because certain Letters, formerly rejected as spurious, are now generally regarded as authentic products of his old age. Unfortunately few of the dialogues can be dated, so that allotting them to particular stages of their author's career is largely guesswork. But it is worth while to attempt a reconstruction of the broad outlines of the story.

Born in the early years of the Peloponnesian War—probably in 428 B.C.—Plato came from one of the wealthiest and most aristocratic families of Athens. His father claimed descent from the legendary last king of the city; his mother could look back with more confidence to Solon as her ancestor. Most of his boyhood was spent in the home of his step-father, a friend of Pericles. It was typical of the trends of the time that during the final disastrous years of the war, when the young Plato was growing to manhood and first showing his intellectual powers, some members of his family turned from its democratic traditions to oligarchy. Plato's uncles, Critias and Charmides, became leaders of the revolution which culminated in the rule of the

'Thirty Tyrants', and invited their brilliant nephew to join them. Many years later, in the document now known as his *Seventh Letter*, Plato tells of his early expectation of a political career, of the invitation and his reaction to it—his hope that 'the Thirty' 'would so manage the State as to bring men out of a bad way of life into a good one', his disappointment at their violence and wrongdoing which made him 'disapprove of their proceedings, and withdraw from any connection with the abuses of the time'. When the oligarchs were overthrown and democracy returned, 'once more', he writes, 'though with more hesitation, I began to be moved by the desire to take part in public and political affairs'. But the sovereign people condemned and executed Socrates, who in these critical years had become the strongest influence on Plato's mind. For the time being he turned his back on politics and concentrated on philosophy—the beginning of that divorce between men of thought and men of action which was to persist and grow in the centuries to come. Says the *Seventh Letter*:

The result was that, though at first I had been full of a strong impulse towards political life, as I looked at the course of affairs and saw them being swept in all directions by contending currents, my head finally began to swim; and, though I did not stop looking to see if there was any likelihood of improvement in these symptoms and in the general course of public life, I postponed action till a suitable opportunity should arise. Finally it became clear to me with regard to all existing communities, that they were one and all misgoverned. For their laws have got into a state that is almost incurable, except by some extraordinary reform with good luck to support it. And I was forced to say, when praising true philosophy, that it is by this that men are enabled to see what justice in public and private life really is. Therefore, I said, there will be no cessation of evils for the sons of men, till either those who are pursuing a right and true philosophy receive sovereign power in the States, or those in power in the States by some dispensation of providence become true philosophers.[1]

[1] 325 d-326b. Tr. Harward (Cambridge University Press).

Development of the thought expressed in the last sentence was to bring Plato back to politics in action as well as in his writings, but his first tendency in this mood of post-war disillusionment was to dwell on the memory of Socrates. To these years many of his shorter works must belong. Some deal directly with the Master's trial and death—the *Apology*, for example, which presents Socrates in court, and *Crito*, which shows him in prison explaining to a young friend his reasons for refusing to escape. Others—the *Charmides*, for instance, or *Euthyphro* or *Laches* or *Lysis*—are dramatic sketches of him amid various company, following his usual methods of conversation and pursuing his search for definitions as he talks. In thought, these early works are concerned with the mental confusions of the plain man, or at any rate of the ordinary well-educated Athenian—problems easily intelligible to the modern reader, though often far removed from his own. In form, most of them take their main framework from Socrates' own practice, considering and rejecting one hypothesis after another and reaching no positive result. But they are not stereotyped. They are literary experiments; and how far Plato advanced in literary skill during this period can be seen by comparing one of the brief and simple sketches with a dramatic masterpiece like the *Protagoras*, in which he sets Socrates among those experts in disputation, the Sophists. Here description is used (Socrates tells the story himself) to give a brilliant picture of the background out of which the Socratic dialogue arose; and as the narrative proceeds not only question and answer fill the pages, but other devices from the Sophists' intellectual stock-in-trade: the telling of a 'myth' to point a moral, with all the eloquence of the new rhetoric; the interpretation—often fantastic—of a passage of poetry. In subtlety of portraiture and craftsmanship as a dramatist Plato never surpassed his achievement in the *Protagoras*. But in depth of thinking and the use of the dialogue form as a vehicle for thought he had much further to go.

About 388 B.C., when he was perhaps forty years old, Plato made a journey to Southern Italy and Sicily. The visit had a twofold effect on his mind. On the one hand a stay at the luxurious court of the great 'tyrant' Dionysius I of Syracuse, described in the *Seventh Letter*, confirmed his disgust with the political and social life of his day. On the other hand, it must have been at this time that he came to know a ruler of a very different stamp: the philosophic statesman or statesmanlike philosopher Archytas of Tarentum, who was then the leading exponent of Pythagoreanism. The doctrines of the Pythagoreans and the Orphic beliefs from which they arose—ideas well suited to one who was turning his back on practical life—were no doubt known to Plato before this Western journey: there are traces of their influence in dialogues probably published earlier than this. But now the growing effect of such ideas on his outlook led him on to a fresh stage in his development as a thinker—the building of a positive philosophy, a metaphysic, on the foundations he had learned from Socrates. With the Socratic emphasis on the importance of the individual soul he combined the Orphic doctrine that the soul is a fallen spirit, temporarily imprisoned in the mortal body, destined ultimately to return to the higher state from which it has come. Socrates had sought to define moral qualities—justice, piety, temperance, and the rest: Plato now concerned himself with the nature and status of these qualities, and saw them as patterns comparable to the numbers in which the Pythagoreans found the key to the universe— 'Ideas' or 'Forms' which (in the words of a recent writer) 'were not class-concepts, but rather Ideals from which human aspiration could derive its force and take its direction'.[1] Here was true reality, compared with which the world of sensation and action

---

[1] Stenzel, *Plato's Method of Dialectic*, p. xxxvi.

was a fleeting shadow. The aim of philosophy, of all true education, must be to get to know this realm of the mind — or rather, to recollect the knowledge which the soul possessed before its embodiment in the flesh. And the driving force in the search for truth must be love, devoted no longer to earthly bodies but to the ideal beauty which only the mind can see.

The growth of this amalgam of rationalism and mysticism as the central feature of Plato's thought had a decisive influence on his life. It led him, after his return from the West, to the foundation of the Academy, where he spent most of his remaining years guiding the thoughts of pupils from all over Greece. It had an equally profound effect on his writings—not only on their content, but also on their form.

Plato's early works have the same negative, destructive quality that seems likely to have been characteristic of the historical Socrates. But the dialogues which (as far as we can judge) follow the visit to Italy and Sicily have a positive purpose—the guiding of the reader towards the vision of reality and truth. As Socrates says in the *Republic*, 'the entire soul must be turned away from this changing world, until its eye can bear to contemplate reality and that supreme splendour which we have called the Good' [1] The question and answer form now often becomes a mere routine, sometimes even an inconvenience. The stock replies which interrupt Socrates' discourse—'Certainly', 'Of course', 'How so?' and a dozen others—are tiresome rather than helpful. Yet except in this superficial sense Plato is not abandoning the Socratic method. The process of thought through which these dialogues take us is a development from Socrates' practice of moving from one hypothesis to another. They do not start from first principles in modern textbook style. Awareness of first principles—the 'ideas'—must be reached by long mental effort, in

[1] 518 c. Tr. Cornford (Oxford University Press).

which discussion plays an essential part. Here is Plato's description of the process in the *Seventh Letter*:

After much effort, as names, definitions, sights, and other data of sense are brought into contact and friction one with another, in the course of scrutiny and kindly testing by men who proceed by question and answer without ill will, with a sudden flash there shines forth understanding about every problem, and an intelligence whose efforts reach the furthest limits of human powers.[1]

As in the earlier dialogues, the starting point of the conversation is still some occasion and problem from the experience of ordinary life. But discussion of this particular issue is now only a means of ascent into the realm of the absolute, where the mind can climb beyond hypotheses 'to something that is not hypothetical, the first principle of all'. Only after this contact with the supreme reality can we take the downward path towards something which Plato's early works never attempted: a final answer to the problem originally posed. The journey is not short or simple. An apparent or approximate solution at an early stage may be rejected with the comment that the real truth can only be learned by following 'a longer way round'. The brief dramatic sketch like the *Lysis* or the *Euthyphro* is now replaced by works of considerable length.

The Socratic method of reasoning, thus developed and formalised, combined with Plato's dramatic skill to provide the main structure of these works of his middle years. But his development had carried him to a point where rational argument was no longer enough, either as guide or as means of expression. Some aspects of the ascent to the world of reality and truth could be shown to the reader only by appealing not to his reason, but to his emotions and imagination. This need affects the dialogues as a whole, giving their drama new power and new depth of purpose. But it also has a particular result—far greater use of a device

[1] 344b. Tr. Harward (Cambridge University Press).

which occurs only twice in works likely to have been written before the visit to the West. When the conversation has reached a stage at which argument must give way to imagination, Plato deserts the question and answer method and makes Socrates or another character tell a story, a *mythos;* a story, for example, of the nature of the soul's existence after death, or of its journey from this world to the realm of pure thought, or of the origins of the universe.

Here also Plato is in a sense following the Sophists, who used fables or myths as allegories to illustrate their teaching. He puts such a story into the mouth of Protagoras—the tale of Prometheus and Epimetheus, possibly quoted from one of the Sophist's own treatises. But Plato's myths are not allegorical. They constitute a return to old ways of thought and expression—the ways of the poets and early dramatists, before the spread of that rational approach to experience of which Socrates was the greatest exponent. Plato did not cease to be a poet when he stopped writing verse. Just as his philosophy now combined rationalism and mysticism, so in his writings he now juxtaposed reasoned argument and the art of the story-teller, the logic of prose and the inspiration of poetry, the new way and the old. Despite his insistence on the conflict between philosophy and the poets—the conflict which we have seen as a vital factor in the growth of Greek literature—he brought both elements together in his greatest works. The man who wanted to ban poets from his ideal state nevertheless wrote the great myth in the *Phaedrus,* one of the most splendid flights of the poetical imagination in all Greek literature. And so here again the development of the content of his thought and a change in the form of the dialogues went hand in hand.

In this way Plato's brilliance as a literary artist reached its highest pitch. Consider briefly two of the outstanding achievements of this phase—the *Phaedo* and the *Symposium*—before turning to its greatest masterpiece, the *Republic*. These two works are very different, yet strangely similar. They present a sharp contrast in occasions, in atmospheres, in subject; yet from opposite angles both are concerned with the same theme, the same line of thought. They appear unlike in form, yet in its own way each follows the same pattern.

The *Phaedo* is a narrative of the scene in the prison at Athens on the day which ended with Socrates' death. Plato makes Socrates employ these last hours just as he used the casual meetings of the gymnasium or the market-place—as an opportunity for conversation with his friends. Here as on more trivial occasions, the starting point of the discussion is a question which arises naturally out of the situation. 'As I am going to another place', says Socrates, 'it is very meet for me to be thinking and talking of the nature of the pilgrimage which I am about to make.'[1] The problem of the proper behaviour of the philosopher in the face of death leads to consideration of his reasons for confidence in the survival of the soul. Socrates, calmer than any of his companions, has still the charm and ironic wit of the earlier dialogues, yet he has changed. Here it is the others, not Socrates, who are doubtful (though the twentieth-century reader may feel their doubts are not carried far enough). Socrates has a positive purpose. Where he returns to his old manner to refute other 'hypotheses' about the soul and its future, it is only as a means to asserting his own confidence in immortality. The various arguments by which he conveys his conviction to his hearers are usually regarded as so many 'proofs' of immortality, some of which are faulty even if we accept his assumptions—and most modern readers will not. But 'proving' immortality is not Plato's aim. His object is to suggest to the reader that separation of soul from body is only one aspect of a division that runs through all experience and sets everything connected with the

[1] 61 d-e. Tr. Jowett (Oxford University Press).

soul apart from everything connected with the body—knowledge from sensation, the 'ideas' from particular things, the eternal from the temporal, heaven from earth. The 'arguments' are a series of variations on this theme, lifting the reader more and more insistently towards a vision of reality in which survival of the soul falls naturally into place. Once this ascent has been accomplished, Socrates' attitude towards death—the point from which the conversation started—is seen to be correct. But to drive his message home Plato uses other means besides discussion. First, an appeal to the imagination, a 'myth', in which the future existence hitherto discussed in abstract argument is pictured as a reality in space and time, brought before the eye of the mind as a tempting vision of supernatural beauty. Second, an appeal to the emotions—a superbly simple narrative of Socrates' own end. These final pages, more effective for the reader of today than all the rest, add an aura to the whole and transform the belief in immortality into something vividly alive. So form and content, dialectical skill and dramatic power, are all moulded together to make the *Phaedo* a single unified work.

The *Phaedo* is a call to asceticism, to denial of the flesh. The *Symposium*, on the contrary, is filled with the praises of a force usually closely associated with fleshly desires: *eros*, love—in particular, the homosexual emotion which flourished in the exclusively male society of the Athenian gymnasium, and which was such a regular concomitant of intellectual discussion in the circles in which Socrates moved that it might well be looked upon as a stimulus urging the mind towards philosophy. Yet although this physical feeling is Plato's starting-point, he does not remain on this level, but turns from bodily love to an *eros* that is purely of the mind. Desire must be reason's servant, not its enemy, as in the tragedies of Euripides. The seeming contradiction of thought between the *Phaedo* and the *Symposium* is superficial.

So also is the apparent contrast between them in form. The narrator of the *Symposium* repeats an account he once heard of a banquet held to celebrate the first victory of the young tragic playwright, Agathon. Some of the most brilliant men of Athens were present (including, of course, Socrates) and the hard drinking that might have followed was replaced by speeches from the guests in praise of Love. This setting, strange to us, contained nothing surprising for Plato's contemporaries. Songs after dinner—one of the many types of literary competition—had been a familiar custom for many generations. The rise of rhetoric put prose in the place of verse, the after-dinner speech in place of the lyric or the drinking-catch. Plato valued the practice so highly that he made it a regular function of the Academy and laid down elaborate rules for such occasions in the *Laws*. It was natural that he should publish a work in this form; natural, too, that the speeches should be in praise of some mythical figure—a favourite theme in fourth-century displays of eloquence. The distinctive feature of Plato's banquet is that it is *Socratic*, not merely because Socrates is the central character, but because the whole pattern and purpose of the book are based on the Socratic method, on the Socratic approach as Plato developed it. The hypotheses which Socrates extracted in conversation from his companions and then demolished have their equivalent here in the first five speeches. He uses question and answer to show the weakness of one, and then—since he himself is no orator—recounts a speech he once heard from Diotima, a 'myth' which raises audience and reader into the sphere of reality and reveals the true function of *Eros* as guide from earth to heaven, from the appetites of the body to the sublime heights of mental contemplation. Not only the speeches fit this general plan. As in the *Phaedo*, the whole picture enhances the central theme, and the personality of Socrates embodies and symbolises Plato's message. Plato gains his effect here by contrast, setting his eulogy of spiritual love against a background of physical pleasure. Opposite Socrates he puts Alcibiades, against the symbol of fixity and steadfastness the symbol of change and unreliability. Amid the hurry on the way to the banquet at the beginning of the dialogue, Socrates stops in a doorway to think, and later Alcibiades relates how he once stood thus for twenty-four hours in camp at Potidaea. Throughout the narrative it is evident that he is superior to the rest of the company because he possesses a secret. His calm, it is implied, is based on that knowledge of 'the other world' which he reveals when his turn comes to speak. As soon as his speech is over, the entry of the drunken Alcibiades casts us headlong from the heights of metaphysics into the chaos of the senses, but he also delivers a eulogy—not of *Eros*, but of Socrates—which vividly illustrates the superiority of wisdom over the flesh. At the end of it all, Socrates alone is still sober and goes quietly about his business. These last pages of the *Symposium* fulfil the same part as the story of Socrates' death in the *Phaedo*.

These two dialogues, concerned with the welfare of the individual soul, seem far removed from the political ambitions and problems of Plato's youth. In the *Gorgias*, written some years earlier, he had emphatically turned his back on politics. Yet his renunciation was far from final. Like almost all his contemporaries, he continued to consider human well-being in political terms, to regard the individual as incomplete without society. His political thinking was not limited to the fifth-century ideas among which he was brought up, but was influenced by all the currents of fourth-century history, whether it moved with them or struggled against the stream: the class struggle between rich and poor; the growth of individualism and decline of loyalty to the city; the increase of specialisation and professionalism, even in the army and in politics; the rise of powerful autocrats in many states; the tendency towards federation.

Plato's mind was swayed, whether towards agreement or opposition, by many of the various trends of thought that we know from Xenophon, Isocrates, and the rest of his contemporaries: their condemnation of democratic politics at Athens; their turning away to the ideals of earlier days, or to other states— Sparta, for example, or Persia; their talk of communism, feminism, and other Utopian plans for transforming society; last but not least, the chief hope of fourth-century critics of democracy—their desire for a leader, their belief that in the education of a single ruler lay the path to better things.

At an early stage, as the *Seventh Letter* shows, Plato decided on his own remedy for the sickness of the body politic, his own version of the concept of the enlightened autocrat: the combination of the man of thought and the man of action, the philosopher-king. As time passed and his philosophy as a whole developed, he elaborated his application of reason to politics. Thucydides had seen the cause of Athens' fall from greatness in her desertion of what he regarded as a rational ideal. Plato wanted to save society by restoring the rule of reason, or rather by imposing on the human community a structure drawn from that blending of reason and mysticism which formed his own metaphysic. But of course other elements entered into the picture besides those drawn from Plato's conception of absolute truth: elements taken from his own worldly experience of contemporary states and contemporary ideas, from the traditions and prejudices of his own family and class. He was concerned not with society in the abstract, but with the form of society in which he had been brought up—the city-state. When the city-state's authority was sapped by individualism and class struggles, he saw these developments not as changes out of which a new world would emerge, but as maladies to be cured. The clock must be put back and in such a way that it will never move forward again. To restore the unity and harmony of the city, property must be separated from power, individualism must be suppressed (yet Plato himself is ahead of his time in his portraiture of individual character!). Class contentment must replace class war. Plato found the means to these ends in an analogy between the constitution of the state and the make-up of the individual. Apart from slaves, who are taken for granted and therefore scarcely considered, the ideal community must be divided into three classes analogous to a triple division of the individual soul: 'craftsmen', the producers and distributors of goods, who can have property but no political power; 'guards', a professional army and police-force, who must have all things—even wives and children—in common; 'rulers', drawn from among the 'guards', an aristocracy of intellect which must control the whole, just as reason should control our individual life. Thus the city is to be reorganised so that its structure and customs are in accordance with nature, and the philosopher—the true and natural ruler—is supreme.

This was the political programme set before Plato's pupils in the Academy. To a wider circle he made it known in the book we now call the *Republic* because the Latin *respublica* was used to translate *politeia*, the Greek word for 'constitution' or 'organisation of the city'. The *Republic* describes Plato's ideal state, but it is not confined to politics. Like his other works, it has a single main theme, but no one single subject. It ranges over the whole of his philosophy. In form it is far from merely descriptive. It is a conversation, narrated by Socrates, between him and characters typical of the social and intellectual atmosphere in which Socrates moved and Plato spent his youth: the rich merchant, Cephalus, and his son Polemarchus; Plato's elder brothers, Glaucon and Adeimantus, with the advanced views of youth; the Sophist Thrasymachus, most advanced of all. Superficially the dialogue has the casualness of conversation, with its digressions and sudden transitions. Sometimes dramatic effect seems to be the author's chief aim. But the real clue to the puzzle which the structure of the *Republic* presents to most modern readers is that this conversation also is *Socratic*. Just as the *Symposium* combines the method of thought which Plato had learnt from Socrates with the custom of making speeches after dinner, so here the same method moulds the description of the ideal state. Ascent from the particular to the general, from immediate problem to first principles, followed by descent to the particular and the immediate, is once again the core of the book, and it is this that mainly determines the stages in which the description is given. Considered from this point of view the 'metaphysical' passages, sometimes regarded as digressions, fall into place as the key to the whole. The net result is complex, even confusing. Yet it possesses one great advantage: it reveals Plato's political views as he himself saw them—as part and parcel of his whole philosophy.

Book I was probably written much earlier than the rest of the dialogue. Like Plato's other early works, it deals with a moral quality: 'justice' is the usual translation, though the Greek word is almost as wide in meaning as the English 'right'. Is justice more profitable than injustice? Is honesty the best policy? A series of hypothetical answers leads to no positive conclusion, except that justice must be *defined*. To facilitate the search for a definition a new hypothesis is introduced in Book II: Socrates' suggestion that justice will be found more easily in a city, because it exists there on a bigger scale. This proposal, with its assumption that state and individual have the same structure, leads to the conclusion that for city and individual alike justice lies in each part performing its own function and thereby ensuring the harmony of the whole. Socrates' hypothesis thus gives us a definition. It also brings forward a description of the ideal city, its division into classes, and especially the life of the 'guards'— their education, their communal existence, their conduct in war.

So nearly half of the conversation passes. But is the ideal

society practicable? This question calls forth a higher hypothesis: to justify the rule of the philosophers, who alone can transform the ideal into a reality, Socrates introduces the distinction between the world of 'ideas', from which they draw their superior wisdom, and the world of sense. Once more deductions are made, but to arrive at the full truth a 'longer road' must be followed, leading still further upward. To deal with the education of the philosopher-kings, Socrates ascends to the ultimate, 'unhypothetical' principle on which the previous 'hypotheses' depend: the 'idea' of 'the good', known not by reason but by mental vision, describable only by metaphors and analogies. Here is the central and culminating point of the whole argument. We have climbed to the top of the ladder, and now we can descend again, reaching definite conclusions about problems to which previously no accurate answer was possible—the training of the philosopher, the comparative merits of different types of state and individual, even the relative happiness of the just man and the unjust. The righteous man.is 729 times as happy as his opposite, the tyrant!

What remains—Book x—begins by relating to the 'ideas' the philosopher's education of the 'guards'. The dialogue ends with a myth of life after death: after all it is not earthly well-being, but the hope of the soul's salvation in the next world, that matters most.

Whether the ideal state can ever be realised in practice is a question raised more than once in the *Republic*, but never decided. 'Perhaps', says Socrates, 'there is a pattern set up in the heavens for one who desires to see it and, seeing it, to found one in himself. But whether it exists anywhere or ever will exist is no matter; for this is the only commonwealth in whose politics he can ever take part.'[1] Yet it is clear that for years after publishing the dialogue Plato cherished the idea of establishing such a

[1] 592 b. Tr. Cornford (Oxford University Press).

city on earth. Artificial creation of constitutions was a familiar concept to the Greeks, with their traditions of great lawgivers and of colonisation, and one function of the Academy was to be a training-school for future makers of laws and founders of cities. The great test of Plato's hopes came in 367 B.C., when Dionysius of Syracuse, whom he had visited earlier, died and was succeeded by his son of the same name. Dion, doubly related to the old 'tyrant' by marriage, had long been a zealous disciple of Plato, and now persuaded the new monarch to invite the philosopher to his court. Plato hesitated, then made the journey—and so began a long and complicated story which ended in disaster. Although he was warmly welcomed at first, and under his influence mathematics became all the rage at the Syracusan court, the young ruler soon turned from enthusiasm to suspicion. Dion was removed into exile and Plato held a prisoner until he gained his release and returned to Athens. Six years later he visited Syracuse again at Dionysius' own invitation, failed once more, and from Athens watched the tragic sequel: the forcible expulsion of Dionysius by Dion, the latter's oppressive rule and assassination. Far from the realisation of Utopia, the tale finished on a note all too familiar in the history of Greek states.

The failure of this venture into practical politics must have confirmed Plato in trends to which increasing years and his life in the Academy were already bringing him, and which leave their stamp on all his later works. As he moved further away from the association with Socrates which had inspired his youth, the quiet Academy, not the lively streets and meeting-places of Athens, became the background of his thought. His earlier writings had always had something of the brilliant amateur about them: now he was the professional philosopher, almost the professor of philosophy. He was no longer concerned with the problems of the ordinary man, but with the puzzles that arose within his own school.

He now turned, as a teacher of intelligent pupils must, to the intellectual difficulties inherent in the views he taught. He developed a new interest in logical method and the use of words, replacing the Socratic approach by a new way—'division'—of arriving at definitions, and discussing such questions as the implications of the word 'is', the significance of negation, the possibility of false statement. Where before he had hymned the praises of knowledge, now he investigated the nature of sensation and its relation to knowledge. Where he had regarded the 'ideas' primarily as ideals, as objects of mental vision, now he considered their number, the connection between them, and their connection with mathematics; most important of all, the bridge between the 'ideas' and the changing world of sense.

Such topics as these make up the content of Plato's later dialogues—the *Theaetetus* and the *Parmenides*, probably written shortly before his first visit to Dionysius II, the *Sophist, Statesman, Philebus, Timaeus, Critias* (an unfinished fragment), and the *Laws*. In form there are corresponding changes from the works of his earlier years. Socrates is sometimes dropped as the chief speaker, and his place taken by a figure obviously representing Plato himself. Because clarity now matters more than dramatic effect, character-drawing is abandoned, and Plato returns to direct dialogue instead of narrative and description. The discussion itself is usually little more than a lecture interrupted by brief expressions of agreement. 'When the other party to the conversation is tractable and gives no trouble', says the chief speaker in the *Sophist*, 'to address him is the easier course; otherwise, to speak by oneself.'[1] Because we are now in the Academy, as it were, we plunge straight into a problem instead of leading up to it from some occasion of ordinary life. Because the Socratic method of ascent to first principles followed by deduction from them is no longer the pattern of all Plato's thought, this ceases to

[1] 217d. Tr. Cornford (Kegan Paul, Trench, Trübner & Co., Ltd.).

282

be the key to the structure of his writings. They are more specialised than before, more confined to a single subject. And although the *Laws*, Plato's last and longest work, is nominally a conversation, and the *Timaeus*, because it describes the world of sense and not the world of knowledge, consists mainly of a 'myth', both are in fact little different from lectures. The Socratic spirit of inquiry has given way to dogmatism. These products of Plato's old age are full of significance for the development of his thought, but as literature they are often as lifeless as modern imitations of the dialogue form, for they too are remote from the living environment from which that form arose.

Plato's students in the Academy followed his example by writing dialogues, taking over the conversational form as the established and natural vehicle for philosophy. Among them was his greatest pupil, Aristotle, who published a number of dialogues during the twenty years which he spent in the school. None of them survives today. From the fragments which still exist and the comments of those ancient authors who read them, it seems likely that most of them were close to Plato in both content and form. Some had familiar titles—*Menexenus, Symposium, Sophist, Statesman*. In style and structure they appear to have imitated various phases in the development of the Platonic dialogue, including the use of myth, although Aristotle also created a new type, destined to become the model for many works in Latin, in which exchange of speech for speech replaced the outworn convention of question and answer. These works were the chief source of Aristotle's literary fame in antiquity, as well as the basis of much of his philosophical influence in later centuries. But he did not remain satisfied with the dialogue form. As Plato had moved away from Socrates, so Aristotle moved away from Plato. The division of philosophy into separate departments, the building of a system of doctrines, the use of technical terms, dogmatic exposition—trends of the time which had already left their mark on Plato's later writings—affected the whole character of Aristotle's mature thought. He now abandoned more literary forms in favour of lectures, and it is notes on these lectures that constitute nearly all his surviving works. Among the subjects which he systematically treated was not only logic—the rules of reasoning—but also dialectic, the rules of discussion. In Aristotles's *Topics* the art of philosophic conversation which had arisen nearly a century earlier was systematised, codified, brought under rule and regulation. And unfortunately it is this dreary textbook, not his dialogues, that we still possess.

The story which began in the streets and gymnasia of Athens has ended in a handbook of dialectic. The sequel—the dialogues produced centuries later by Plutarch and especially by Lucian— lies outside the scope of this book. In his attacks on pretence and sham, cant and pedantry, Lucian showed much of the Socratic spirit, and combined it with a whimsical fancy almost worthy of Aristophanes. Some of his writings are remarkably close imitations of the language and manner of Plato's early works. But no later composer of literary conversations, Greek or Roman, could fully recapture the life and vigour which had once flowed into the dialogue form from the personality of Socrates and the atmosphere of democratic Athens.

CHAPTER X

AFTER ALEXANDER

GREEK literature did not come to an end when Alexander's campaigns transformed the Hellenic world. Far from it. If production statistics had been known in antiquity, the graph for literary output would have shown a rise in these later centuries. Never had there been so many writers at work, so many books published. A complete survey of the subject would now go on to cover several further phases of development: the closing years of the fourth century B.C., during which Athens was still pre-eminent; the brilliance of Alexandria in the third century under the Ptolemies, which gave the name 'Alexandrian' to all the writings of the time; the comparatively unfruitful period of domination by Rome until Greek literature enjoyed an Indian summer in the second century A.D.; the move to Byzantium and the rivalry between Christian authors and the last exponents of Paganism. If any one date can be selected, it is the reign of Justinian, nearly nine hundred years after Alexander, that brings the story to a close. Although time has been even less generous here than earlier, and most of the authors belonging to these final stages are known to us only through brief fragments or the comments of others, there are a number of considerable figures still to come whose works we can read at any rate in part: at Athens, Menander and Theophrastus; at Alexandria, Callimachus, Apollonius, Theocritus, Euclid; under the supremacy of Rome, Polybius, Epictetus, Plutarch, Lucian, Marcus Aurelius. These and a score or more of others make the old age of Greek literature far from feeble or undistinguished.

To deal with all these in this volume is impossible. A halt

must be called somewhere. And since my main object is to describe the development of literature against the background of Greek history, it seems logical to stop at the point at which events in the Greek world began to be overshadowed and dominated by the rising power of Rome; to continue, in short, until something has been said of the 'Alexandrian' period, and to go no further than the beginning of the second century B.C.— although it may be added that the remains surviving from these 150 years reveal features and tendencies which were to last until the whole tale was told.

What are those remains? No very extensive addition to our book-case of Greek literature. In prose there are a number of textbooks, but little that could claim any literary merit. In verse we have no more than will go comfortably into a single volume: parts of several comedies, but no complete play; one long narrative poem in the epic style and several short ones; a few 'hymns'; a number of 'idylls' and 'mimes'—brief sketches of country or town life; a lengthy monologue; a didactic poem on astronomy and the weather; a few score epigrams. In comparison with the fifth century B.C. the prospect is barren, and would probably be little different even if more than this small fraction of the original output had survived. There is no great masterpiece here, no writer of the stature of Pindar or Sophocles or Plato (though some would place Theocritus on that level). Nor is there any striking innovation in form: such novelties as do occur are secondary or subsidiary, adapted or derived, additional offshoots from the great branches which the tree had already put out by the close of the fourth century B.C.

At first glance there is a paradox here, an apparent break in the connection between the history of literature and the development of society. Alexander's conquests and their sequel transformed the environment in which Greek literature was produced— extended its boundaries, altered its relations with non-Greek peoples, changed the nature of its politics, vastly increased trade, travel and industry. Books were now produced in greater quantities and more cheaply than ever before. Greek culture and the Greek language spread where they were hitherto unknown. If social change was previously the main driving force behind the growth of literature, if earlier developments in the organisation of society led to new advances in the literary sphere, why were the great events of the close of the fourth century B.C. followed by the production of works mostly so mediocre in quality, so lacking in inspiration, so close to the old conventions in form? 'Exhaustion of the Greek genius' is no answer to the problem. The explanation still lies in the relationship between literature and society, but closer examination is necessary in order to see how that relationship had changed.

In the earlier stages of Greek history literature was deeply rooted in the life of the city-state, part and parcel of the existence of the community, or at any rate the dominant section of the community. Often it was bound up with the common religion, nearly always with social occasions, great or small. It was usually produced for public recitation or performance rather than for private study. Epic, choral song, drama, oratory, dialogue, nearly all the types of literature drew their life and vigour from the life and vigour of the city—its traditions and ambitions, its internal struggles, its rivalry with other states. This was the forcing-house in which literature grew and flourished up to the beginning of the Hellenistic Age.

The transformation brought about by Alexander removed this creative power of the city-state, and it was never restored. Nor was any adequate substitute put in its place.

Cities, of course, continued to be the normal form of local organisation—not only the cities of earlier days, but the many new ones scattered over what had once been the Persian Empire. These cities possessed varying degrees of nominal independence.

Assemblies, councils, magistrates still went through the motions of government and administration. The external manifestations of city culture were maintained in the old centres and established in the new—festivals and ceremonies, for example, complete with contests and recitations, often more spectacular than ever before. But these municipal towns of the Hellenistic kingdoms were not the sovereign city-states of the old days. Their life provided no such inspiration for literature as there had been in fifth-century Athens. The old motives and themes had gone. Local patriotism and competition between cities, though they continued on a petty level, had little genuine meaning where all real power was in the hands of military autocrats and economic and social life were dominated by a wealthy middle class which was everywhere more or less the same. War and politics were now the concern of specialists. The old religious traditions were now no more than a dead mythology to the educated Greek.

Not only had the city become a poor shadow of its earlier self, but the place of literature in the city's existence had also changed till it played no such integral part as in the past. In the new towns in 'barbaric' lands Greek culture was confined to the Greek section of the population and those natives—a small minority—who became Hellenised. To the Greek-speaking inhabitants of old and new cities alike, acquaintance with literature came primarily through books and was largely the privilege of those who could afford to buy books—that well-to-do middle class which formed the respectable society of the Hellenistic world. There is no really popular literature among the remains that survive from this period, though the mime, spoken and sung, may have had large audiences and some prose works—miscellaneous collections of information or gossip or anecdotes—may have reached a very wide public. Most authors now catered for the well-educated few, and even for them literature was what it is for most people today—a pastime apart from ordinary existence. Specialisation was now coming into its own, and literary specialists, professional men of letters, wrote books for readers who looked upon the enjoyment of literature as a separate department of their lives. Art for amusement's sake, even art for art's sake, were replacing art for the city's sake. We are near to the study armchair, far from the days when Aeschylus fought in the Persian Wars and dramatised for the victors of Salamis the sequel to their success.

The life of the educated urban middle class, mainly concerned with drawing the maximum profits from slave labour and exploiting the new commercial possibilities which Alexander's campaigns had opened up, clearly contained little that was likely to inspire great literature, even though it at first provided the driving-force for spectacular advances in science and mathematics. But they were the public for whom most literature was produced, the section of society from which most authors came; and their outlook inevitably left its stamp on the writings of the time. Their materialistic love of fact—one cause of progress in the scientific sphere—found its literary reflection in concentration on factual detail and in realism: Hellenistic literature keeps close to the ground, rarely soars into the realm of imagination. Their individualism, carried to unprecedented lengths in a world where individual enterprise mattered more than common effort, had its counterpart in portrayal of scenes from private life, in emphasis on personal emotion. The expression of individual feeling now became a commonplace, and romantic love, so shocking to the Athenians when they watched the plays of Euripides, was now an accepted and familiar theme. Hand in hand with individualism went cosmopolitanism, the acknow-ledgement of a common humanity transcending any city walls.

These were some of the 'modern' trends. But all the modernity of these later times was accompanied by a clinging to the past, a fresh conservatism which replaced the old conservative traditions of the city. The heritage of earlier culture which now gave the educated middle class its intellectual status was treasured as never before. Not only were the old works preserved in book form, classified, catalogued, annotated; imitation of them kept conventions in being, even revived conventions long since dead, in circumstances very different from the origins which gave them life and meaning. Greek literature after Alexander presents a strange combination of modern and ancient, an interesting study of the adaptation of old forms to new needs and new points of view.

One result of this concentration on the past was a revival of verse. We shall find writers at Alexandria and elsewhere not only returning to verse, but imitating verse forms which had long since fallen out of use. Consider only the extant remains of the literature of the day, and it would seem that although the fourth century B.C. had brought prose to the forefront, the third, like earlier centuries, was an age of poetry. But the impression is false. The verse revival was a temporary phase, appealing chiefly to only a small, highly educated minority of the reading public. The main current of literature continued to be prose, now the ordinary medium of expression, as it is in modern times. Philosophy, science, geography, grammar, mythology, and a dozen other subjects were dealt with in prose works now lost. Typical of the growing homogeneity of the Greek world after Alexander was a development in which Xenophon had been a pioneer— the adoption of a 'common dialect', drawn mainly from Attic, which replaced the variety of earlier days. Yet so far as we can judge from the existing remains, the simplicity of Xenophon was rarely reproduced. The influence of rhetoric was still strong, especially in the writing of history. There was a general tendency towards heaviness, towards the use of too many abstract or technical terms. Hellenistic prose was written mainly for readers, and the vividness of style which had appealed to the audiences of earlier days was now a thing of the past.

So much can be said of the general background of literature after Alexander. But look at the surviving remains more closely, and it becomes clear that in the Hellenistic world generalisation is almost as dangerous as in earlier times. Distinctions must still be drawn between the particular places in which literature came into being. The main dividing line lies between the old cities and the new, and on each side there is one example far more important then the rest: among the old, Athens; among the new, Alexandria.

Let us glance at Athens first. Superficially, Athenian life was little different now from what it had been in the city's more glorious days. Not only her appearance was the same: the same activities continued—the great festivals, the meetings of Council and Assembly. But Athenian politics now meant little in terms of effective action, and even in commerce she no longer held the lead. Her sole claim to pre-eminence lay in the sphere of culture and intellect, and here she retained the foremost place until the close of the fourth century, and yielded it only to Alexandria in the third. Her dialect was now the accepted language of the Greek world. Her past achievements in literature and art formed a great part of the heritage treasured by educated Greeks everywhere. She had now become what Pericles (according to Thucydides) claimed her to be—'the school of Hellas'; and she had the distinction and the limitations of an old university town. Above all she was respected and visited as the home of philosophy. The intellectual vigour once devoted to imperial ambitions and political dispute was now spent on philosophical discussion. To Plato's Academy and Aristotle's Lyceum were added the Porch of Zeno, founder of Stoicism, and the garden of Epicurus, and the whole city rang with the battle of the schools. From all this two documents of literary value are still extant, both typical in different ways of the trends of the day. From Theophrastus, head of the Lyceum, whose scientific repûtation rests on two long botanical treatises in the Aristotelian manner, we have a little book of *Characters*—a series of brief prose pictures of the types to be seen in contemporary Athens. Individual portraiture had never been so subtle or so realistic. From Cleanthes, head of the Stoic school in the third century, there survives a *Hymn to Zeus*—the first Greek poem that is religious in the modern sense, the first great example of devotional literature, as its opening lines show:

> O God most glorious, called by many a name,
> Nature's great King, through endless years the same;
> Omnipotence, who by thy just decree
> Controllest all, hail, Zeus, for unto thee
> Behoves thy creatures in all lands to call.
> We are thy children, we alone, of all
> On earth's broad ways that wander to and fro,
> Bearing thine image whereso'er we go.
> Wherefore with songs of praise thy power I will forth shew.[1]

Time has been a little more generous with the other form of literature for which Athens was now famous: 'New' Comedy, the type of drama which Roman playwrights were to imitate and hand down to modern times.

The development of Attic drama, of course, had not been at a standstill between the end of the fifth century B.C. and the closing decades of the fourth. The dramatic contests went on, and hundreds of new plays, all now lost, were performed. In tragedy even before 400 B.C. innovations had been tried which carried further the trends of Euripides: a fictional plot, for example, and choral songs which were mere interludes. But they failed to give the art of tragedy new life. Spectacle, music, and acting became more important to the audience than the play itself. The

[1] Tr. J. Adam in *The Vitality of Platonism* (Cambridge University Press).

old fifth-century masterpieces far outshone contemporary efforts, and revival of them became a regular practice. It was comedy that retained something of its old vigour and succeeded in adapting itself to the changing environment. The comedies of the time of Demosthenes and Aristotle were far removed from the *Peace* or the *Birds*. The process of coming down to earth which we find in Aristophanes' last plays seems to have continued in the works of his successors, who often followed in the footsteps of Euripides rather than of Old Comedy. Obscenity of both language and costume disappeared. Attacks on personalities became less frequent. Partly through burlesque of myth and of tragedy, placing gods and heroes amid the trivialities of normal human existence, partly through portrayal of contemporary types, the poets moved towards imitation of ordinary life, representation of ordinary character, use of ordinary prosaic language. So the 'New' Comedy which confronts us when drama partly emerges once more from obscurity towards the end of the century is realistic comedy, comedy of manners.

Fifty years ago New Comedy was known only from numerous brief fragments and the Latin plays in which Plautus and Terence imitated the Greek originals—how closely, it was impossible to tell. Since then discoveries in Egypt and the patient work of scholars have restored large parts of three plays by Menander, the New Comedy playwright whom ancient commentators admired above all others and placed among the greatest authors of antiquity. The gaps can be reasonably filled by conjecture—Professor Gilbert Murray has recently published reconstructions of two of the plays under the titles *The Rape of the Locks* and *The Arbitration*—and some idea can be formed of the best that New Comedy had to show.

How does Menander compare with Aristophanes? The structure of comedy has almost entirely changed. The *parabasis* and other peculiar features have gone. The chorus has been reduced to a stage-direction, or rather to something strangely reminiscent of the original *komos;* the dialogue, still in iambic verse, is interrupted by interludes in which bands of revellers sing and dance to keep the spectators entertained—the beginning of the modern division into acts. At or near the opening of the play stands a prologue in the manner started by Euripides, sometimes spoken by a divine figure (perhaps invented for the occasion) and sometimes placed after the first dramatic scene. In *The Rape of the Locks* an explanation of the situation by 'Ignorance' follows the first 'act'.

Some notion of the nature of Menander's work may be gained from two typical passages from this play. In the first, Pataecus urges Polemon to get his mistress back by persuasion rather than by force:

Pataecus	Now, Polemo,
	If this occurrence was the sort of thing
	You and your friends describe; or if again
	The girl in question were your lawful wife ...
Polemo	Pataecus! What a thing to say!
Pataecus	You know,
	It makes a difference.
Polemo	Sir, I regard
	That lady as my wife and always have!
Pataecus	You need not shout. Who gave away the bride?
Polemo	Gave her to me? Who? She herself.
Pataecus	Quite so.
	No doubt at that time she was pleased with you.
	Now she is not. She has left your house because
	You did not treat her suitably.
Polemo	What's that?
	That hurts me worse than anything you have said.
	I only want her to come back to me.
Pataecus	Oh, you're in love, I know. But don't you see
	That makes this conduct all the more demented?
	What is it that you're aiming at? What slave
	Is it you claim to take possession of?

The lady you pursue is her own mistress.
The only course open to one like you,
In love and trouble, is to plead with her.[1]

Here another character complains of his lot:

Moschio   Of all the unlucky devils now alive—
And there's a bumper harvest of them now
In every town of Hellas, God knows why!—
I don't believe there's one in all the lot
As miserable as me. When I got home
I did none of the things I always do,
Didn't go near my mother, didn't call
Anyone in the house to speak to me;
I went straight to my bedroom, thinking hard,
And lay down flat. Then I sent Davus in
To tell my mother that I'd come—just that,
And nothing more. He found them all at lunch
And stayed there, gorging. So I waited on,
And told myself: 'At any moment now
Mother will come from that delightful girl
And tell me on what conditions we may meet.'[2]

Clearly we are far away from Aristophanes. There is no laughter
here, although a piquant situation or a neat phrase may raise a
smile. The keynote is realism—nothing, perhaps, to impress the
modern reader who is accustomed to realistic drama, but so
unprecedented in ancient times that a commentator[3] exclaimed:

Menander! Life!
I wonder which of you has copied which?

The Athenian audience no longer see John Citizen leaping over
the bounds and restraints of ordinary living. They watch a
reflection of their own existence. The stage is peopled by characters such as can be met any day in the streets of Athens, some

[1] Ll. 363-76. Tr. Murray (George Allen and Unwin, Ltd.).
[2] Ll. 409-27. Tr. Murray.
[3] Aristophanes of Byzantium.

of whom reappear in Theophrastus' book. Slaves have a prominent part, as they do in the life of the period. So do courtesans. Dominant in the play, as in the city, is the well-to-do middle class, and most of the other characters are its dependants—slaves, courtesans, cooks, nurses, spongers, and the rest. Politics and events in the larger Greek world are ignored. Private life and personal feelings provide the poet's material now; above all, love between man and woman. There is plenty of moralisation in the comedies, typical of contemporary Athens. Menander is said to have learnt philosophy from Theophrastus. Most of the familiar themes of the time are there, often crystallised in neat epigrammatic form. Cosmopolitanism, for example:

> No honest man I call
> A foreigner; one nature have we all.[1]

Or emphasis on man's weakness amid the somersaults of Fortune:

> We live, not as we choose, but as we can.[2]

If any particular outlook is dominant, it is Epicureanism. But the values and assumptions that really count in the plays are those of the urban middle class. Money and respectability are the twin essentials of the inevitable happy ending. Apart from these New Comedy has few or no morals. Aristophanes is a strict moralist compared with Menander.

Not only are characters and their actions far more realistic than in Old Comedy, but also the language they speak, though Menander does not go to the same extremes as the modern realistic novel. There is nothing fantastic or obscene in his dialogue. He carries the trend which we find in Euripides to its logical conclusion. His verse, except that it scans, might as well be prose. His diction is simple and pure but not colloquial Attic—the educated speech of his own day, subtly adapted to the different characters who use it.

[1] *Fr.* 602.   [2] *Maxims*, l. 190 (Meineke).

Realism, I have emphasised, is the keynote. Yet it was a strangely limited realism. The old circumstances and methods of presentation continued—the huge open-air theatre; the restriction to three speaking actors, all male; the use of masks, now differentiated to suit the various character types, but still grotesque and exaggerated. Apart from these theatrical conventions, there is a limitation of plot probably more obvious to the twentieth-century reader than to the ancient audience—a limitation not merely due to the narrowness of middle-class life in Athens, nor to the necessary silence of the poet on political affairs. New Comedy gives us not a complete picture of the private life of the well-to-do Athenian family and its dependants, but only a narrow selection from the adventures which they may undergo. There is a strange similarity in all the plots of Menander that we can partially reconstruct—something as stereotyped as the modern Boy meets Girl, Boy loses Girl, Boy gets Girl, but not so universal. In New Comedy the Boy has usually already lost the Girl, and the play tells how he regains her; but the circumstances of loss and restoration are also stereotyped, repeatedly involving items foreign to modern experience—abandoned infants, birth-tokens, the intrigues of an ingenious slave, the recognition of a courtesan as a free-born and marriageable woman after all.

Why this limitation, these many variations on this particular theme? Convention, it would seem, was still strong enough at Athens to restrict drama to subject-matter of a type already often used in the theatre. The elements of the stock Menander plot can be found in Euripides—in his *Ion*, for example; they were made familiar during the fourth century by the comic poets' repeated parody of tragedy. Like other Hellenistic literature, New Comedy, for all its newness, looked back to the past. Such a limited and stereotyped form of drama, such a strange mixture of realism and convention, had a limited appeal. Despite attempts to transplant it elsewhere, New Comedy flourished only at Athens, and there not for long. Even at Athens its best days were over by 250 B.C., and in the second century, when imitation of Menander and others was giving comedy a new lease of life in Italy, in Greece it showed the same symptom of decline as tragedy—the performance of 'revivals' of earlier plays.

So much for Athens. Of the new cities, several became centres of culture: Alexandria, Pergamum, Antioch, Tarsus and others. But easily the most outstanding was Alexandria, and it is there that we find in the most pronounced form the tendencies which were shared to some extent by all.

Alexandria was something new in history, something quite different from Athens and the other old towns of Greece proper —a city ten miles round, with broad main streets, spectacular buildings, and a lighthouse on the adjoining island of Pharos. Within a few decades of its foundation it was the world's chief market and one of its greatest manufacturing centres. Egyptians, Jews, Greeks—every race was there. The upper class which dominated trade, industry, banking, administration and the professions was Greek in language and outlook, if not always by birth. In control of all, of course, were the Macedonian Ptolemies and their court.

In such a motley population there could be no national or popular culture. To the majority Greek culture and literature were alien and unknown. But they were strongly encouraged by the Ptolemies, who were not only anxious, like the 'tyrants' of earlier days, to add artistic and literary lustre to the brilliance of their regime, but also wanted to prove that Macedonian 'barbarians' were as civilised as anyone of true Hellenic stock. To promote their aim they followed the example set by Plato's Academy and still more by Aristotle's Lyceum, and established in the royal quarter of the city a 'Hall of the Muses' which far outstripped both in magnificence. This famous 'Museum' of

Alexandria, with a 'priest of the Muses' shrine' as its president, included a dining hall, botanical gardens, an observatory, and a zoo. Nearby stood the great Library containing hundreds of thousands of papyrus rolls, all the literary wealth of the past now stored up in book form. A contemporary moralist[1] scornfully described the Museum as 'the hen-coop of the Muses', but to scholars and scientists it offered a tempting refuge from the disorders and disturbances of the time. The royal invitation drew them to Alexandria from Samos, Cos, Rhodes—from everywhere except Athens. A list of some of the most famous men of letters who came there shows the variety of their origins. From Cyrene, further along the African coast, came Callimachus, most typical of all Alexandrian writers, and Eratosthenes, scholar and poet as well as the outstanding geographer of antiquity. From Syracuse in the West came Theocritus, greatest poet of the Alexandrians; from Chalcis in central Greece, Lycophron, the most obscure. The scholar Aristophanes originated from Byzantium, and Aristarchus from Samothrace. The only leading figure on the list born in Egypt was epic poet Apollonius, who spent part of his life at Rhodes and was known as 'the Rhodian'. Most of these men were Librarians. All the members of the Museum, perhaps a hundred in number, depended on the patronage of the Ptolemies and received an official allowance. Together they formed a coterie of intellect and learning, a closed society attached to the court but little connected with the rest of the town.

An institution in which learning and scientific investigation stood at such a premium naturally produced many books of prose—not oratory or philosophy, but technical and specialised disquisitions and handbooks: the *Elements* of Euclid, for example, Eratosthenes' *On the Mensuration of the Earth*, the treatises on lexicography and grammar by Aristophanes of Byzantium. Even those now known only for their poetry, like Callimachus and

[1] Timon, in Athenaeus 1, 22d.

Apollonius, wrote scholarly prose works as well, and after a few generations the poets disappeared and only scholars and scientists remained. But it is Alexandrian verse, or rather a small part of it, that has survived. Needless to say, the poetry of these librarians and other members of the Museum was in no sense popular. They did not draw their inspiration, such as it was, from Alexandria or Egypt, which left little mark on their work; nor from events in the wider Greek world, though these contained dramatic and poetical material in plenty; nor from their royal patrons, though they eulogised them with flatteries unprecedented in the days of the city-state. They were scholars writing for scholars and for a narrow circle of cultured laymen, concerned with preserving the heritage of the past rather than exploiting the full possibilities of the present. And so it was mainly to the past that they looked for inspiration and material— not so much to the fourth or fifth century B.C., the era of Athens' greatest achievements, but to still earlier days, to Homer, Hesiod and the other early poets whom as scholars they edited with so much care. They took over the language and diction of their models, using whichever dialect was traditionally correct for the form they imitated. They filled their poems with myth and legend, especially local legend—tales which they did not believe. The gods and goddesses whom they use as celestial machinery are either lifeless reproductions of the deities of early epic, or divine reflections of the rulers or the Greek upper class of Hellenistic times. One learns little or nothing from these Alexandrian poets about the religion or philosophy of their own day. The being presented to us in Callimachus' *Hymn to Zeus* is a powerful and wealthy monarch surrounded by a brilliant court and with an army at his command: we are very far from the poem of the same name by Stoic Cleanthes.

Because the Alexandrians reached their public mainly through the bookseller and wrote for readers rather than an audience, they could throw simplicity to the winds and indulge to the full their natural scholarly bent. In both content and language they were pedantic, sometimes even deliberately obscure. There is no more cryptic piece of verse in Greek than Lycophron's *Alexandra*, which reports in 1474 enigmatic lines how the prophetess more commonly known as Cassandra foretold the results of Paris' visit to Sparta. Yet all this dry-as-dust archaism was strangely mingled with modern elements, with a deliberate striving after novelty and originality. Although most of the language of Alexandrian verse was archaic, new words and usages were mixed with the old. Ancient legend was frequently given an up-to-date flavour—an atmosphere of romantic love, for example—which is sometimes incongruous, but sometimes brings an otherwise dead narrative to life: the Alexandrians, like most earlier Greek writers, are most readable when nearest to the realities of their own time. Similar combinations of old and new governed their use of verse forms—the same forms which convention had long since stereotyped, but completely separated by now from their original accompaniment of music or dance or both, and adapted to purposes often far different from those they had once fulfilled. Two of these forms cover most of the surviving remains—the epic hexameter and the elegiac couplet.

A strange amalgam of old and new in epic verse was the *Phaenomena* of Aratus, who looked back to Hesiod and Empedocles and Parmenides and used hexameters instead of prose for his astronomical textbook. The poem had a double appeal to his contemporaries: it gave them facts, and it imitated the old masters. But Aratus was a scholar, not a scientist. Unlike the Roman Lucretius, he had no conception of the grandeur of science, no grasp of universal principles, to lift his book out of the rut of monotonous detail. Today it is a literary curiosity, interesting only as a reflection of its age. More readable—in parts—is Apollonius' *Argonautica*, earliest extant specimen of the literary epic. Apollonius too was a scholar, perhaps even Librarian at Alexandria. Certainly his account of the Argonaut's voyage is a scholar's work, a collection of material drawn from many books and woven together with much skill but little imagination. It has all the typical Alexandrian vices: pedantic display of learning, excess of detail, unreal deities, spineless human characters. Yet in the third of its four books a new note enlivens the ancient story: Apollonius' romantic picture of Medea falling in love with Jason is nearer to the sentimental modern novel than to Homer or Hesiod. Here are a few lines, with an astronomical simile strangely embedded in the middle:

> Even now Medea could not alter
> Her mood for all her singing, and no song
> Of those she tried to play with pleased her long,
> But she would fail and falter;
> And not among her maids her gaze she kept
> At rest, but scanning every distant road
> She turned her cheeks abroad,
> With heart that broke each time she seemed to hear
> A sound of wind or footfall running near.
> But soon he showed before her waiting eyes
> High striding, much like Sirius ascending
> From Ocean: loveliest he, far-seen to rise,
> But dismal ruin to the flocks impending.
> So lovely to her sight came Aeson's son.
> But when she saw, he hurt her with desire,
> The heart sank from her breast, a mist drew on
> Over her eyes, her cheeks went hot as fire.[1]

Although the *Argonautica* is only half as long as the *Odyssey*, its length was bitterly attacked by Callimachus, and led to another product of the Alexandrian spirit—the earliest literary quarrel, typically concerned with a question of form and technique. Aeschylus had fought the Persians, but Callimachus and Apollonius battled in epigrams over the proper size of an epic

[1] III, ll. 948-63. Tr. Allen (*O.B.G.V.* 538).

poem. Many of their contemporaries evidently sided with
Callimachus, for not only he but others joined in creating a
fashion for miniature epics—brief narratives of a few hundred
lines each. Not far removed from these are Callimachus' *Hymns*,
dreary displays of learning modelled mainly on the *Homeric
Hymns*, partly on Pindar, and really concerned more with
glorification of Ptolemy than of the Olympian gods.

Most Alexandrian poets wrote some hexameters. But their
favourite metre was the elegiac couplet, now far removed from
its flute accompaniment and its limitation to themes of feasting
and war. Often it was used like the hexameter, for narrative and
description. In shorter poems it became the recognised vehicle
of personal feeling; and although pedantry and artificiality left
their mark here too and love poetry was often written in elegiacs
by authors who were not in love, it is here that once again, as
three or four centuries earlier, the individual speaks. The
Alexandrians naturally excelled in using the form in which
scholarly wit and precision were most at home—the elegiac
epigram, produced in great numbers by poets from now on
throughout Hellenistic and Roman times. From the *Palatine
Anthology*, in which the epigrams of more that 320 writers were
brought together in the tenth century A.D., and from other
sources we have a few hundred out of the thousands published in
the Alexandrian period. Many of the best are by Callimachus.
An epitaph on a boy, for example:

> Philip's Nicoteles, a twelve-year lad,
> Lies buried here: the hope his father had.[1]

Or a poem to a dead friend, familiar to English readers in Cory's
translation:

> They told me, Heraclitus, they told me you were dead;
> They brought me bitter news to hear and bitter tears to shed.

[1] *Palatine Anthology* VII, 453. Tr. Ensor (*O.B.G.V.* 516).

I wept, as I remember'd, how often you and I
Had tired the sun with talking and sent him down the sky.
And now that thou art lying, my dear old Carian guest,
A handful of grey ashes, long, long ago at rest,
Still are thy pleasant voices, thy nightingales, awake,
For Death, he taketh all away, but them he cannot take.[1]

The scholar-librarian could show humour at times:

A boy was adorning his stepmother's grave
With a wreath ('twas a low-standing stone),
And thinking that with the departure of life
Her nature must also have gone.
But the headstone fell flat on the boy as he crouched
And crushed him before he could fly;
And the moral for stepsons is this: 'Twill be best
If you let sleeping stepmothers lie.[2]

Many others are by Asclepiades of Samos, who thus appeals to a coy mistress:

Why hoard your maidenhood? There'll not be found
A lad to love you, girl, under the ground.
Love's joys are for the quick; but when we're dead
It's dust and ashes, girl, will go to bed.[3]

Perhaps most remarkable of all is a poet of a very different stamp from whom we have about a hundred epigrams—Leonidas of Tarentum, a wanderer who lived in many parts of the Hellenistic world and subsisted by writing dedications or epitaphs for a small fee. He bids the mice begone from his poor hut:

Hence! Out! Begone in scuttering flight,
Ye little people of the night!
This is a poor man's hut. Too thin
The store in Leonid's bread-bin
To share with mice! Little indeed
Will furnish all the old man's need—

[1] *P.A.* VII, 80. Tr. Cory (*O.B.G.V.* 513).
[2] *P.A.* IX, 67. Tr. Furness (Jonathan Cape, Ltd.).
[3] *P.A.* V, 85. Tr. Furness (*O.B.G.V.* 525).

Some salt, two barley cakes, may be,
Coarse-ground; with that content and free
He lives in those hard noble ways
His fathers' law school'd him to praise.
Therefore, my lickerish friend, what gain
To ransack all his spare domain,
Peer, poke, and find no morsel, nay,
No broken remnant brush'd away?
Flit fast to other houses: there
A mouse may light on lordlier fare.[1]

The most striking feature of Leonidas' work is one which scarcely emerges in translation: his themes are usually drawn from the life of the poor, yet his style and language are strangely mannered and artificial. Though he did not live at Alexandria, the humble content and elaborate diction of his poems form a paradox which is thoroughly Alexandrian.

One literary form used by the Alexandrians brings us still nearer to the life of the age: the 'mime'. There is evidence that mimes, both spoken and sung, were performed by travelling players throughout the Hellenistic world. But the specimens we now possess were never intended as popular entertainment. They may portray common folk, but like other Alexandrian poetry they were written for a small, highly educated audience; still more, for highly educated readers. Miniature comedies were a literary fashion, like miniature epics, and they also present a strange mixture of modern and ancient—the up-to-date realism of New Comedy expressed in metre and language borrowed from the early days of Greek literature.

From Herodas, who probably visited Alexandria but was never one of the inner circle of scholars, an Egyptian papyrus has given us eight mimes more or less complete. Their characters and themes show us more of the seamy side of the Hellenistic period than anything in Menander: a brothel-keeper, for example,

[1] *P.A.* vi, 302. Tr. Bevan (Oxford University Press).

brings an action for assault against one of his patrons; a truant schoolboy is caught and flogged; a mistress orders a beating for her unfaithful slave-lover. Yet the vocabulary and verse-form of these realistic sketches are archaic and the sentence-structure is often distorted to fit the metre—artificialities which make them remote from the actual conversation of the day.

A far more brilliant mime-writer than Herodas was Theocritus, generally regarded as the greatest of all the poets of the Hellenistic Age. Theocritus is often singled out from his contemporaries as a genius with an invention and achievement of his own—the creation of 'pastoral poetry'. Yet in many ways he was true to the Alexandrian type. We gather from his poems that he spent his life in several of the literary centres of the day: Syracuse, Cos, Alexandria. Like others, he looked to patronage for his means of livelihood, and two pieces are concerned with it out of the thirty (apart from epigrams) which are ascribed to him: a frank appeal (apparently unsuccessful) to Hiero of Syracuse, and a tedious eulogy of Ptolemy Philadelphus. All his 'little songs', as he called them, or 'idylls' ('little poems'), as ancient grammarians described them, fit easily enough into the general picture of the time. As the names suggest, they have a brevity of which Callimachus must have approved: the longest is only 280 lines. Two favourite Alexandrian forms are well represented, for there are four short epics on legendary themes and some twenty epigrams. If Theocritus stands out above his fellows, it is mainly because he rarely lets the characteristics which he shares with them spoil the balance or the beauty of his poetry. He is a scholar, but does not often display his erudition. He describes works of art at length, but the descriptions are usually relevant. His language is archaic, but boldly adapted to present needs. It is he who carries furthest the tendency towards novel combinations of elements drawn from the past: he mixes dialects; if *Idyll* VIII is really his, he combines elegiac couplets with hexameters; he brings together spoken verse and song, epic narrative and dramatic dialogue. Of all the Alexandrians he is the least bound by conventional rules of form and style.

The mime is the chief sphere in which all this artistry found expression. About a dozen of Theocritus' poems are mimes, written—like those of Herodas—to be read or recited, not acted. Two of the most effective are drawn from town life. One is the passionate monologue of Simaitha, first trying to regain her lover by magic rites, then telling her story. The other, *The Syracusan Women at the Adonis Festival*, is the most brilliant extant illustration of Hellenistic realism, although it includes flattery of the Ptolemies and a song near to the worst Alexandrian style. Here are the opening lines in which Gorgo comes into Praxinoa's house from the crowded streets of Alexandria:

Gorgo   Praxinoa at home?

Praxinoa   Dear Gorgo, at last! Yes, I'm at home.
The wonder is you've come at all. Eunoa, fetch her a chair,
And throw a cushion on it.

Gorgo   Pray, don't trouble.

Praxinoa   Do sit down.

Gorgo   What a giddy, madcap thing to do! I've scarce got
                               through alive,
Praxinoa, what with all that crowd, and all those
                           four-horsed cars.
Everywhere soldiers' boots, everywhere troopers in fine cloaks!
And the street's endless. Really, my dear, you live too
                           far away.

Praxinoa Yes, for that lunatic needs must come to the ends of the
                           earth and take
This hole—one can't call it a house—on purpose to prevent
Our being neighbours—all for spite as usual, the jealous wretch!

Gorgo   You musn't say such things, my dear, about your
                           husband Dinon,
When the boy's listening. Do take care. See how he's
                           staring at you!
Never mind, Zopyrion, sweet pet. She doesn't mean papa.

Praxinoa By our Lady, the child understands.
Gorgo   Yes, he's a nice papa.
Praxinoa The other day that papa of his—yes only the other day
          We said, 'Daddy, go to the shop and buy some rouge
                                                and soda,'—
          Well, back he comes to us with salt, the great thirteen-foot
                                                lout![1]

Here we are fairly close in theme, though not in quality, to
Herodas. But more often Theocritus turned the mime to a new
purpose—the representation of scenes from country life. It was
to this that scholars gave the name of 'pastoral' or 'bucolic' verse.
No doubt the poet was led towards this development by various
influences: by his fellow-poets on the island of Cos, by his own
Sicilian origin and background, by his familiarity with the
Sicilian and Coan peasant and countryside, by the traditions of
Sicilian comedy and mime. He borrowed and adapted the traditions of popular rustic poetry and folk-song, like the singing-
match and the refrain, and because of this his pastoral scenes have
a vitality which the other Alexandrians lack. But Theocritus does
not know his peasants as he knows Gorgo and Praxinoa. Most
of his portraits of them are far from the photographic realism
to which he approximates when he brings his Syracusan women
to Alexandria. His approach to them is literary and romantic,
typical of the sophisticated man of letters looking at the life of the
countryside. They have no houses, no families, no problems of
making a living. The sole topic which he selects from their
existence is love, and the 'pastoral poems' are a series of variations
on this theme, from passion and jealousy to parody and caricature,
from the simple backchat of Milon teasing the love-sick Bucaeus
(*Idyll* x) to the grotesque charm of giant Polyphemus voicing
his longing for sea-nymph Galatea (*Idyll* xi). Mythical figures
like Daphnis and Menalcas are introduced as well as peasants.

[1] *Idyll* xv, ll. 1-17. Tr. Trevelyan (Cambridge University Press).

Theocritus' countryside is a place where reality and legend merge together to form a single romantic whole. To conclude this chapter I will quote a brief passage from one of the 'pastorals', in which a goatherd vainly serenades his Amaryllis:

> I will go serenading Amaryllis, while my goats,
> With Tityrus to herd them, go browsing o'er the hill.
> My well-beloved Tityrus, pasture my goats awhile,
> And to the spring-head lead them, my Tityrus: but beware
> Yon tawny Libyan he-goat's tricks, else he'll be butting you.
> O beautiful Amaryllis, why no longer from your cave
> Do you peep forth to greet me, your beloved? Do you hate me
> then?
> Can it be I appear snub-nosed, dear nymph, when seen from close?
> A jutting-bearded Satyr? You will make me hang myself.
> See here ten apples I have brought you, fetched down from the tree
> From which you bade me fetch them. I will bring ten more
> tomorrow.
> Look on my heart-tormenting grief. Would that I might become
> Yon booming bee, and enter so your cavern, steering through
> The ivy and the feathery fern, wherein you lie embowered.
> Now I know Love. A cruel god is he: a she-lion's breasts
> He sucked, and in a forest his mother nurtured him,
> Since with slow fire he burns me thus, smiting me to the bone.
> O beautifully glancing—but all stone! O dark-browed Nymph!
> Around me, your own goatherd, fling your arms, that I may kiss you.
> Even in empty kisses there is a sweet delight.
> Soon you will make me tear this garland into little shreds,
> This ivy wreath, dear Amaryllis, that I keep for you,
> Twining it with rose-buds and sweet-smelling parsley leaves.[1]

As we have seen, these various verse writings of the Alexandrian scholars did not constitute the main bulk of Hellenistic literature. Yet they throw much light on the trend of the time. In earlier chapters we have watched the emergence of reason out of more primitive ways of thought, and have seen its importance for authors as different as Euripides, Thucydides and Plato. It is

[1] *Idyll* III, ll. 1-23. Tr. Trevelyan.

significant that the Alexandrians looked back to models earlier than the rise of rational thinking: as we read their lines, we feel that the retreat from reason which characterised the later history of the Graeco-Roman world has already begun. Greek literature dawned with the surge and thunder of the *Odyssey*. Now, in its late afternoon, Theocritus bids us sport with Amaryllis in the shade. The brilliance of midday is past and gone, and twilight seems not very far ahead.

INDEX

References to works are given under their authors.